GH01005383

Europe and
the Middle East

Studies on the European Polity

BRENT NELSEN, SERIES EDITOR

Europe and the Middle East:
In the Shadow of September 11
Richard Youngs

Sustaining European Monetary Union:
Confronting the Cost of Diversity
Tal Sadeh

The Europeans:
Political Identity in an Emerging Polity
David Michael Green

Europe and the Middle East

In the Shadow of September 11

Richard Youngs

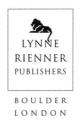

LYNNE
RIENNER
PUBLISHERS

BOULDER
LONDON

Published in the United States of America in 2006 by
Lynne Rienner Publishers, Inc.
1800 30th Street, Boulder, Colorado 80301
www.rienner.com

and in the United Kingdom by
Lynne Rienner Publishers, Inc.
3 Henrietta Street, Covent Garden, London WC2E 8LU

Library of Congress Cataloging-in-Publication Data
Youngs, Richard, 1968–
  Europe and the Middle East : in the shadow of September 11 / Richard Youngs.
     p.   cm. — (Studies on the European polity)
  Includes bibliographical references and index.
  ISBN-13: 978-1-58826-476-3 (hardcover : alk. paper)
  ISBN-10: 1-58826-476-9 (hardcover : alk. paper)
  1. Europe Union countries—Foreign relations—Middle East. 2. Middle East—
Foreign relations—European Union countries. 3. National security—European
Union countries. 4. International relations. 5. International economic relations.
I. Title. II. Series.
JZ1570.A55Y68 2006
327.4056—dc22
                                                            2006011924

British Cataloguing in Publication Data
A Cataloguing in Publication record for this book
is available from the British Library.

Printed and bound in the United States of America

       The paper used in this publication meets the requirements
  ∞   of the American National Standard for Permanence of
       Paper for Printed Library Materials Z39.48-1992.

  5 4 3 2 1

Contents

1 European Challenges in the Middle East
   After September 11   1

2 Iraq: Europe's Nemesis   31

3 Iran: The End of the Affair   67

4 The Maghreb and Mashreq: New Directions   95

5 Palestine: State Building in Hard Times   145

6 The Gulf and the Arabian Peninsula:
   Not-So-Benign Neglect   171

7 Turkey: Success and Its Malcontents   197

8 Conclusion: Europe in the Middle East   221

Bibliography   233
Index   245
About the Book   255

1

European Challenges in the Middle East After September 11

The terrorist attacks of 11 September 2001 on New York and Washington have been widely interpreted as a watershed moment in international relations, and in particular in the West's relations with the Middle East. These attacks prompted Western governments to reassess their security strategies globally, but most especially in the countries of the wider Middle East. In the aftermath of 9/11, debate ensued over whether the West should seek to fashion a qualitatively different relationship with the Middle East. To many it had become apparent that alliances with authoritarian regimes in the Middle East had not served to protect Western interests. Many analysts urged that greater attention be paid to the underlying roots of discontent and instability in the political repression prevalent across the Middle East. A link was widely proclaimed between this region's lack of democratic governance and international terrorism, as the latter generated a steady stream of attacks and threatened actions after 9/11; many analysts conversely questioned this hypothesized connection. That serious new challenges presented themselves as much to Europe as to the United States was demonstrated in most sobering fashion by the bombs that exploded in Madrid in March 2004 and in London in July 2005. These attacks revealed a wider and more amorphous network of radicals in Europe than previously suspected, with a complex mix of political, religious, and Iraq-specific motives.

Apparently reflecting a new understanding of security imperatives, in the wake of 9/11 the US and European governments committed themselves to encouraging processes of political liberalization in the Middle East. A plethora of new reform-oriented initiatives were introduced by international organizations, the United States, and the European Union (EU). The issue of political reform in the Middle East, and the role that Western states might play in the region's possible democratization became a defining issue of post–September 11 international relations.

If generic reassessments were forthcoming after 9/11, policy was also confronted by more specific challenges in the Middle East. Most obviously, as Iraq emerged to dominate the international agenda after 2002, further debate was triggered on the propriety of moves away from containment-based security doctrine, and subsequently on the rightful nature of international involvement in nation building. Other long-simmering issues also reached pivotal moments. Tensions deepened between Israel and the Palestinians, and a little over a year after Yasser Arafat's death Hamas won a watershed electoral victory in January 2006. Crunch time approached on Iran's alleged development of nuclear weapons, just as conservatives reasserted their grip on the country's political system. And crucial decisions fell due in Turkey's long and arduous journey toward hoped-for membership in the European Union. In sum, a general reassessment of relations with the wider Middle East and "Islamic fundamentalism" combined with a series of more specific flashpoints in the region. The dynamics that drove the latter were distinctive, but also fed into and were themselves affected by changes to the international environment occasioned by 9/11. This combination of issues rendered the Middle East the most strategically challenging of arenas for European foreign policy. Perceptions were widespread that the Middle East represented a primary source of increasing security risk—stemming from international terrorism, the effects of migration, and weapons of mass destruction (WMD) escalation.[1] These coalesced around a direct set of planned responses to 9/11, which in turn conditioned the backdrop to challenges specific to different parts of the region.

This book examines European Union policies—understood as the strategies of European governments nationally and those of the EU collectively—in relation to the challenges emanating both from the individual parts of the Middle East and from the overarching changes to the post-9/11 security environment. It focuses on one specific aspect of European policy in the Middle East, namely that relating to the issue of political reform. The aim is to analyze the balance between two strands of policy—the commitment to political reform versus traditional counterterrorist and containment-oriented cooperation—and how far understandings of strategic interests really changed after

2001. The book also assesses what variation there was between different European governments; between European and US approaches in the Middle East; and in EU policies toward different parts of the Middle East. An underlying theme is to draw from the study of European policies an appreciation of how the relationship between political Islam and the West and "Western" norms evolved as a result of the international context conditioned by 9/11. In exploring these substantive and strategic debates, the book also examines what light the case of the Middle East sheds on the nature of the EU's international "actorness."[2]

The book assesses European policies from the vantage point of a critical juncture in relations with different parts of the Middle East. By early 2006 the EU was just beginning to reengage in Iraq and consider possible ways of assisting this country's nascent democratic process in the wake of the December 2005 elections. In Iran, the EU found itself obliged to reassess a decade-long effort of rapprochement after conservative candidate Mahmoud Ahmadinejad emerged victorious from June's presidential elections, with European states finally voting to refer Iran to the United Nations Security Council when it resumed nuclear activities in January 2006. In the Maghreb and Mashreq discussion ensued over how to revitalize the Euro-Mediterranean Partnership (EMP) as this most distinctive of EU policies celebrated its tenth anniversary in November 2005. In the Palestinian Territories, the EU sought to encourage President Mahmoud Abbas along the road of democratic reform, while facing the challenge of responding to the rising popularity of Hamas, prior to the latter's electoral win in January 2006. In the states of the Gulf Cooperation Council (GCC), the EU deliberated on a new strategic partnership aimed at correcting its erstwhile neglect of this region—this as Gulf states came to occupy part of the front line in international counterterrorist concerns, while also benefiting from dramatic rises in oil prices. And in Turkey, just when accession negotiations were finally opened in October 2005 after many years of problematic relations between the EU and Ankara, the rejection of the European constitution by French and Dutch voters led many observers to suspect that the very principle of Turkish accession would be revisited.

Reacting to September 11

For many years Western policies worked to install and maintain in power autocratic regimes across the Middle East. This trend began with

the process of decolonization, in which departing European governments accorded power to authoritarian leaders and powerful security
forces. Colonial powers left legacies of arbitrarily drawn boundaries
and of states incorporating a complex mix of ethnic, religious, and tribal
groupings. Sometimes European powers left minority groups to take
over the reins of power, and these quickly assembled the instruments of
firm state control in protection against majority ethnic and religious
constituencies.[3] Historical variation in the process of state formation in
different Arab states moved toward a common suppression of political
rights.[4] These biases deepened as Western powers supported friendly
authoritarian states during the Cold War. The logic of Cold War containment was compounded in the Middle East by the judgment that authoritarian regimes should be backed additionally as a bulwark against a
resurgent political Islam—the latter invariably perceived to be fundamentally hostile to the West and to democratic norms.

Western perspectives on the Middle East were slow to change
after the end of the Cold War. While policies seeking to encourage
democracy and human rights were developed throughout the different regions of the world, their emergence was conspicuously tepid and
selective in the Middle East. The European Union enticed the Maghreb
and Mashreq into a new partnership ostensibly predicated upon a
commitment to political pluralism, but the Euro-Mediterranean Partnership in practice occasioned no more than a partial and extremely
cautious shift in European security strategies. Dialogue on political
reform was developed with these Arab states, and a number of human
rights and cultural initiatives were funded to a modest extent. European governments had begun to inch toward a less exclusively containment-based approach to the Middle East, but the substance of
their policies suggested they did so with little urgency or priority.
External powers continued to exhibit a reluctance to engage with
Islamist civil society organizations. Both US and European governments favored engagement and enhanced economic cooperation with
Arab regimes, even as many of these tightened their control over domestic dissent. Preserving the apparent momentum that was then developing in relation to the Middle East peace process militated against
pressuring the Arab regimes committed to the Oslo accords. Open conflict in both Palestine and Algeria led European states in these contexts
to back increasingly repressive security forces. If the EMP's approach
to political reform was cautious, such a focus was even more circumspect and ad hoc in the states of the Gulf Cooperation Council and

Iran. Policy toward Iraq in the wake of the Gulf War was avowedly based on containing Saddam Hussein. A focus on human rights entered Western discourse in the region, but strategic interests were still seen in a most immediate sense through the lens of intensified, traditional security cooperation with Arab governments.

Responses to the attacks of 11 September 2001 pointed toward a far-reaching reassessment of Western policies. Critics located the source of rising Islamic radicalism and instability besetting the Middle East in the region's lack of democracy. It was widely agreed that political Islam had merely been bolstered by its political prohibition. While external powers sought to shore up pro-Western autocrats as a defense against radical Islam, political Islam's very radicalism was at least in part a product of those same Western policies. Far from successfully containing the Islamist revival, Middle Eastern autocrats had fueled anti-Western feeling and played to Islamist opinion in order to shore up the precarious legitimacy of their own rule. A vicious circle had taken hold: regimes had often played up the dangers of radical Islamism to justify to the West their own repressive powers, which merely served further to foment that very radicalism. Instability was judged by some to be a response to political repression more than to economic deprivation.[5] Analysts suggested that peaceable Muslims required greater political autonomy to speak out and reclaim Islam from extremists, to temper a prevailing social forbearance of radicalism in the region. The lack of democracy in the Middle East was also seen by many to have been a factor driving migration, an increasingly politicized issue within Europe itself. The United Nations' seminal Arab Human Development Report 2002 explicitly linked the region's lack of democracy to its economic and social travails; its 2004 report was even more candid in unpacking the ills of the Arab world's democratic shortfalls.[6] In a shift away from the "big power" WMD security logic of the Cold War, counterproliferation strategies were now seen to be hindered mainly by regimes' lack of transparency and their fomenting of substate actors. Some analysts proffered an association between liberalism and the tempering of Arab nationalism. In sum, it was suggested that the post–September 11 war on terrorism required a new "civic front," linking global democracy to a range of deepening challenges.[7]

A new logic quickly appeared in some of the rhetoric of a number of Western governments. US Secretary of State Colin Powell argued after the 9/11 attacks that "we will continue to advance our

fundamental interests in human rights, accountable government . . .
for we believe a world of democracy . . . is a world in which terrorism cannot thrive."[8] In his November 2003 speech at the National
Endowment for Democracy, President Bush acknowledged that
"sixty years of Western nations excusing and accommodating the
lack of freedom in the Middle East did nothing to make us safe."[9]
The president's rhetoric became even more "forward leaning" after
his reelection, regularly reinforcing the stated commitment to spreading democracy.

In Europe, External Relations Commissioner Chris Patten argued
that "fostering human rights should become an integral part of the
fight against terrorism."[10] British prime minister Tony Blair opined in
2003 that "the best security we can have . . . is through our values,
the spread of our values."[11] In his main 2004 foreign policy speech,
Blair asserted that "lasting security against fanatics and terrorists
cannot be provided by conventional military force but requires a
commitment to democracy, freedom and justice."[12] EU foreign policy
high representative Javier Solana argued that even if political change
could not be expected immediately to assuage the most implacable of
terrorists, it was significant that the latter had been "nourished by a
pool of disaffection."[13] In March 2005, then French foreign minister
Michel Barnier suggested that strategic policies should be guided by
recognition that "a more democratic world is the guarantee of a more
secure world."[14] Rarely a week passed without a European minister
delivering what became an almost standard stock speech advocating
a broader approach to security in the Middle East, embracing economic development, political liberalization, and cultural cooperation.

A plethora of new initiatives and policy documents were elaborated that purported to offer support for political reform in the Middle East. The United States introduced a Middle East Partnership Initiative (MEPI), which made available $264 million for the period
2002–2005; by 2004, nearly a third of this had been spent on political aid projects, while an additional $800 million had been allocated
for democracy and governance projects from the United States Agency
for International Development (USAID).[15] The budget of the National
Endowment for Democracy was increased by nearly a third, specifically for reform work in the Middle East. The new US National Security Strategy committed the administration to link democracy promotion and security interests more systematically.[16]

All major European donors initiated new democracy, governance, and human rights aid programs in the Middle East, most parts

of the latter having been conspicuously absent from the expanding field of political reform activity during the 1990s. The German government created a Task Force for Dialogue with the Islamic World within the Austwärtiges Amt (Foreign Office), while the development ministry devised a more comprehensive and governance-oriented aid program for the region. The British government introduced a new Arab reform strategy, restructuring foreign office departments around this thematic issue. It also created a fund for the Engaging with the Islamic World Program, which grew from £1.5 million in 2003 to £8 million allocated for 2005, channeling funds in particular to reform projects run by international organizations such as the United Nations Development Programme (UNDP) and the Organisation for Economic Cooperation and Development (OECD) and seeking to "mainstream" the development of such projects in UK diplomatic posts within the region. Denmark launched a Wider Middle East Initiative in June 2003 with €15 million available for democratic reform programs, and Sweden introduced a new €5 million governance allocation into its Middle East and North Africa program. In October 2004, Spain's new center-left government launched plans for a reform-oriented Alliance of Civilizations and designed a new strategy for extending the scope of its democracy assistance projects.[17] The French development ministry similarly elaborated a new strategy to enhance its profile in democracy assistance, extended to a number of priority Arab states.[18] Several European governments enjoined their respective political party foundations to establish a profile of reform work in the Arab world.

Commitments also accumulated at the European Union level, in this case building on some of the initiatives and discourse established during the 1990s. The EU's new Security Strategy agreed upon in December 2003 asserted that (in a subsequently much-quoted phrase), "The best protection for our security is a world of well governed democratic states."[19] A new strategy paper on the Arab world drawn up at the end of 2003 by Chris Patten and Javier Solana urged that more effort and thought be invested in the issue of promoting democracy in the Middle East.[20] This paper developed into the Strategic Partnership with the Mediterranean and Middle East, adopted in June 2004, which committed the EU to strengthening its efforts in the region beyond the Maghreb and Mashreq, as well as to widening its range of civil society interlocutors in the Middle East. By 2004, the European Neighbourhood Policy (ENP) was also taking shape, providing a new framework under which reform-oriented "action plans" were being negotiated with individual Maghreb and Mashreq states. In early 2005, the European Initiative on Democracy and Human Rights (EIDHR), managed by the European Commission, increased from four to fifteen the number of Middle Eastern states identified as "target countries."[21]

Reform commitments and initiatives introduced by the US and European governments were soon drawn into the tensions occasioned by the US-UK invasion of Iraq in March 2003. After the introduction of the MEPI, the Bush administration had proposed a Greater Middle East Initiative, aimed at better transatlantic coordination in the promotion of political change in the Middle East. This proposal met with a hesitant response from European governments who objected to the US failure to consult with actors in the Middle East in drawing up the initiative. This European unease was compounded by a more general concern that cooperation with the United States would sully European reputations in the region, at a juncture when the scale of US difficulties in Iraq was becoming painfully evident. However, a revised and scaled-down Broader Middle East and North Africa Initiative (BMENA) was agreed at the G8 meeting in Sea Island in June 2004. This referred to the "political modernization" rather than "democratization" of the Middle East, and incorporated systematic consultation with Arab governments. While European governments resisted a pooling of EU and US resources into a common democracy fund, the BMENA contained a number of significant initiatives to enhance reform dialogue in the Middle East and facilitate better transatlantic coordination. Italy assumed joint chairmanship, with Turkey and Yemen, of the Democracy Assistance Dialogue group created under the auspices of the BMENA. When ministers inaugurated the BMENA's Forum on the Future in Morocco in December 2004, the commitment to encourage political change in the Middle East appeared to have been consolidated at the highest political level. At the November 2005 meeting of the Forum on the Future in Bahrain $50 million was allocated to create an independent foundation to fund democratic reform projects. In June 2004, the North Atlantic Treaty Organization (NATO) launched its Istanbul Cooperation Initiative, which purported to extend the framework of the organization's Mediterranean Dialogue to Gulf states and included a commitment to intensify the as yet limited focus on strengthening civilian control over military forces in the Middle East.

In short, from much analysis and formal policy commitments it appeared that there had been something of a paradigm shift in the wake of 9/11. Some analysts feared the shift in thinking was too radical and absolute.[22] If perspectives had previously been unduly containment-oriented, they suggested, the new assumption that efforts to democratize the Middle East would provide an antidote to terrorism was overly simplistic. Caution was required in extrapolating from evidence of democracy's virtue in managing context-specific, low-level societal tension to a conviction that governance reform was rightfully the central strand of efforts to combat the qualitatively distinct threat of Al-Qaida. Many lamented that the international agenda was being driven by a disproportionate focus on one specific kind of international terrorism, when deficiencies in economic development and human security were still far more pervasive in their effect. Political change was, skeptics argued, in danger of being conceived in too instrumental a fashion through the lens of Western self-interest. Some critics judged post-9/11 democracy promotion efforts in fact to be a recipe for further instability and violence.[23] Others observed that the radicalism of Muslims within Europe rarely derived from conditions in the "home" countries of the Arab world, but rather reflected the more generalized phenomena of alienation.[24] It seemed that in many countries there were small committed bands of extremists operating so far beyond generally accepted rules and norms that their grievances were unlikely to be assuaged by any change in political regime. In these highly charged political debates nuanced views often seemed absent, charting a middle course between such skepticism, on the one hand, and the uncritical advocacy of democracy as panacea, on the other hand.[25] As a new policy discourse embedded itself, the question remained whether Western commitments to encourage democracy in the Middle East would prove calibrated in proper measure to the diversity of challenges at hand.

The Dam Bursts? Politics in the Middle East

The longevity of the Middle East's nondemocratic regimes certainly rendered these new commitments highly ambitious. Freedom House scores were regularly cited to show that the nineteen Middle Eastern states suffered the lowest level of political freedom of any region in the world, and that the Middle East was the only region where the overall level of freedom had declined since the 1970s. There was still no full-fledged Arab democracy.[26] Yet the apparent and longstanding ossification of Middle Eastern politics seemed during 2004 and 2005 to give way to an unleashing of reform potential. The prospect of a tipping point of change crystallized in the early months of 2005. January 2005 witnessed in short succession the holding of democratic elections in the Palestinian Territories and Iraq. In February, the assassination of former prime minister Rafik Hariri unleashed civil protest in Lebanon, which was soon dubbed the "Cedar revolution." In the same month a change in the Egyptian constitution was authorized to provide for multicandidate presidential elections. By the middle of 2005, few reports on the region neglected to allude to the blossoming of an "Arabian spring."

A more gradual dynamic of change had in fact been accumulating in the Middle East for some years. Most notably, after taking office in 2002, Turkey's Islamist-oriented government expanded Kurdish cultural rights and introduced measures to temper the military's political preeminence, inching Turkey toward fully developed democracy. Reforms had begun to be implemented particularly in the region's monarchies, most notably Morocco, Jordan, Kuwait, and Bahrain, whose regimes were judged by some to enjoy a legitimacy that gave greater scope for reform than in secular republics. After Mohammed VI assumed the throne in 1999, Morocco made significant progress on a range of human rights issues, most notably through a new civil rights code that strengthened women's rights in issues relating to marriage, custody, and inheritance, and through the opening of investigations into past human rights abuses. After an Equity and Reconciliation Commission presented its findings at the beginning of 2006, King Mohammed committed his government to introducing new human rights measures. On the back of similarly liberalizing measures, the Jordanian government elaborated a national agenda for reform, and a more reformist government was appointed in mid-2005.

In Egypt lively debate erupted on democratic change. Opposition parties formed a democratic alliance, which included informal coordination with the Muslim Brotherhood, before the government of Hosni Mubarak decided in October 2004 to grant its first license to an overtly oppositional party, the al-Ghad (Tomorrow) Party. The 2005 constitutional change permitting multicandidate presidential elections was followed by the emergence of an outspoken opposition movement, Kifiya (Enough), while Egypt's judges pushed for a more independent process of electoral scrutiny. While Mubarak predictably won the September 2005 presidential elections, open debate on reform had taken a firm hold. Parliamentary elections at the end of 2005 handed the Muslim Brotherhood a significantly increased share of seats to the detriment of the ruling National Democratic Party (NDP).

As the violence of Algeria's civil war subsided, Islamist groups bought into peaceable political process, the remnants of the Front Islamique du Salut (FIS) were increasingly marginalized, and the army stepped tentatively back from day-to-day political life. As President Abdelaziz Bouteflika removed a number of military hardliners in the autumn of 2004, the twin (and mutually stoking) entities opposing democratic reform—the army and violent Islamist groups—seemed less overwhelming than they had for many years. In Iran, reformers' calls for democratization became increasingly unrestrained after the late 1990s. In Saudi Arabia Crown Prince Abdullah bin Abdul Aziz launched a national dialogue on political reform in 2003; human rights demonstrations took place; and in early 2005 elections were held for municipalities. The Bahraini parliament was reinstated in 2002, after a 27-year suspension; the Kuwaiti parliament established itself as a lively chamber of genuine political debate; and a wave of elections spread through the Gulf monarchies after 2002. In Kuwait, the autumn of 2004 saw the reformist Sheikh Sabah take over the functions of the ailing crown prince; the government issued its first license to a human rights nongovernmental organization (NGO); and in 2005 women were granted the vote. At the end of 2005, the United Arab Emirates, the only Gulf state still not to have held elections of any type, called indirect elections for half the seats on its parliament-like Federal National Council. President Yasser Arafat's resistance to political liberalization had already sparked unprecedented democracy protests in the Occupied Territories prior to his death in November 2004. And while violence still wracked Iraq, by early 2006 the country had navigated three national votes—for a transitional government in January 2005, for a constitution in October 2005, and for a permanent administration in December 2005.

The Arab League adopted a 13-point reform action plan in May 2004. In February 2005 a number of Arab states signed up to a new OECD-UNDP Initiative on Good Governance for Development. In 2004, a series of pro-democracy gatherings—albeit sanctioned by official authorities—were held in Sana'a, Alexandria, Istanbul, Beirut, and Doha. At the end of September 2004, Arab civil society activists presented their blueprint for reform to the BMENA's Forum on the Future. Key Arab civil society figures argued that new reform activity was both significant and more firmly rooted than often presumed, as such trends revived the Middle East's previous "liberal age" of the late nineteenth and early twentieth centuries.[27] Many liberals suggested that the new international discourse on democracy had left them feeling emboldened. Much evidence indicated growing support for democracy among Muslims. Numerous polls showed that citizens in Middle Eastern countries strongly and increasingly endorsed democratic ideals.[28] There was no poll suggesting that Arabs actively opposed democracy. Arab responses to the international focus on democracy were replete with contradictions: there was simultaneously resistance to the hegemony of "Western" political forms alongside citizens' apparent desire to be part of a wealthy and democratic international cultural order.

As the dynamics of change accumulated, however, the limits to political opening also became apparent. Several polities in the Middle East remained resolutely closed. Syria's "Damascus spring" of apparent opening under Bashar Assad was almost immediately reversed and hardliners regained ascendancy, orchestrating new clampdowns against democracy activists. A further, brief respite early in 2003 was followed by another period of political tightening, explained by the regime as a response to Syria being adversely affected by the United States–led invasion of Iraq. The last of the political salons that had opened in Damascus was finally closed down in May 2005. Tunisia was perhaps the most spectacular "backslider," with the Bin Ali regime widening its repression of Islamists to a general curtailing of autonomous civil society activity: Tunisian elections in October 2004 showed no movement toward freer political competition, rubber-stamping an originally unconstitutional fourth term for Bin Ali.

Notwithstanding the emergence of vibrant debate, the extent of concrete change in Egypt remained limited. The September 2004 congress of the National Democratic Party ruled out a lifting of emergency law or the granting of greater freedoms for civil society organizations. The *Cairo Times,* a leading liberal paper, was closed down. Even as the al-Ghad party was granted a license, its leader, Ayman Nour, was imprisoned, and the Mubarak government postponed its holding of a group of eight major industrial democracies (G8) conference on political reform. The decision to allow multicandidate elections was interpreted as a means of the regime simply preempting pressure for meaningful liberalization: nominations to stand against Mubarak were still controlled by the NDP, while the Muslim Brotherhood was still denied official recognition.[29] Indeed, in the early months of 2005 nearly two thousand supporters of the Muslim Brotherhood were arrested and harsh clampdowns followed against Kifiya-led demonstrations. Parliamentary elections later in the year were subject to familiar tactics of manipulation and voter intimidation, with secular-liberal democrats failing to win any notable representation.

Saudi Arabia's incipient system of consultation was extremely cautious and arguably simply increased the Al-Sauds' patronage-based influence. The Saudi regime thwarted democracy demonstrations in December 2004 with customary brutality. Across the Gulf, reforms were pursued in a highly top-down fashion, with the aim of shoring up the declining legitimacy of ruling emirs. In September 2004, the Bahraini government closed the Bahrain Center for Human Rights; reformers were arrested; a proposed independent human rights commission was rejected; and dashed hopes for reform provoked a reemergence of tensions between the dominant Sunni minority and the politically excluded Shia majority. In Kuwait, even reformers in parliament resisted calls to include in the government representatives from outside the ruling family. Leadership successions in Saudi Arabia, Kuwait, and the United Arab Emirates in a short period of time at the end of 2005 and early 2006 raised new questions over the future of Gulf regimes. Yemen suffered a gradual tightening of political space from the late 1990s under the Saleh government and what was increasingly the dominant party system of the General Popular Congress. And, of course, the challenges remained especially acute in Iraq. Quite apart from its crippling levels of violence, and despite the development of a formally democratic political process, Iraq still lacked basic state-institutional capacity and national civic organizations to underpin the introduction of democratic politics.

Even in the most reformist states, political liberalization occurred within tightly controlled parameters. In Morocco, the palace retained control over key areas of policy, clamped down on journalistic freedoms, and continued to proscribe the biggest Islamist organization, Justice and Charity, from the political arena. Political *alternance* allowed for limited contestation among broadly status quo–oriented political parties, which in fact served to broaden the consensus behind the monarchy's continuing dominance. The king's intervention to choose a coalition government following elections in 2002 was seen by many as an attempt to retain a malleable governmental team. A dramatically reduced turnout for these elections suggested increasing dissatisfaction with the lack of genuine political alternatives in Morocco. After the 16 May 2003 bombings in Casablanca, the government tightened restrictions on Islamists and removed many critical clerics; gave security forces sweeping new powers to detain suspects; brought forward plans to control political party activity more tightly; and reputedly pressured the mainstream Islamist Party of Justice and Development to compete in only a limited number of seats in municipal elections.

In Jordan, soon after taking power in 1999 King Abdullah II moved to suspend parliament and postpone new elections. While elections were later held in 2003, limited political reform was accompanied by deliberate gerrymandering to disadvantage both the Islamist opposition and Jordan's Palestinian majority. Reform was conceived as a vehicle for legitimizing the Jordanian regime through direct plebiscitary links between the government and tribal independents; it precluded support for countervailing institutions and parties. Change was directed in a heavily top-down fashion from the king, with most of the cabinet remaining politically illiberal. This dynamic of control was manifest in signs of a clampdown on the Jordanian Muslim Brotherhood in September 2004, and in restrictive provisions covering the activities of professional associations and political parties introduced in early 2005. The terrorist attacks in Amman on 9 November 2005 led to a new security focus on the part of the government, despite the king's reiterating his rhetorical commitment to political reform. The cases of Jordan and Morocco suggested that even against a backdrop of increasingly competitive elections, parliaments were often coopted into reform processes instrumentally circumscribed by regimes.

In Algeria it remained unclear whether President Bouteflika was committed to using his consolidated power vis-à-vis the army and violent Islamist groups to democratize Algeria fully. Key journalists remained imprisoned and the party system subjugated, while Bouteflika deliberately stoked division in the ruling National Liberation Front Party to shore up his own position. The 2004 elections were fought not on the basis of distinctive party political platforms, but with Bouteflika in effect standing against the crisis-ridden party system. Presidential power increased over regional governors, the judiciary, and parliament. Bouteflika and the army had negotiated an implicit deal whereby the latter withdrew from day-to-day involvement in politics in return for Bouteflika's guarantee of a robust approach to counterterrorism. A new amnesty law was widely seen as offering impunity to the military for excesses committed during the 1990s. The president's approach seemed to be based on a direct pro-peace appeal to the Algerian population that bypassed intermediary institutions. In

March 2005 reforms to family law left highly conservative provisions intact in order to appease Islamist parties.

During 2004, Syrian control over Lebanon tightened, through manipulation of local elections, increased troop deployments, and intervention to extend the term in office of pro-Damascus president Emile Lahoud. The withdrawal of Syrian troops from Lebanon in May 2005 represented a necessary step toward the restoration of Lebanese sovereignty, but also revealed that the country's consociational democracy had failed to transcend denominational divisions. Stability had depended on the sharing out of spoils to different factions. Reform to the electoral law, necessary to ensure that new elections did not simply replicate the same sharing out of power, was not agreed in the wake of Rafik Hariri's assassination. And indeed the elections held during May and June 2005 duly produced a familiar distribution of posts between pro- and anti-Syrian factions, with little renovation of the Lebanese political class.

While protracted democratization appeared strongly embedded in Turkey, some observers feared that the continuing prevalence of a nationalist Turkish security culture constituted a barrier to full democratization. Frequent skirmishing over second-order issues was witnessed between the Recep Tayyip Erdogan government and the army, and some questioned the breadth of support behind the Justice and Development administration's efforts to remold the country's military-guaranteed constitutional order. In Iran, conservative clerics fought to reestablish control after reformers gained ascendancy in parliament after 2000, and they excluded several hundred reformist candidates in the January 2004 legislative elections, which guaranteed the return of a conservative-dominated *majlis*. This served as a prelude to the June 2005 presidential elections, from which most reformist candidates were also barred and which, of course, returned the hard-line conservative victor, Mahmoud Ahmadinejad.

More generally across the Middle East, democratic dynamics were tempered by the general persistence of rentier-based economic structures. In the late 1980s, economic internationalization appeared to open the door for reform; regimes judged it necessary to offer political liberalization as a means of underpinning unpopular economic adjustment. However, the rigors of economic liberalization subsequently encouraged regimes to strengthen executive primacy over possible opposition to painful reform measures. During the 1990s, incremental, if halting, economic reform failed to engender significant diversification that would relieve economies from dependence on the rents accruing to regimes from natural resource exploitation. Investment was largely limited to the oil and other natural resource industries, and these remained isolated enclaves within Middle Eastern economies. By 2004, 98 percent of Algeria's export earnings came from hydrocarbons; foreign direct investment inflows remained the lowest of all developing regions, at 0.2 percent of gross domestic product (GDP); and even in states like Jordan, well over half the workforce remained in public sector employment.

Indeed, patrimonial-style rule actually intensified as regimes took it upon themselves to allocate the benefits of new market and regulatory activity. Regimes skillfully built up cross-cutting alliances among economic actors, bureaucracies, and unions, playing these off against each other to retain relations of dependency.[30] Across the region, observers saw the relative lack of reformers within economic and political elites as differentiating conditions in the Middle East from those that had produced consensual, pacted transitions in other parts of the world.[31] It was argued that, unlike in Latin America and Asia, in the Middle East neither the working class nor the private sector was sufficiently organized to act as the agent necessary to ensure that economic opening could be used to increase pressure for political liberalization.[32]

The fluidity and variety in the region's political trends were additionally both reflected in and effects of the changing nature of political Islam. The development of political Islam was widely interpreted as the reincarnation of an older Arab nationalism, dressed in more indigenous language and belief systems.[33] Across the region strands of political Islam professed firm commitment to democratic norms, while mainstream Islamist parties in Morocco and Jordan self-denyingly aligned themselves with partial processes of reform. Even in Saudi Arabia some detected the emergence of more reformist Salafi currents. Such trends were interpreted as part of Islamists' "return to modernism."[34] Polling suggested that citizens' attitudes toward Islam had no negative bearing on views regarding democracy.[35] Crucially, these Islamists became both more accepting of the nation-state and keen to develop political agendas that would accord them influence within national political processes. Some detected powerful new pro-reform alliances between Islamists, leftists, and nationalist opposition forces.

Conversely, illiberal currents of Islam remained powerful, for example within Jama'a al-Islamiyya, Hamas, and Wahhabi groups. Trenchant critics insisted that feelings of subjugation, limited concepts of individual human rights, and historically rooted pride continued to militate against the emergence of a genuinely democratic, pro-Western political Islam.[36] The vast majority of analysts rejected Orientalist claims that the Middle East was unsuited to democratic norms, but some cautioned that the recognition of context as influential should not be seen to reduce political Islam's more problematic elements to mere epiphenomena of economic and social difficulties. Questioning perceptions of a pro-democracy drift in political Islam, one expert judged that the highly politicized post-9/11 international environment had in fact favored the fortunes of more radical strands.[37]

Many self-styled Islamist modernizers advocated liberalism but not democracy, seeing religious development as requiring better protection for individual rights of the sort not well preserved through majority rule.[38] Even where they adopted platforms broadly in favor of democracy, Islamist groups invariably declined to militate for specific reforms.[39] Islamists came to advocate free elections, but often implied that these should take place within parameters that prevented the complete separation of state and religion. In states where Islamists gained parliamentary representation—Morocco, Jordan, Algeria, Kuwait—they pushed many illiberal agendas. In both Kuwait and Algeria, for example, Islamists blocked government proposals to extend women's rights. Even if the political agendas of Islamist organizations had unquestionably evolved, some observers doubted that a committed and coherent constituency for democracy could yet be detected in the Middle East.[40]

Indeed, a prominent social reformist strand of Islam, focusing on marrying textual study with grassroots social activity, brought with it a degree of disengagement from debates over political structures.[41] Some argued that this apolitical strand, rather than political Islam as such, provided the soil in which conservative fundamentalism had most strongly taken root.[42] Moreover, it was this form of social Islamism—which governments had sought to incorporate into political institutions, seeking to provide a seamless shift to a more Islam-sensitive semiauthoritarianism—that threatened to bypass democracy as the mechanism of change toward broader social inclusion. Whatever the changes in Islamists' political manifestos, in practice relations with secular liberals remained strained in many countries. It was suggested that divisions within Islam had come to express underlying class structures, the newly pro-democratic strands of the Islamist middle classes having failed to take the young urban poor with them on their journey toward more Western liberal norms.[43] One observer noted that Arab intellectuals and activists had focused so overwhelm-ingly on resisting pernicious governmental repression and attaining the most basic of rights that there remained a need for the relationship between Islam and political modernity to be fully worked through.[44]

A final factor pervading all levels of debate in the Middle East was the impact of violent conflict within the region. It was widely argued that the failure to secure a final settlement between Israel and the Palestinians made "selling" democracy harder and diverted the energies and focus of Middle Eastern civil society. Democracy had not become a more potent rallying cry and motivation for action in the Middle East in part because so much protest instead focused on reacting to Israeli heavy-handedness in the Palestinian Territories and perceived Western support for Israel. Ensuring greater civilian dem-ocratic control over militaries in the Middle East was complicated by the legitimacy bestowed upon militaries by the lack of resolution of the Israeli-Palestinian conflict. By 2003 the Arab-Israeli dispute was joined by the Iraq conflict in conditioning broader political debates across the Middle East. Many feared that US intervention in Iraq risked compromising the appeal of democracy throughout the region. Shia-inspired instability in Iraq was soon used by incumbent Sunni regimes as further justification for their own reluctance to cede power. As the Sunni-led insurgency then intensified, events in Iraq appeared significant in their re-igniting of the Sunni-Shia split as a major factor in Middle East politics. The UNDP 2003 Arab Human Development Report opined that "the issue of freedom in Arab coun-tries has become a casualty of the overspill from the Anglo-American invasion of Iraq" and that, because of conflict in Iraq, democracy's predicament was "even graver than before."[45] Even as Iraq moved haltingly toward the creation of a sovereign, democratic government in 2005, any positive longer-term impact of the post-2003 experience of Iraq for the broader region remained to be demonstrated.

What Potential for Effective European Action?

In sum, this was the background of unresolved tensions and diversity within the Middle East against which European governments, individ-ually and collectively as the EU, committed themselves to developing a more effective and reform-oriented strategy in the region. This com-mitment evoked debates over the nature and extent of European capa-bilities to realize the declared objectives. Even if they were genuinely minded to support reform dynamics in the Middle East, could European governments individually and the EU collectively muster the influence to make a significant and favorable impact? If Europe had failed the test set by the Balkans wars, the most strategically prominent issue of the 1990s, was it now ready and willing to contribute more effectively to a new approach to security in the Middle East, widely seen as the most important international challenge a decade on?

Throughout the period of the Cold War, the Middle East proved to be the least auspicious arena for developing effective, coordinated European action. In the 1970s, Organization of the Petroleum Exporting Countries (OPEC) decisions drove a wedge between European states and were among the primary causes of a general atrophy in European integration. OPEC expressly sought to split European states, targeting sanctions and production cutbacks specifically at Germany and the Netherlands, the states deemed most pro-Israeli. France was widely seen as most influential in seeking to reposition European policy in the Middle East. It was after the oil crisis that the EU as a group created the Euro-Arab Dialogue and issued the Venice Declaration supporting Palestinian self-determination. In large part at the behest of the United States, however, the EU then excluded issues relating to the Arab-Israeli conflict from the Euro-Arab Dialogue; as a result the dialogue was in effect suspended, and periodic attempts to resuscitate it failed.[46] Perhaps more than anywhere else, in the Middle East France was judged to "see itself as a soloist backed up by the rest of European orchestra."[47] The incremental development of the Euro-Mediterranean Partnership in the late 1990s indicated elements of a more united, Europeanized approach, but this continued to be offset by barely disguised differences and national primacy in relation to Iraq, Saudi Arabia, Libya, and many aspects of strategy toward the Arab-Israeli conflict. The "duality" of EU foreign policy making—divided between Commission-managed "external economic relations" and an intergovernmental diplomatic strand—continued to hamper Middle East strategy severely, reducing the EU to a "clearinghouse of different interests" devoid of common direction.[48] With European pretensions to a more effective Middle East policy resting on these fragile foundations, many critics of course doubted that Europe was institutionally and conceptually equipped to meet its post-9/11 aspirations.

Familiar debates continued on the question of how effective a process of foreign policy coordination had developed among European governments. How far the EU possessed the mechanisms to benefit from the combined weight of its member states was a matter of long-standing analysis. By the beginning of the new century, few analysts adhered to entirely minimalist or realist interpretations of EU foreign policy cooperation. The EU had, it was widely argued, moved slowly and incrementally to avail itself of new policy instruments and improved processes of coordination. Reforms to the EU's Common Foreign and Security Policy (CFSP) after the late 1990s included the creation of a "high representative" for foreign policy with his own planning unit and the possibility of more qualified majority voting in foreign policy decisions. In January 2005 High Representative Javier Solana additionally appointed a personal representative for human rights to coordinate reform-oriented strategies. The new European Security Strategy provided a clearer articulation of post-9/11 strategic aims, while the draft European constitution proposed an EU foreign minister to combine the twin posts of high representative and external relations commissioner, as well as a common diplomatic service. Although by the end of 2005 this constitution looked unlikely to survive, diplomats from some member states intimated that the new foreign policy provisions were one area that might be extracted and implemented separately. Commitments to create a European Security and Defence Policy (ESDP) were judged by many to be adding a vital piece of hard power to the array of EU instruments and driving a convergence of operational methods among European security forces.[49]

Most analysts of European foreign policy coordination attested to a deepening reflex of foreign policy cooperation between EU member states. The CFSP, national foreign policies, and Commission-managed economic dimensions of EU external relations were seen as increasingly melded together in a deeply interconnected "European foreign policy system."[50] The outcomes of successive efforts at coordination had come to constitute a constant "feedback" into the policymaking process, driving enhanced determination to achieve effective cooperation.[51] Within a framework of multilevel governance, national interest formation could no longer be conceived as separate from the CFSP process itself; national adaptation to EU foreign policy norms was increasingly significant; and a dynamic of shared "problem solving" now usurped standard interest-bargaining competition.[52] It was suggested that such policymaking dynamics had ensured a gradual "ironing out of national foreign policy idiosyncrasies."[53]

As US strategies in the Middle East intensified after 9/11, much commentary focused on the widely perceived differences between

European and US approaches and capacities. As transatlantic divergence appeared to widen, the Middle East routinely served as the most significant backdrop against which EU-US differences were played out. The Middle East was defined by one prominent diplomat as the defining "fault line" between Europe and the United States.[54] It was often assumed that while the United States saw 9/11 as an attack on "Western values," Europeans saw it as an attack on US policies and judged the main security issues relating to the Muslim world to be far less direct in nature.[55] During his April 2005 visit to Brussels, President Bush suggested that, for Europe, 9/11 had represented a "passing moment" and not a trigger for the kind of fundamental change visited upon US foreign policy.

A prominent assumption was that Europe was less heavy-handed and unidimensional than the United States in the use of its international influence. The eschewal of a crudely instrumental use of power was routinely conceived as an important and pervasive aspect of EU foreign and security policy coordination. Many analysts of European foreign policy judged a focus on human rights and mutually beneficial democratic power sharing to flow from the EU's own experience and identity.[56] It was such a dynamic that was seen to have invested European actions with both value and effectiveness in post–Cold War Eastern Europe and at the end of the 1990s in Kosovo.[57] If the EU had gained influence, it was as a point of reference for governance standards, a model to help temper conflicts through its philosophy of "multiple rather than exclusive identities."[58] The nature of "social learning" in the evolution of European identity and deliberative European democratic space was seen as having provided the key to taking the EU beyond power-interest dynamics to enjoy significant standing as a conveyor of democratic norms.[59] The centrality of normative values had, it was suggested, deepened a European foreign policy *system* into a foreign policy *society*.[60] A commitment to promoting democracy and human rights had been central to the EU's collective identity, which provided the enabling conditions for coordinated European foreign policy action.[61] As *The Economist* opined: "The EU is comfortable talking about values, but uncomfortable talking about interests."[62]

For some, such dynamics heralded a welcome postmodern form of international relations. In contrast, the most widely cited post-9/11 critique of the EU saw such notions as a self-serving cover for Europeans' own weaknesses. It was asserted that the EU had inappropriately moved "beyond power into a self-contained world of laws and rules and transnational negotiation and cooperation," and that the European approach was merely and naively to seek "to bind nations together" through trade, diplomacy, inducements, compromise, and social interdependencies.[63] Whether such sweeping statements merited the enormous attention and notoriety they subsequently acquired was widely debated; but they undoubtedly galvanized debate. One leading European thinker-practitioner shared the concern that while such postmodern logic might work internally, the EU needed to recognize that rougher "laws of the jungle" would often be appropriate beyond its own borders. In this sense, European effectiveness required the EU to move beyond the illusion of a strategy based solely on expanding the geographical range of a "cooperative empire" predicated on Europe's internal dynamics.[64] After having incorporated southern and then eastern European states into the EU, dealing with the next ring of neighboring states would be more challenging. Notwithstanding incipient change in the Middle East, this was an area where the EU would still often be working against, rather than with, third country governments.

The EU was widely seen as lacking a culture of assuming ultimate and full responsibility for international problems, knowing that whatever European governments' criticisms of the United States, European forms of soft engagement would not be sustainable without the security guarantees provided by Washington. Many feared a repeat in the Middle East of the Eastern European experience: despite the extensive EU engagement linked with enlargement, many liberals in this region still judged the United States to have been their strongest ally in the moment of democratic breakthrough. One nuanced study of the EU's role in Eastern European democratization concluded that Europe had been slow and initially reluctant to act, contributing mainly to underwriting democracy once the big, determinant decisions had already been taken in the region.[65]

One angle on EU foreign policy dynamics placed more emphasis on exploring the complex coexistence of identity and interest, and the role of identity formation as part of the EU's calculus of self-interest. Some agued that far from being a policy bereft of power, the EU's use of norms and values had exhibited some strategic purpose.[66] This might be seen as constituting the foundations of a European concept of power, not as a dereliction of instrumentalism. The gradually accumulating EU partnerships incorporated regularized cooperation on a wide range of subjects, with the stated aim of encouraging far-reaching economic, political, and social change in third country partner states. EU partnerships with developing regions across the world structured a similar form of holistic engagement with the goal of transformation, purporting to fashion a deeply intrusive, embedded, and proactive international influence. The use of conditionality established itself as a central element of the EU's concept of engagement, with third country agreements incorporating clauses relating to economic reform, democracy and human rights, cooperation on combating illegal migration, the readmission of migrants, and counterterrorism cooperation. Approximation by stealth and politicosocial "surveillance" were the leitmotifs of this intensely European form of strategic engagement.[67] For Chris Patten, this took European policies far beyond mere "liberal mush."[68]

The EU could then be seen as inching toward a concept of transformative power. This was reducible to neither hard nor merely soft power, but sought to cut across this routine dichotomy in embracing a more comprehensive conjunction of material policy instruments, long-term inducements, and cognitive identity formation. A commonly forwarded view was that the United States remained more inclined than the EU to focus primarily on the symptoms rather than the causes of terrorism and international instability.[69] US forms of engagement were often seen as more sporadic, less institutionalized, and less consistent, aiming at particular problems only when their symptoms assumed urgency. Self-styled neoliberals in the United States berated the Bush administration "neocons" for exhibiting too general a predisposition toward direct social engineering, and for adhering to such an instrumental perspective on political reform that they were disinclined actually to follow through on democracy promotion in any sustained or comprehensive fashion.[70] Rather than revealing the EU's marginality to overwhelming US power, the post-9/11 environment could be interpreted as showing the real problem to be US *weakness*—this being reflected in Washington's inability to secure support from others for aspects of its new security agenda. Against this background, the question arose of whether a European approach to international relations could itself be uniquely suited to the aim of assisting a fundamental transformation of Middle Eastern politics and societies (in a way that recognized the necessarily primary role of domestic actors in any such change), or whether the familiar tensions and lowest common denominator dynamics of EU foreign policy would predominate as post-9/11 strategies took shape.

Challenges for European Policy in the Middle East

This range of issues provides the backdrop for the analysis of European Middle Eastern policies developed in this book. With the apparent reassessment of EU approaches to security after 9/11 and in response to political developments in the Middle East, issues of both political will and capacity presented themselves.

A first set of questions related to political will. How far did approaches toward the Middle East really change after 9/11? The potential strategic value of democratization, in providing for the more peaceable articulation of interests and compromise, was a well-entrenched point of agreement among many analysts by the end of the 1990s. But, as pointed out, doubts remained that the nature of political regimes was really a prime determinant of international difficulties. European statements sometimes claimed to enunciate a strategy that fell between the two extremes of, on the one hand, seeing political reform as inevitable panacea and, on the other hand, seeing in democratization only a danger of more radical governments assuming power. As the concrete substance of European strategies in the Middle East evolved, it became necessary to ascertain what in practice was the balance struck between these extremes. Precisely what form of change did European governments seek to encourage? Some advocated improved respect for basic rights as a means of actually helping to head off the uncertainties of regime change and full democratization, in a context of Islam's deepening hold on the region.[71] Did this view find an echo in European approaches, or were efforts to encourage reform in the Middle East more far-reaching? Did European policy promote no more than a very limited degree of political liberalization? Were European governments more or less equivocal than Washington that traditional policies toward the Middle East really did have to change? Was it really the case that the EU focused effectively on the underlying root causes of terrorism in a more sophisticated and less knee-jerk fashion than the United States? Was the EU able to combine a long-term and genuinely transformative engagement with interjections aimed at securing more direct, short-term strategic results, on issues such as WMD proliferation, the Middle East peace process, and energy supply guarantees?

As outlined above, variation between Middle Eastern states increased, with reform opportunities emerging in some states but more intense obstacles persisting in other countries. This raised the question of whether the EU was able to elaborate policies capable of both assisting incipient reform dynamics and pressing to temper resistance to liberalization. Were the variations in Middle East reform processes adequately reflected in European policies, and in what way did the EU seek—if at all—to approach the very precise challenges and characteristics of Middle Eastern politics? In light of the account offered in this chapter, it is necessary to explore whether the EU sought adequately to address the subtleties of reform dynamics in different places in the Middle East or whether an inappropriately uniform approach was applied across the region.

A second set of issues touched on the EU's capacity to react to and influence political trends in the Middle East. It was notable that new US policy initiatives attracted significant attention, with European strategies seeming to have adopted an increasingly secondary role: was EU influence really so marginal as this implied?[72] While the EU complained about US heavy-handedness, it appeared to many that the stated US commitment to democracy promotion in the Middle East did foster debate in the region in a way that the EU's longer-standing discourse and presence singularly failed to do. Others insisted that the United States' lack of credibility in the region afforded European purchase greater legitimacy and potential. But was the EU's internal model of identity formation really able to be used effectively as an external instrument on its immediate periphery? Did the EU cleverly and surreptitiously weave itself into the fabric of Middle Eastern societies to affect profound cognitive change, or did European forms of engagement merely soak up differences and indulge illiberalism? If the EU failed to attain the political clout merited by its aid and trade presence, and if economic and social engagement failed to transmit themselves into effective political change, it was necessary to explain and assess the effect of these blockages.

The book explores these questions through a detailed analysis of the policies followed by the European Union in different parts of the Middle East since 9/11. Successive chapters chart policy developments:

- in Iraq, as the EU struggled to move beyond the divisions over military invasion, through the transfer of formal sovereignty to an Iraqi government, toward an effort to play some degree of role in the country's political and economic reconstruction
- in Iran, as the EU's policy of engagement encountered problems, negotiations over nuclear activities intensified, and conservatives reasserted their pre-eminence in Iranian politics
- in the Maghreb and Mashreq, as the Euro-Mediterranean Partnership failed to deliver on its political objectives, but where the EU's presence and influence deepened to a greater extent than in other parts of the Middle East
- in Palestine, as the EU developed its most notable institution-building program while seeking to contend with the effects of the new intifada, but struggled to mitigate either the undermining or backsliding from democracy of the Palestinian Authority
- in the countries of the Gulf Cooperation Council, along with Yemen, as the EU tried after 9/11 to reverse a legacy of limited political engagement, and as countries such as Saudi Arabia presented new challenges in terms of security, energy supply, and political change
- in Turkey, as debates over accession to the EU evolved and the entwining of Turkish and European politics become more marked, leading to the opening of entry talks with Ankara in October 2005.

Drawing from these case studies, the book's conclusion elucidates a number of key findings: the nuanced impact of 9/11 on European strategy, relative to trends specific to different national contexts in the Middle East; the extent to which efforts to promote political change became more notable, but were not the most strongly intensified area of EU policy after 2001; the emergence of significant variation between different parts of the Middle East, in terms of both the general level of European commitment and the types of strategy employed; the way in which strategic competition with the United States colored European approaches to issues of political reform; and the contrasting balance between European governments' national policies and EU-level instruments in different areas of the Middle East. The conclusion in this sense provides an overview of how the changing nature of political challenges in the Middle East sheds new light on the EU's reactive capacity as an international actor, suggesting qualification to some of the assumptions commonly made about European foreign policy.

Notes

1. As evidenced in a survey of European policymakers, Kirchner and Sperling, "The New Security Threats," p. 437. On the gathering "mini arms race" in the region, see M. El Baradei and J. Rutplat, "Time to Act on Middle East Arms," *Financial Times,* 2 February 2004.

2. The case studies presented in the book draw information from over one hundred interviews with European policymakers in the European Commission, European Council, and European Parliament; and representatives of the governments of Denmark, France, Germany, Italy, the Netherlands, Spain, Sweden, and the UK, based both in European capitals and in the Middle East. These interviews were carried out on condition of anonymity and are thus not cited individually.

3. Hinnebusch, *The International Politics.*

4. Enhali and Adda, "State and Islamism," pp. 66–76.

5. Hafez, *Why Muslims Rebel.*

6. United Nations, *Arab Human Development Report 2002,* chapter 10; United Nations, *Arab Human Development Report 2004.*

7. Barber, "Democracy and Terror."

8. Powell, "A Long, Hard Campaign," p. 51.

9. www.whitehouse.gov/news/release/2003/11/20031106-2.html.

10. Speech, *European Commission Weekly News Digest,* 14–20 July 2003.

11. Press conference with President Bush, London, 20 November 2003.

12. Mansion House speech, November 2004.

13. *Financial Times,* 25 March 2004, p. 13.

14. *Le Monde,* 2 March 2005.

15. Council on Foreign Relations, *In Support of Arab Democracy,* appendix F, p. 65.

16. US Department of State, *The National Security Strategy.*

17. Youngs, *Survey of European Democracy Promotion Policies 2000–2006.*

18. Ministère des Affaires Etrangères, *Pour une Gouvernance Démocratique.*

19. Council of the European Union, *European Security Strategy,* p. 11.

20. Commission of the European Communities, *Strengthening the EU's Relations.*

21. Commission of the European Communities, *EIDHR Programming Document 2005–2006,* C(2004)4474.

22. Carothers and Ottaway, "Middle East Democracy"; Gause, "How to Reform Saudi Arabia."

23. Hobsbawm, "Spreading Democracy."

24. Roy, "Islam in the West."

25. Youngs, "Democracy and Security in the Middle East."

26. Brumberg and Diamond, "Introduction."

27. Ibrahim, "Reviving Middle Eastern Liberalism," pp. 9–10.

28. World Values Survey 2001–2005.

29. Springborg, *Multiple Candidate Elections in Egypt.*

30. Brumberg, "Liberalization Versus Democratization."
31. Schnabel, "Democratization and Peacebuilding," p. 36.
32. Bellin, "The Political-Economic Conundrum," p. 10.
33. Burgat, *Face to Face with Political Islam,* p. xiv.
34. International Crisis Group, *Islamism in North Africa,* p. 2.
35. Tessler, "The Influence of Islam."
36. Lewis, *The Crisis of Islam,* p. 21.
37. Fuller, "Islamists in the Arab World."
38. El-Affendi, "The Elusive Reformation," p. 35.
39. Hawthorne, "Middle Eastern Democracy," p. 13.
40. A. Hamzawy, "The Tortuous Path of Arab Democracy," *Daily Star,* 2 April 2005.
41. Roy, *The Failure of Political Islam,* p. 195.
42. International Crisis Group, *Islamism in North Africa,* p. 14.
43. Kepel, *Bad Moon Rising,* p. 17; Kepel, *Jihad.*
44. Noyon, *Islam, Politics and Pluralism,* p. 28.
45. United Nations, *Arab Human Development Report 2003,* pp. 31–32.
46. For overview, see Dosenrode and Stubkjaer, *The European Union and the Middle East,* pp. 85–103.
47. Leveau, "France's Arab Policy," p. 14.
48. Monar, "Institutional Constraints," p. 229.
49. On the latter, see Griegerich and Wallace, "Not Such a Soft Power," pp. 163–182.
50. White, *Understanding European Foreign Policy.*
51. Ginsberg, *The European Union.*
52. Smith, "Toward a Theory," pp. 740–758.
53. Everts, *Shaping a Credible European,* p. 5.
54. C. Bildt, "The Middle East: Fault Line in a Transatlantic Rift," *Financial Times,* 29 April 2003.
55. Fukuyama, "The US vs. the Rest," pp. 8–24.
56. Manners and Whitman, "The 'Difference Engine,'" pp. 380–404; Diez, "Constructing the Self," pp. 613–636.
57. Smith, "The EU, Human Rights."
58. Noutcheva et al., "Europeanization and Secessionist Conflicts," p. 26.
59. Checkel, "Why Comply?" pp. 553–588.
60. Tonra and Christiansen, "The Study of European Union Foreign Policy," p. 8.
61. Sedelmeier, "Collective Identity," p. 131.
62. *The Economist,* 13 March 2004, p. 48.
63. Kagan, *Of Paradise and Power,* pp. 3, 5, and 58.
64. Cooper, *The Breaking of Nations,* pp. 62, 78, and 160.
65. Kubicek, *The European Union,* see concluding chapter by Kubicek.
66. Schimmelfennig, "The Community Trap"; Matlary, *Intervention for Human Rights.*
67. Leonard, *Why Europe Will Run the 21st Century.*
68. Patten, "Engagement Is Not Liberal Mush," pp. 36–38.
69. Booth and Dunne, "Worlds in Collision," p. 18.

70. R. Asmus and K. Pollack, "The NeoLiberal Take on the Middle East," *Washington Post,* 22 July 2003.

71. Indyk, "Back to the Bazaar"; Norton, "Political Reform in the Middle East"; Sarsar, "Can Democracy Prevail?" p. 47; Langhor, "An Exit for Arab Autocracy," pp. 116–122.

72. Among the considerable number of works on changes to US policy, examples include: Khan, "Prospects for Muslim Democracy," pp. 79–89, which highlights the United States' lack of credibility in conveying a democratic message to the region; Takeyh, "Uncle Sam in the Arab Street," pp. 45–51, which focuses on the short-term costs to US interests of a democracy promotion effort, but sees such a strategy as desirable over the longer term; and Cofmann Wittes, "The Promise of Arab Liberalism," pp. 61–76, which reveals the limited substance of US democracy efforts under the Middle East Partnership Initiative.

2

Iraq: Europe's Nemesis

The most prominent Middle Eastern issue on the international agenda was, of course, one whose direct link to 9/11 European governments rejected. By the beginning of 2006, nearly three years after the US-led toppling of the Saddam Hussein regime, Iraq remained wracked by insurgent violence, while making halting progress toward sovereign and democratic government. The formal transfer of sovereignty from the occupying Coalition Provisional Authority (CPA) to an interim Iraqi government took place in June 2004; elections in January 2005 produced a transitional Shia-led administration; and after an extended period of negotiation, in May 2005 a government was formed that shared out key positions between Shia, Sunni, and Kurdish representatives. In October 2005, after further protracted interethnic negotiation, agreement was reached on a new constitution, which won popular assent in a referendum. Elections in December 2005 paved the way for the formation of a new administration, again delicately sharing out portfolios between Iraq's three main sectarian groups. Quite apart from the continuing violence, the foundations of Iraq's incipient democracy remained fragile: much basic state-institutional capacity was absent; Iraqi security forces were insufficiently resourced and trained; civil society and political parties were fragmented largely along sectarian lines, with few national-level organizations having emerged; and the extent of Kurdish pressure for increased autonomy was a persistent source of tension. Beyond the celebration of Iraq's installing a democratically elected government, the country looked no less benighted—if for different reasons—than it had been under Saddam Hussein's rule.

The purpose of this chapter is not to offer an account of the military invasion of Iraq, the WMD-related debates that preceded it, or the Western intelligence failings that subsequently emerged. Exhaustive coverage has been given to these issues and to debates over the rights and wrongs of the UK-US invasion that took place in March and April 2003. Rather, the purpose here is to chronicle principally the evolution of European positions in relation to Iraq's postinvasion policy challenges. The chapter offers an account of European diplomacy in the run-up to the transfer of sovereignty in June 2004; of the EU's cautious and qualified moves toward greater engagement after Iraq's January 2005 elections; and of the concrete European initiatives undertaken in relation to security issues and Iraq's economic and political reconstruction. This exposition reveals the inability of both the European governments that opposed the invasion and those that participated in the US-led coalition to exert any meaningful influence on the direction of US policy. It also uncovers the paucity of European deliberations and policy initiatives pertinent to the very specific dilemmas conditioning Iraq's postinvasion democratic development, reflecting a persistent tendency to approach Iraq through the lens of the transatlantic relationship. The chapter outlines how new European initiatives, introduced during 2004 and 2005, fell short of constituting a comprehensive and committed EU strategy toward Iraq.

Containment Between the Wars

During the 1990s a philosophy of containment prevailed in European policies toward Iraq. The conditions imposed on Iraq after the 1991 Gulf War related to the cessation of weapons development and specifically excluded issues of internal political reform and human rights improvements.[1] European governments were widely judged to be intent on avoiding abrupt regime change that would unleash instability and risk Iraq fracturing into three—with, it was feared, the southern Shiite region seeking to align itself with Iran, and with Iraqi Kurds in the north looking toward an alliance with Turkish Kurds. Whatever their other differences with the United States, European governments adhered to this logic as much as Washington. Aid flows remained limited, with Iraq receiving a total of only $122 million in 2001—even if it was the European donor community that provided nearly all this basic humanitarian assistance, with Iraq's biggest aid donations coming from Germany, Britain, Norway, the Netherlands, the European Commission, and Sweden.

US policy was initially also based on containment, with US forces stepping away from backing the 1993 Shia uprising against Saddam. Divisions with Europe began to appear, however, when the Clinton administration passed the Iraq Liberation Act in 1998; released $100 million of support for Iraqi opposition groups, principally the Iraqi National Congress; and stepped up direct operational military support for opposition forces in the late 1990s.[2] The terrorist attacks of 11 September 2001 galvanized what was an already present desire within the Bush administration to focus in a more concerted fashion on regime change; significantly, this meant that even before the dramatic divisions that developed over military intervention, European governments had begun to bridle at intensified US efforts to boost and organize anti-Saddam political forces. European donors openly expressed concern over US support for exiled opposition figures lacking any local base or support in Iraq. A December 2002 conference of leading exiles had to be moved from Brussels to London due to European states' caution.

European unity also gradually dwindled as the 1990s progressed. One senior Common Foreign and Security Policy official lamented that on Iraq there had been only "intermittent superficial discussions and the occasional minimalist declaration."[3] Member states feared that Iraq would "break the back" of the incipient CFSP, and therefore expressly kept it outside this forum. Not only were there growing differences between European governments, but positions were discussed first in the UN rather than EU forums.

Differences emerged on the lifting of sanctions. French companies visited Iraq, preparing themselves for the possible lifting of sanctions; British firms were not allowed to do so. Contracts were awarded to French companies at this stage. Winning $3 billion worth of deals, France was the largest beneficiary of the UN Oil for Food program, although Paris did at the end of the decade support the United States and UK in seeking to prevent Saddam from widening the scope of exchanges permitted in return for oil exports.[4] After the fall of the Saddam regime Paris was initially more reluctant to assent to the lifting of sanctions and the disbanding of the Oil for Food program, in part as such moves would invalidate the contracts already won by French companies. French authorities were later accused of—but denied—complicity in the corruption that occurred under the

Oil for Food program, gaining cheaper oil supplies in return, it was alleged, for turning a blind eye to proceeds flowing directly into Saddam's coffers. As was later revealed, the scale of kickbacks offered under this program played a crucial role in shoring up the Baathist regime. European governments would also later admit that during the 1990s they turned a blind eye to the smuggling that they knew to be undermining the effect of sanctions.

The new Blair government did not develop any concerted democracy promotion strategy in Iraq. In the years following Labour's 1997 electoral victory there was virtually no discussion of Iraq in cabinet. In the brief military engagement of Operation Desert Fox in 1998—which took place after Saddam withdrew cooperation from UN weapons inspectors—the UK was the only European state to join the United States in carrying out bombing raids. Blair would later claim that he became seized of the need to develop a broader Iraq policy after 2001, when the impact of 9/11 was compounded by the increasing disrespect of sanctions against Iraq. However, in practice, government spokesmen acknowledged that policy was still aimed at containing, not removing, Saddam, and that post-9/11 British intelligence reported unambiguously that no link could be found between the Baathist regime and the attacks on the Twin Towers.[5] Indeed, the UK had chosen to focus more tightly on WMD, as the issue most likely to secure broad international backing and legitimacy. Most British diplomatic activity focused on elaborating UN resolution 1441—under whose provisions the United States agreed to another round of UN inspections—which the UK government saw as its main contribution to bridging the divide between the United States and European states. This resolution proved, of course, ambiguous over the question of whether further noncooperation with weapons inspectors from Saddam would automatically trigger military action. Blair argued after the invasion that he had been "uncomfortable" with the implication of resolution 1441 that cooperation on weapons inspections would have enabled Saddam to stay in power; this was, however, the only line that the prime minister judged would win support from the Labour Party.[6]

British contact with Iraqi opposition groups was sporadic, with the UK declining to offer the latter any direct support. There was, in the words of one British diplomat, no policy of "regime change for the sake of regime change." Even in the run-up to the military intervention of 2003, the UK distanced itself from active US efforts to mold opposition forces into a more coherent force.[7] Proactive UK political work was relatively limited, selective, and cautious. The Foreign Office guided the Westminster Foundation for Democracy to support the Iraq Institute for Democracy in Kurdish-controlled northern Iraq in generating ideas for democratization across Iraq. But it avoided the kind of direct political engineering increasingly typifying US initiatives at this stage. Whatever the dynamics between the UK and United States on the broad question of military intervention, on the issue of Iraq's internal politics London appeared largely passive and reactive to the Bush administration. As Chris Patten would later assert, the UK along with other coalition members "stumbled across the case for democracy when their other justifications for the war crumbled."[8]

The focus of most debate was on the differences that emerged in particular between Britain and France on the military invasion; but what was significant beyond these differences was the common prioritization, on the part of all European governments, of the WMD issue. Member states reached different conclusions on how much additional time to grant UN weapons inspectors—and different ministries within these states read different meaning into intelligence reports—but all subjugated to the WMD focus any strategy concerned with the nature of Iraq's internal political regime per se. As noted, had Saddam changed his attitude toward weapons inspections, in London, Rome, Madrid, Copenhagen, and The Hague—even if not in Washington—the focus might indeed never have shifted to Iraq's democratization.

The UK was subsequently accused of having inadequately planned, during this period, for Iraq's postconflict challenges. An interdepartmental Iraq Planning Unit was established, incorporating Foreign Office, Ministry of Defense, and Department for International Development (DfID) officials. The head of the Foreign Office recognized, however, that this was "too ad hoc" in addressing guidelines for postconflict reconstruction and drew little from lessons learned in peace support operations carried out elsewhere. Some divisions emerged between ministries, but these were not as marked or determinant as the well-publicized split between the Pentagon, the State Department, and USAID in Washington. The treasury was most skeptical of the UK channeling money though the UN, the Department for International Development most insistent on UN backing for preparing postinvasion aid projects. Britain's ambassador at the UN during this time, Jeremy Greenstock, admitted that in terms of Iraq's internal political restructuring, "there was a wider remit" in Washington than in London.[9] Whatever the true nature of postconflict planning and prognosis in London, as with the State Department's long-running Future of Iraq program, this was soon overridden by the Pentagon. Moreover, it became clear in the postinvasion period just how far the UK's participation in the US-led military action was driven personally by Tony Blair, without broad "buy-in" from Whitehall.

The Transfer of Power

After the invasion had succeeded in dislodging Saddam from power and the Coalition Provisional Authority had assumed control, perspectives on the transfer of power to a new sovereign Iraqi government shifted back and forth during 2003 and 2004. Three separate but connected issues engendered debate: the timing and pace of power transfer; the relationship between the recuperation of Iraqi sovereignty and the holding of democratic elections; and the role of the United Nations in the design and piloting of Iraq's nascent democratic process.

In the initial aftermath of military operations, US administrator Jay Garner was keen to hand over political power relatively quickly to an Iraqi administration; this objective reputedly reflected the positions of most Pentagon officials and President Bush. Replacing Garner, Paul Bremer sought to slow down these plans; he supported a merely consultative interim Iraqi council and assumed a more direct role in appointing public officials. With antipathy to CPA occupation increasing, by the end of the summer of 2003 the process was once more hastened, and the Iraqi Governing Council (IGC) was given more authority than Bremer had originally intimated. By the autumn of 2003 the notion had taken shape of transferring sovereignty to an interim Iraqi government relatively quickly, based on some form of popular consultation that would provide a degree of representativeness without having to wait for the convening of full democratic elections. The United States sought to organize representation around US-selected regional caucuses that would choose members of a national assembly. After the UN opposed such caucuses, the formally sovereign interim Iraqi government created at the end of June 2004 exhibited much continuity with the US-selected IGC and was subject to relatively limited scrutiny from a national assembly, in a context where the United States was perceived to have retained considerable political power. This shifting context dominated political strategy and was well chronicled during 2003 and 2004. But what was the European input on these issues?

As partners in the CPA, the British government took control of four governorates, three in the south and one in Kirkuk. Jeremy Greenstock, by then the UK's representative to Iraq, suggested that the whole rationale for UK involvement was precisely to assist in and have some purchase on the postconflict political process.[10] British officials exhibited some sympathy with US concerns over the risks of a precipitate transfer of power, fearing the effects of factional infighting, the lack of local parties to compete with returning exiles, and the better short-term preparedness of extremist parties. The UK shared, and indeed strongly espoused, the basic premise that a constitution was first needed, to enshrine agreement on basic political norms and procedures and to reduce the divisiveness of elections. A primary feature of British efforts was, however, to push the United States into ceding more responsibility to the UN and to agree to a clearer timetable for the end of occupation. British officials in Iraq pressed Bremer to widen the authority of the IGC and argued that responsibility for selecting its members should rest with the UN. In the summer of 2003, UK envoy John Sawers was advocating elections by mid-2004 and stressing the need for "an Iraqi led timetable for the constitution"—at a time when Colin Powell was already suggesting that full elections would be inadvisable before 2005.[11]

The UK declared itself particularly uneasy with Pentagon "minimalists" apparently intent on simply placing US-backed figures in power.[12] London was increasingly exasperated that the Pentagon and State Department were backing their own competing client groups, the Iraqi National Congress and Iraqi National Accord, respectively—although it was not completely averse to supporting its own favored figures, such as UK-based Shia moderate Abdul Majid Al-Khoei. UK officials acknowledged that there was no significant difference with the United States over the policy of de-Baathification, if only on the practical judgment that many Baathists had themselves begun to melt away and were unwilling to engage with the CPA. However, a modest difference lay in the UK's greater willingness to include lower-ranking Baathists within municipal administrations. At the local level, UK officials perceived themselves as more flexible than their US counterparts in using local "notables" to organize broadly representative structures; a declared UK priority was to focus on the practical delivery of services rather than pristine democratic procedure. Indeed, military officials occasionally stepped in to allocate competences where they deemed the organization of local elections to be going awry.[13] As the UK's senior representative in the south of Iraq suggested, "participation" should be the immediate aim rather than democracy. Broadly representative bodies covering relatively mundane technocratic issues could help build trust by incorporating traditionally competing groups to discuss issues of daily relevance over which communal cooperation was required.

Other European views were more unreservedly focused on hastening the US departure from Iraq. Europeans were perhaps most vocal in their criticism of de-Baathification policies. A common admonishment heard from European chancelleries was that the CPA had been too ready to dissolve state institutions and isolate the very national-level officials who did think of themselves as Iraqis. This contrasted with Europeans' criticism of the United States for *not* sufficiently clearing away "old guard" elites after its other military interventions.[14] The Europeans' preference was for the UN to assume full control and for elections to be held in the short term. By August 2003 President Chirac was calling for a transfer of power "without delay."[15] The immediate formal transfer of power, in Chirac's vision, would then be followed six to nine months later by a full transfer of substantive policymaking power, following elections.[16] French foreign minister Dominique de Villepin insisted that elections be held by the spring of 2004. The French and other governments were reluctant to back UN involvement that served merely to endorse a US-designed process—for example, by the UN simply selecting names to an interim administration whose whole authority was already set by the United States. While in Kosovo the French had been one of the strongest supporters of a postconflict period of joint administration between the UN and local representatives, in Iraq they opposed such an option, believing that the UN would be unable to lever genuine autonomy from the United States. Most Europeans other than the UK backed a division of labor according to which the CPA would confine itself to law and order issues, the UN would take charge of the political transition, and the Governing Council would assume full control of day-to-day issues.[17] The primary aim of ousting the United States was undisguised; elsewhere in the world the French were known to be firm supporters of gradual democratization, but in Iraq they led the charge for rapid elections. In their advocacy of quick elections the French also found themselves pushing against the views of the IGC. Most Europeans were also somewhat more interested to see the UN assume a greater role than was the UN itself—while the UN, moreover, did not appear to enjoy unmitigated legitimacy among ordinary Iraqis.

The British government frequently presented itself as attempting to mediate between the US and European governments. While pressing the United States into a firmer commitment to expedite the transfer of sovereignty, the UK argued that the Franco-German call for a tightly fixed timetable was too rigid and failed to mesh with fast-changing conditions on the ground in Iraq. Part of the British aim in pushing for a primary UN role was to win European support for the internationalization of reconstruction efforts. A UN resolution eventually won passage that asked the IGC to produce a timetable for elections by 15 December 2003. Agreement emerged after France and Germany dropped their insistence on an immediate transfer of sovereignty in return for tighter UN control over the timetable for the transfer of power—although both governments subsequently claimed they were in fact not satisfied and that this agreement would not suffice for them to offer any concrete positive support to the political process.

After the UK had worked hard to push the United States into speeding up the political process, positions changed as 2004 progressed. Concern grew within the British government over the transfer of power being, in the words of one diplomat, "shoehorned" into a US domestic timetable. A particularly strong criticism was that the Bush administration's decision to bring forward to June 2004 the formal transfer of sovereignty risked cutting across long-term, grassroots aid programs being funded by the UK in the south. British officials became more frustrated that, whatever justifiable grounds there might be for not rushing into elections, little was being done in practical terms to make elections more feasible—for example, in exploring the use of existing ration cards to make practicable some form of cursory identification. It was perceived that it rather suited Bush not to allow for the possibility of a Shia victory in a genuinely democratic Iraqi election during the United States presidential campaign. Ambivalent toward the concept of US-selected caucuses, the UK pressed in favor of the UN's proposed system of more open "cascading caucuses," in which participatory community meetings would themselves select representatives up to each successive level of administration. Focusing on such local-level forums would, it was argued, provide legitimacy-strengthening participation while "avoiding the uncertainties of democracy." In this sense, "manipulated indirect elections" would provide the best compromise prior to full democratization in 2005.

The UK saw another of its roles as mediating between the United States and the UN to get the latter involved in bringing influential Shia cleric Grand Ayatollah Ali al-Sistani into the process of sovereignty transfer.[18] UK officials acknowledged that they expended much negotiating capital pressing the United States to allow the UN to pronounce (unfavorably) on the feasibility of elections—this being seen as necessary to convince Sistani to drop his insistence on immediate elections. The UK worked through intermediaries to push a compromise with Sistani in which there would be some form of elected representation, but with Shias accepting a lower percentage on the assembly than merited by their demographic dominance, in order to placate Kurds and Sunnis.

The UN opined in February 2004 against both caucuses and interim elections, enabling a deal whereby Sistani accepted a delay to elections and the United States dropped its proposed system of caucuses. The UK pushed for UN primacy in selecting the interim Iraqi government; this caused increasing tension with Paul Bremer, who was engaged in drawing up the United States' own list of preferred names. The perception that the United States remained intent on micromanaging the political process was cited by many in explanation of the escalation in violence after April 2004. British diplomats professed irritation with the US effort to preempt the handover of formal sovereignty in June 2004 by pushing through a host of decisions prior to end of June. Notwithstanding these differences, the UK accepted that the interim government could have only limited powers, mainly to prepare for the transfer to a fully elected government; otherwise it would itself be seen as lacking legitimacy. In short, British officials claimed that they were pushing the United States on some of the very issues that had become a source of concern among the wider international community—although it appeared that the UK then invariably followed lines along which the United States showed little willingness to compromise. On these detailed political strategies, one senior US official in Iraq lamented that the British presence had been a mere "adornment" and a "humiliating" experience for routinely ignored UK officials.

The French government insisted that the pushing back of elections to 2005 should not delay the transfer of sovereignty. According to de Villepin, sovereignty had to be transferred in "accelerated" fashion, and whether or not "the process is complete."[19] The French were by this stage pushing the notion of a "national conference" of the type sponsored by France across francophone Africa as a preparatory mechanism to democratic transition, to serve as the basis for a national unity administration until 2005 elections. The French vision was of a *loya jirga* equivalent, a broad conference selecting an interim government, a "national roundtable" exploring a range of possible arrangements for post-June. As 30 June approached, France warned that there must, in the words of one diplomat, be a "radical rupture," not a situation where the United States simply selected a slightly expanded IGC. The need was for an Iraqi "strongman" to take over quickly, not a gradual CPA-mediated, bottom-up development of democracy. In debates at the UN, the French pressed for a predetermined timetable for CPA withdrawal, while German views became a little more accommodating. The delays to elections were still cited by most Europeans as grounds for not engaging more systematically on questions of political process. Reports from French sources themselves revealed that this reluctance was increasingly blackening French and other European states' credibility within Iraq.[20]

Far from narrowing transatlantic differences, the formal transfer of sovereignty to an interim Iraqi government at the end of June 2004 seemed to open a further round of European criticism. With the French government again assuming its role as lead protagonist, Europeans complained that the interim Iraqi government lacked anything close to full sovereignty and that, contrary to UN special envoy Lakhdar Brahimi's aims, it resembled in large measure a continuation of the US-appointed IGC. (One US adviser held the opposite view, that Brahimi had obtained most of the personnel he had sought.)[21] One common fear was that the deal had ensured the worst of both worlds: a loss of international control without any concomitant increase in governmental legitimacy. The French model had been for a national conference to select a government; ultimately, such a gathering was called after the government had been selected and was accorded only a limited role. In addition, Europeans pointed to the very limited powers of the constitutive assembly set up to monitor the interim government. The United States was criticized by one influential organization for raising unrealistic expectations in trying to sell a notion of "sovereignty" being imminently transferred;[22] yet it was precisely the advocacy of such sovereignty transfer that represented the most prominent position adopted by those European states that were not part of the coalition.

Toward Elections and European Engagement?

Notwithstanding such criticisms, in June 2004 the EU approved a new strategy paper for Iraq. This struck a more positive and constructive tone, observing that Europe had an even greater need than the United States for Iraq to succeed, not least to help stabilize Turkey—with Iraq potentially soon to be an immediate neighbor of the EU—as well as to encourage the return of the large number of Iraqi exiles in Europe. It was pointed out that engagement in the development of standards and legal frameworks familiar to European investors would be important if the latter were not to find themselves excluded from the Iraqi market. The strategy argued that the EU's own experience would enable it to play a particularly strong role in fostering processes of national reconciliation and consensus building and the development of federalism and decentralization. The new strategy committed the EU to entering into dialogue with the Iraqi government on the rebuilding of political processes; to considering security sector support; and to developing a more significant role in judicial reform and strengthening the rule of law. The EU would also use its engagement with other Middle Eastern states to push these into more constructive partnership with the new Iraqi government. The strategy suggested that the EU would invite Iraq to participate in the EU's new Strategic Partnership with the Mediterranean and Middle East; push for Iraq's entry into the WTO; and reinstall the EU's Generalized System of Preferences (GSP) trade provisions, which ceased to apply in Iraq after the Gulf War.[23] A troika meeting with the Iraqi interim government was arranged in September at the United Nations in New York.

External Relations Commissioner Chris Patten stated that the EU would now invest priority effort "to work for a better future in Iraq whatever the bitterness of past disputes."[24] The notion of working to incorporate Iraq into a regional framework was accorded particular importance and was seen as the added value of an EU contribution. Encouraging a more positive and proactive involvement on the part of Iraq's neighbors was seen as crucial to moving beyond the treatment of postconflict debates, in the words of one European diplomat, "as a transatlantic issue." In this light, Javier Solana met in Cairo with the Conference of Neighboring Countries of Iraq in September to push forward these ideas.

EU officials lamented the limited impact of this new strategy. The latter had been able to define long-term goals in a more coherent

fashion, and for the first time since the invasion, without internal differences paralyzing discussions; but short-term priorities remained
uncertain. Indeed, the strategy had expressly focused on the long-
term structure of EU-Iraq relations to avoid short-term controversies.
Member states had declared a desire to engage symbolically, through
increased visits and regular dialogue with the Iraqi government, and
the "big three" states had leaned heavily on the Commission to elaborate new strategies in this regard; but diplomats acknowledged that
governments remained "confused" over more practical involvement
on the ground in Iraq. National diplomats recognized that many key
questions had not been addressed under the strategy and that on many
of the most difficult political issues the EU continued, in the words of
one diplomat, "to put things off." A number of member states admitted
to having reined back the scope of the new strategy, concerned at the
ambitions for EU policies pressed by coalition member governments.
Diplomats opined that the strategy's main impact was to force member states for the first time into more substantive debate on Iraq's
political development. Insiders claimed that by this stage discussions
were finally beginning to move beyond the replay of familiar differences toward US policy, while acknowledging that far-reaching consensus on proactive engagement remained absent.

EU discussions focused on possible assistance for Iraq's elections. An EU "scoping mission" in September 2004 recommended this
as an area for potential European action. Germany also introduced
plans for election training in Jordan. However, many member states
were still reluctant to move forward with concrete plans and financial
commitments until it became clearer that the election timetable
would be adhered to. A number of member states complained that the
scoping mission had been precipitate and unrealistically ambitious,
pushed too heavily forward by the presidency now held by a coalition member, the Netherlands. Moreover, plans centered on only an
indirect contribution to monitoring elections. The prospect of an EU
observation mission being deployed to Iraq, let alone a more significant role in the direct organization of elections, was ruled out. On the
one hand, European governments expressed concern with the prospect of elections being delayed and thus allowing new prime minister Ayad Allawi to consolidate his hold on power—and for US influence thus to be prolonged. On the other hand, member states also
berated the United States for taking a heavy-handed approach to
security in order to "save face" and show that elections were possible
by the January deadline.

The creation of an EU envoy or special representative to Iraq and the opening of an EU office in Iraq were options advocated by some member states but still blocked by other governments. Member states still refused to engage in serious discussion of coordinated debt relief for Iraq, with France in particular resisting talk of anything over 50 percent relief. While new discussion took shape on more detailed institution-building challenges at official levels, ministerial meetings still failed to engage on these less high-profile issues. Diplomats acknowledged that Europe saw itself continuing to play a role only "at the margins." In striking contrast to elsewhere in the Middle East, there was no push from member states to ratchet up EU commitments in order to match US influence. Intimations of Iraq's inclusion in a possible wider Middle East framework were in fact not welcomed enthusiastically by the EU's Euro-Mediterranean Partnership partners, who were concerned with the prospect of European resources being diverted to Iraq.[25]

The limit of EU ambitions was to assist in ad hoc areas of peace support and institution-building work within a framework set by the UN, in large part so as not to be excluded from Iraq completely over the longer term. Any attempt to delineate a "grand vision of Iraq's politics" was eschewed within EU forums, but rather, in the words of one official, "taken as given" from the primary domestic and international players in Iraq. Amid the further Najaf Shia uprisings of August 2004, a common EU position on radical Shia leader Moqtada al-Sadr was conspicuously absent. Most European policymakers presumed themselves to be more eager than the United States to see al-Sadr incorporated into the political process, but nothing was done to influence this. Issues relating to the CPA were expressly excluded from EU discussions.

While the French supported the new EU strategy, they remained at arms' length in many discussions and events, often pointedly not turning up at many workshops and civil society initiatives. Some diplomats argued that, in its relentless focus on sovereignty transfer, the French government had found it difficult to react when sovereignty was indeed handed over in June 2004, explaining fluctuating and slightly uncertain positions in the months following the formation of the Iraqi interim government. When the Iraqi president toured European capitals in September, his visit to Paris was cancelled by the French government, reportedly in response to Allawi's swipe at France's "neutrality" on the terrorism sweeping Iraq. Rumors abounded that Paris was instrumental in the president's visit to the European Parliament also being cancelled.[26] Spain's new Socialist government declared a "hands-off" policy toward Iraq; the circumstances of the March elections in Spain (immediately after the Atocha bombings) rendered this a highly controversial topic domestically.

The caution in engaging on overtly political issues was also presented as a form of conditionality. After some internal discussion it was decided that the EU would offer Iraq a somewhat comprehensive agreement that would require approximation to democratic and human rights norms over the medium term, rather than a relatively symbolic trade and cooperation agreement that could be concluded immediately. European governments complained of Allawi's autocratic style, the government's reintroduction of the death penalty, and the suppression of media freedoms during the summer of 2004. One aim of bringing Iraq into the same network of standards and conditionalities applying to other states was to address these concerns. Significantly, those states least keen on EU political conditionality elsewhere in the Middle East were most interested in its being applied in Iraq. For many, this appeared to be the wisest approach, as security continued to deteriorate: the EU setting out its stall, offering partnership in the long term, while nudging Iraq along the path of democracy by clarifying the reforms expected for this to materialize.

Further European criticism was directed at the Iraqi national conference that took place in August 2004, and from which 1,300 delegates selected a 100-member assembly dominated by the bigger parties represented in the government.[27] The EU inched slowly forward, introducing plans at a 5 November meeting to "prepare the ground" for talks with the Iraqi government on a trade and cooperation agreement, and looking at ways of providing the technical capacity that would enable Iraq to administer its current GSP trade provisions with the EU. Complaints arose from some member states that the incentives offered to Iraq were perceived to be extremely limited—trade preferences, when Iraq was not exporting, and involvement in the EU's strategic partnership with the Middle East, which was itself devoid of content. An issue of additional tension emerged in relation to the conference that gathered Iraq's neighboring states and other members of the international community in Cairo in November: France pushed for insurgent groups to be invited to this event, in opposition to Washington.

As the focus gradually switched to preparations for the January elections and debate centered on the prospect of Sunnis boycotting these elections, the European Commission opined that even partial, imperfect elections would be preferable to delay.[28] In the context of the increasingly violent insurgency, such thinking was not entirely different from UK-US reasoning that the holding of elections, even if not under ideal conditions, would represent a large step toward departure from Iraq; in the December 2004 words of Tony Blair, "The exit strategy is a democratic Iraq." There were European criticisms that the United States looked set to ensure that the elections produced a coalition dominated by the "safe" parties already included in the interim administration. But the EU was also eager for elections to take place as soon as possible. The EU committed €31 million to support the elections, but in the form of assistance for the UN and the training of Iraqi observers, not the deployment of a standard EU electoral mission.

The elections prompted further European deliberation. Diplomats suggested that the January polls had increased the willingness of many member states to contemplate more concrete forms of engagement and cooperation. In February, ministers committed themselves to opening a systematic political dialogue with the new Iraq government and announced the launch of EUJUST, a new EU integrated rule of law mission. Agreement was at this stage reached on the opening of an EU delegation in Iraq. The EU agreed to join with the United States in cosponsoring an international conference on Iraq, which took place in June 2005. In the run-up to this conference, Javier Solana suggested that "the international consensus that has eluded us in Iraq is now in place." During this period a particular European concern was with strengthening Sunni participation in the new Iraqi administration; ministers called for a "genuine national dialogue" and the inclusion of all sectors of society in the political process. Protracted negotiations among Iraqi factions delayed the formation of a government until May, with many members of the victorious Shia alliance reluctant to cede key posts to Baath-linked Sunnis. The EU sought to encourage new prime minister Ibrahim al-Jafari to grant significant Sunni representation, to a degree that compensated for the wide-ranging Sunni boycott of the elections. Jafari agreed that this was desirable but saw in international pressure a vision of power sharing that would "compromise parliamentary democracy."[29] European policymakers claimed that they had insisted on an increased number of Sunni seats on the constitutional drafting committee as quid pro quo for talk of new engagement; the United States had also allegedly pressed for the number of Sunnis included in the 55-member parliamentary committee responsible for drafting the new constitution to be increased from two to fifteen.[30] When Sunni representatives rejected the draft constitution at the end of August 2005, the EU and the United States intervened in similar fashion to persuade Shia and Kurdish representatives to cede greater political influence to the Sunni community. Two other issues identified as distinctive European concerns were broadening the security focus away from terrorist attacks toward low-level crime, and ensuring that the trials of former regime members followed the "due process of justice."[31]

If European positions on the EU's general level of engagement in Iraq were in a process of evolution, a degree of familiar reticence remained. Some EU diplomats lamented that French representation at the June conference and a range of other discussions remained either low-level or absent. It was widely agreed that the June conference was valuable primarily in terms of symbolizing a new European willingness to reduce tensions with the United States, but that it was limited in concrete substance. Despite UK pressure, the decision was taken not to send an EU electoral mission to monitor the December 2005 elections; reported manipulation in these elections complicated the subsequent formation of a government. Conversely, in December 2005 the EU did finally agree to open trade talks with Iraq and to set in motion procedures for opening the EU delegation in Baghdad. It was reported that the UK government had provided logistical support for the (unsuccessful) campaign headed by Ayad Allawi—seen as the main hope for cross-sectarian, secular politics in Iraq[32]—but in general the European presence in and around the electoral process was negligible. After the December elections there were European calls for the formation of a national unity government, closely echoing US statements.

Compounding the general political ambivalence on the part of many European donors, no clear state-building strategy took shape. European governments and the EU institutions criticized the United States for leading Iraq toward a system of ethnofederalism and of "undoing the Iraqi nation" in its approach toward ethnicity.[33] But no proactive strategy was elaborated aimed at stemming the drift toward ethnically based politics or actually facilitating any alternative political model. There was no European engagement with or support for secular-ideological parties, cross-cutting in terms of their ethnic makeup. No policy initiatives or diplomatic engagement took shape on a range of political issues: the strengthening of relatively secular Shia parties as alternatives to the Iran-based Supreme Council for Islamic Revolution in Iraq (SCIRI); the development of a secular Sunni party, to fill the gap left by the Baath party; cooperation with other secular, national parties, like the Iraqi Communist Party; or the design of an electoral system best able to mitigate ethnic exclusivity. Within European policymaking circles there was still a striking and conspicuous absence of detailed strategy relating to the types of political model most appropriate for Iraq, reflecting a judgment that EU policy could have little bearing on such debates.

Security Roles

Concerns were, of course, most acutely dominated by the issue of security. In the aftermath of Saddam's overthrow, it quickly became apparent to observers that the most serious barriers to building Iraqi democracy were related directly or indirectly to security.[34] A commonly expressed European view was that the United States had focused too much on designing a political system around its favored exiles and consequently initially failed to think through its strategy for dealing with the more urgent law and order imperatives. The most immediate spillover from divisions relating to the invasion was the limited European willingness to commit troops to assist with postconflict security challenges. In addition to the UK's 11,000 men, by mid-2003 eight other European states were contributing just over 6,000 troops—2,800 from Italy, 1,300 from Spain, 2,400 from Poland, plus a smaller number from Denmark, the Netherlands, Bulgaria, the Czech Republic, and Norway. These contributions represented relatively modest shares of an overall coalition deployment of 155,000 troops, itself proportionately a far more limited force than had been present in the Balkans. (It was estimated that scaling up the Balkans deployment numbers on a comparable basis to account for Iraq's greater size would have required a mission of half a million troops.)

Much focus was of course on the absence of French and German troop commitments. In April 2003, French defense minister Noelle Lenoir referred imprecisely to the possibility of an EU rapid reaction force being deployed to Iraq, but President Chirac quickly reined her back.[35] Initially France also demonstrated a willingness to contemplate

NATO involvement, as a means of defusing tension with the United States and a possible means of linking the assembly of a multi-national force to UN political primacy.[36] Official sources claimed that France did begin to consider unblocking some form of European engagement because of its growing isolation within the EU, where a majority of member states claimed that they did genuinely want to contribute more positively toward security challenges.[37]

A significant EU force failed to materialize, however. The lack of European unity was painfully apparent at the Thessaloniki summit in June 2003, which after acrimonious debate was unable to welcome the fact that some member states were contributing to efforts to improve security and stability in Iraq. Under the terms of a defense agreement with Poland, the German government delayed the latter's assumption of command over one of the military zones carved out by the United States. The influence of the Iraqi conflict on internal European security debates was greater than the European impact on Iraq. It was largely in response to events in Iraq that in April 2003 France, Germany, Belgium, and Luxembourg met to devise plans for a separate EU military command, pointedly crossing one of the most significant red lines drawn by the UK in its conversion to a European Security and Defence Policy.

Increasingly, the issue became less one of massively strengthening European troop deployments and more one of preserving those contributions that had been made. Most conspicuously, the change of government in Spain in March 2004 led to the withdrawal of Spanish troops. When the United States pleaded for additional troop commitments after the April 2004 Shia uprising, only the UK responded positively. By June 2004, even the British government had reconsidered, deciding to send additional troops to Afghanistan rather than Iraq. In accounting for their increasing uncertainty over sustaining troop commitments, several European states cited what they judged to be US heavy-handedness in responding to the lynching of US civilian contractors and the renewed violence triggered in April 2004. The United States itself was increasingly adamant that it was less interested in securing European troop commitments than in having Turkish, Pakistani, and other Muslim forces present in Iraq. Demonstrating the frequent tension between security aims and the transfer of sovereignty, it was the increasingly assertive Iraqi Governing Council that blocked Paul Bremer's efforts to negotiate a role for Turkish troops. In this skirmish, noncoalition European governments leaned on Turkey not to send troops, with some accused by Turkish officials of making threatening linkages to Turkey's EU accession prospects.

Europeans were themselves susceptible to Iraqi assertiveness; some members of the IGC discounted the notion of European troops offsetting the US military and suggested that an EU military presence would be as problematic as the US occupation. Nor did the June 2004 transfer of formal sovereignty suffice to depoliticize European positions on security strategies. While declaring an unwillingness to commit troops themselves, several European governments pushed for UN language that would ensure greater operational autonomy from the United States for any prospective multinational force. This issue was fudged in UN Security Council resolution 1546, but it was significant that this was another issue on which the UK government confronted the United States and sought to mediate between Washington and European capitals, in particular with a view to gaining Paris's assent to the resolution. London also distanced itself from US insistence that US and British ambassadors have a formal role in Iraq's posttransfer security council.

These debates also filtered into European approaches toward the reconstituting and preparation of Iraqi security forces. While urging a rapid end to CPA occupation, nonparticipating European governments berated the United States for speeding up its army training programs in a way that overlooked human rights issues. The US moves at the end of 2003 to bring forward the development of a 40,000-strong Iraqi army from three years to one year were criticized and not supported in any concrete fashion by the majority of European governments. The British government also admitted that on human rights standards in the Iraqi army there was "some haste creeping in." The UK saw its distinctive emphasis in the security sector as being to encourage Sunni recruitment to the national army, judging itself to enjoy greater legitimacy than the United States in drawing disgruntled Sunnis away from the resistance into official security and intelligence roles. Senior UK officials insisted they had expended considerable effort in pushing the United States to extend and speed up the loosening of the ban on Baathists participating in the security forces.[38] Also deemed necessary to complement the US concentration on practical immediate security provision, UK efforts and resources in 2004 turned to the much-delayed creation of a multiethnic defense ministry. While UK advisers were dispatched to work on this challenge,

British officials recognized that the focus on the defense ministry had been tardy—the latter being the last governmental department established—and that by 2004 broadly legitimate civilian-dominated defense policy making was "still a long way off." Indeed, the precise detailed content of UK funded projects revealed a strong orientation in security sector reform toward quantitative rather than qualitative aspects, with the provision of equipment, hardware, and additional capacity prevailing over the focus on developing mechanisms of civilian control.

There was initially some nuanced difference between the US and European forces present in Iraq on the issue of militia forces. The United States adopted a relatively hard line, ordering the dissolution of all militia forces—with the exception of the Kurdish *peshmergas*—although in practice these strictures were not followed as irregular forces were increasingly relied upon to help suppress the insurgency. European positions were from the outset less clear-cut. UK and other European officials found it difficult to engage with Shia paramilitaries in the south but were reluctant to push hard to disband these groups, arguing this would be a sensible objective only in the long term. The danger of the Iraq Civilian Defense Corps becoming a permanent quasi-military presence was recognized, but the UK was keen to benefit from the additional capacity this provided in the short term. European forces were reported to be engaged with Moqtada al-Sadr's Mehdi army from the beginning of 2004. Of course, the United States' own approach on this issue became more pragmatic. Indeed, when the United States struck a deal with Sunni militias to end the April 2004 standoff in Fallujah, several participating European governments complained that this risked undercutting their own work with the incipient Iraqi army, which angrily feared a weakening of its own position against militia forces. After their withdrawal in the spring of 2004, Spanish generals complained that on such issues they had failed to gain any kind of hearing from their US counterparts.

Amid the growing turmoil, the importance was widely recognized of developing Iraqi civilian policing capacity. The possibility of an EU police mission was discussed. However, most European states insisted that this should only take place after the end of military occupation. The United States was itself skeptical over the idea of a European police mission. British diplomats also doubted that an EU police mission would be ready for what would necessarily be a far tougher policing mandate than had applied in the Balkans. National contributions developed on an ad hoc basis. A group of Italian police trainers were killed in November 2003, compounding other states' reluctance to engage in security sector cooperation. In March 2004 Germany launched a training program for Iraqi policemen, but in the United Arab Emirates. Denmark ceased police training proper to focus on "more qualitative" aspects of security sector management, particularly around Basra. France promised use of a police training school, but only after sovereignty had been fully returned. Diplomats acknowledged a lack of internal European coordination on security sector reform work and a failure to incorporate systematically into Iraq strategies the lessons learned from policing missions in other postconflict scenarios. In opposing a renewed US push for NATO engagement at the June 2004 G8 summit, France, Germany, and Spain reinforced their refusal to provide police and army training on any significant scale or inside Iraq. Many Iraqis criticized this obfuscation, and also berated the Europeans for pushing the reversal of de-Baathification while many Iraqis were still uneasy with the notion of former regime officers resuming security functions.

This was an area where some of the most significant divergences between the UK and US appeared. Rumors abounded that the UK was increasingly unhappy with the Pentagon's militaristic imprint on policing doctrine. While British diplomats denied major differences, by February 2004 the UK had imprisoned only 65 insurgents in the south, compared to the US incarceration of over 9,000 men.[39] The UK's most senior police officer in Iraq admitted to major differences over plans for an international police force, with Britain and other European states insisting this fall under UN command, while the United States insisted on CPA primacy.[40] The UK pushed the United States hard from early on to allow the Governing Council to develop an internal security role, while Department for International Development funding supported the creation of a UN security office and coordinator within Iraq.

British officials lamented that the CPA had been slow to move toward "police primacy," as initially the instinct was to focus on army capacities. A pool of 200 British volunteer police officers was eventually established, with a view to maintaining 100 of these deployed to assist in the reform of the Iraqi police service. Of £19 million allocated to Iraq for 2004 under the UK's Global Conflict Prevention Pool (GCPP), nearly £10 million went to security sector reform work. By the end of 2003, a Transformation into Policing (TiP) program was up and running, focusing on human rights, corruption, civilian control, mentoring, and monitoring. Such training provisions were mandatory under this program but were still implemented mainly by the military. UK-run training was based mainly in Jordan, where 50 UK officers were stationed; in March 2004, the UK sent a group of 24 civilian police training officers for the first time into Basra. British officers were also placed to monitor the chief of police in Baghdad, and subsequently to fulfill similar roles in the southern governorates. It was recognized that a lack of manpower limited monitoring provisions under the TiP program, which had a dampening effect on efforts to improve human rights standards in policing. A growing UK concern was that the June 2004 timetable for transferring sovereignty was unduly compressing police training, in the rush to hand over responsibility for policing to Iraqis. British officials also defined their approach as distinctive in its focus on policing that was embedded within local communities, arguing that the stated US aim of creating an ethnically mixed national police force risked "going against the Iraqi grain." The limitations of these policing initiatives were seen after the renewed insurgencies of April 2004, when many Iraqi police officers refused to confront their countrymen. Indeed, by mid-2004 only 13,000 out of approximately 90,000 Iraqi police officers had received training, while shortfalls in basic equipment persisted.[41]

Within the UK government it was acknowledged that security sector work needed now to move away from, in the words of one British diplomat, the priority given to "quantity over quality," the emergency need simply to get men into uniform with a basic policing capacity.[42] New programs planned at this stage aimed to target "the broader institutional context of policing" and the overall political management of the Iraqi police force. Issues of independence, public access to the police, and the quality of senior management began to predominate. Funds under the GCPP, reduced to £8.5 million for 2005, began to be diverted from the security sector into a human rights strand, in particular for minority rights training programs and support for Iraq's special tribunal. However, critics still charged the UK with imposing less stringent entry conditions than the United States on new police recruits and with too leniently handing security posts in southern governorates to known al-Sadr sympathizers.[43]

The issue of security force training was one of the areas in which a greater European engagement was taking shape by 2005, but again subject to significant limitations. Germany moved to increase the scale of its police training program in the United Arab Emirates. The Danes moved back toward reinitiating police training proper, and the Spanish government also announced plans to offer new police training courses. France, Germany, Belgium, and Spain held up agreement on a proposed NATO training program for the Iraqi army. Agreement to establish the center was eventually forthcoming, but the French government insisted on diluting its size and mandate and refused to offer funds. Indeed, France remained the principal spoiler. The French government not only refused to make any significant contribution in the short term to security training but it very openly used networks from outside the country in trying to secure the release of French hostages, bypassing Iraqi security forces.[44] President Bush returned disappointed from his visit to Brussels in February 2005 after France, Germany, and Spain had agreed to a merely symbolic commitment of a few thousand euros to train Iraqi officers, still outside Iraq.

At the same time, debates persisted over troop deployments. By 2005 this was a question of the pace and extent of reductions to existing force levels. France used the November 2004 conference in Cairo to call again for the withdrawal of US troops, reiterating its own firm opposition to any military deployment—although it was rumored that plans were being drawn up in Paris to contemplate some greater form of engagement if John Kerry won the US elections. Germany pledged €4 million to the prospective UN protection force, the biggest European contribution; yet a decision to send German armored vehicles to Iraq engendered domestic opposition. By the end of 2005, Hungarian troops had left Iraq; Dutch, Ukrainian, and Italian force levels were being wound down; and Poland's remaining contingent of 1,700 troops was due to be reduced gradually during 2006. In these cases leaders faced pressure from their respective parliaments to accelerate troop withdrawals. In April 2005, Denmark extended for eight months the mandate for its contingent of 500; at the beginning of 2006, however, Danish opposition parties withdrew their backing for a further prolongation beyond mid-2006. While Tony Blair reportedly shelved plans for a reduction in British troop levels, pressure on the British government increased in the wake of tensions between UK forces and the Basra police that flared in September 2005—tensions that confirmed the extent of Sadrist infiltration into the very security forces being trained by British personnel and the apparent weakening in trust between the latter and the Basra population. The year 2006 commenced amid a swirl of rumors that a timetable for pulling out UK troops had indeed been elaborated.

State Building and Reconstruction

The security situation discouraged European donors from disbursing significant amounts of aid for postconflict state building and reconstruction. The relative paucity of European funding was apparent at the Madrid donors' conference in October 2003. Out of a total $33 billion committed at this conference, $20 billion came from the United States, $5 billion from Japan, $1 billion from the UK, $300 million from Spain, and $1.5 billion from other EU states and the European Commission. The French government declined to make any commitment. A key European demand was that more money be managed by a UN fund, to which the United States would have limited access.[45] The German development ministry was eager to channel aid through the UN as a means of depoliticizing its potential contribution in Iraq by sheltering it from German public opinion. One EU diplomat also highlighted governments' increasingly acute concern not "to be associated with a failure." The lack of European funding was a bitter disappointment to many international—and particularly Arab—NGOs who wished to accept only European and not US funds after the military invasion.[46]

At least until mid-2004, European aid that was forthcoming was to an overwhelming extent earmarked for purely humanitarian purposes. Even coalition members limited most of their funding to basic emergency relief and reconstruction. EU development commissioner Poul Nielsen rejected US proposals to coordinate the deployment of European humanitarian aid with US postconflict efforts, strongly resisting a politicization of humanitarian aid.[47] Moreover, US decisions to exclude a number of countries from US-funded reconstruction contracts reduced European contributions to infrastructure projects. Such discrimination also further weakened European unity: while US congressmen specifically targeted French and Germany companies, UK trade ministers won some exceptions to the rule that only US companies could bid for USAID reconstruction contracts. Alcatel and Siemens won large-scale private contracts to supply Iraq with mobile phone technology, but such successes did not engender increased public commitments from European governments.[48]

Some European diplomats alluded to their concern with striking a fine balance between, on the one hand, keeping clear of a "US-created chaos" and, on the other hand, the need not to be completely excluded from Iraq and a potentially reshaped Middle East over the longer term. Until the end of 2004 it was the former tendency that predominated within most European governments. The French government made a point of not even attending the World Economic Forum in Jordan in June 2003 so as to stress its disassociation from reconstruction and reform projects due to be debated.[49] At the end of 2003 members of the IGC, visiting Paris to urge Chirac to rethink his reluctance to contribute toward rebuilding Iraq, received a cool response. When Iraqi foreign minister Hoshyar Zebari met with his EU counterparts in July 2004 to ask for European assistance, he received few formal commitments. Indeed, by this stage, several European governments were intimating that Iraq's reintroduction of the death penalty might further discourage new EU funding.

More politically oriented aid work was particularly limited. Any focus on political forms of aid was kept off the agenda at the Madrid conference, in large part at the behest of European donors. Of the €230 million committed by the European Commission, €30 million was channeled through UNDP; priority sectors were water, health, and education. The Commission insisted that its reconstruction aid be managed independently of the CPA.[50] Debate ensued over funding for Iraq from the European Initiative on Democracy and Human Rights. Initial proposals—for projects on torture, a truth and reconciliation committee, women's rights, and the media—met with some coolness by national diplomats and other parts of the Commission. At the end of 2003, EIDHR allocated €3 million to assist the UN in building local institutions, the judicial system, and advocacy NGOs, and an additional €8 million was made available under the EU's Rapid Reaction Mechanism to help initiate the UN presence in Iraq. The stated logic of this funding was to fill the perceived gaps left by the United States, which focused mainly on infrastructure and security forces training. In reality these sums amounted to a small percentage of US democracy aid; the United States was developing a number of democracy projects with local civil society as well as its largest ever single US political party assistance program through the National Democratic Institute and the International Republican Institute.[51] Moreover, the disbursal of EU political aid was held back, awaiting agreement on a more prominent UN role in Iraq's political process. Moreover, for 2004–2005 only €10 million was set aside for governance and human rights work, out of a total Commission commitment of €200 million.[52]

Among member states, Sweden developed the most forward-leaning profile of political work, within a €54 million aid package announced early in 2004. Denmark also allocated €50 million to Iraq for 2003–2004, split evenly between humanitarian aid and reconstruction, the latter including some projects on democratic and judicial capacity building. During 2004 Germany and the Netherlands both developed small programs, of €7–8 million, offering training related to democracy and good governance.

One senior EU official lamented that divisions over military intervention continued to "paralyze long-term thinking" on Europe's concrete contribution to the political restructuring of Iraq. The Brussels institutions accused the UK and other coalition members of sending their own governance advisers to Iraq unilaterally and without exploring a possible EU contribution. Policymakers admitted that substantive debate was subjugated to questions of process, with many European governments concerned overwhelmingly with pressing for postconflict work to be run by the UN to temper US autonomy. One diplomat observed that the EU was "leaning on the UN in the absence of a clear European policy" in relation to allocating resources; others revealed that some states had blocked internal EU discussions on Iraq's political options until a UN resolution had provided for a clear timetable toward the end of US occupation. One group of experts urged the EU not to make its institution-building engagement conditional on multilateral control of the political process;[53] yet this appeared to be precisely what had happened.

Britain was the one European state that did develop a relatively comprehensive range of state-building work. In the first year after the fall of the Saddam regime, the UK's Department for International Development spent £544 million in Iraq. Spending on institution building was acknowledged to have been the slowest element of this aid package to develop, however. Officials lamented that the political tensions over military intervention between Tony Blair and the UK's development minister—"the Clare Short problem," in the intra-Whitehall shorthand of 2003—had delayed planning for postconflict governance work. By August 2003, only £1.7 million had been spent on setting up the UK's four governance teams in the south.[54] UK funding was a small fraction of the $87 billion package agreed by the United States in the autumn of 2003—an allocation within which spending on democracy building rose to $458 million in the run-up to the June transfer of power. The British government committed a further $442 million over two years from January 2004. DfID's Country Strategy Paper for Iraq was agreed in February 2004, ten months after the formally declared ending of hostilities.

UK priorities were consciously elaborated to fill what were judged to be the gaps left by US funding. With the United States prioritizing large-scale infrastructure projects and macrolevel political process, the UK focused on small-scale technical assistance for economic and social reforms. UK—and particularly, DfID—officials revealed that both their conceptual thinking and their project development were focused more on fostering the basic foundations of civil society at a local level than on definition of the overarching political system. Organizations supporting citizens' mobilization around service delivery were favored, with Iraq's rationing system no longer in existence and radical clerics moving in fast to meet basic social needs. Local elections, in a basic form, were organized in Basra in the spring of 2004—although CPA officials in Baghdad vetoed UK plans for direct elections in the south.[55]

Guided by the new Iraq Country Strategy, a number of new institution-building programs developed during 2004. Complementing local-level civil society priorities, UK funds supported a range of institutional development. The three top priorities under DfID's governance budget were defined as civil governance, legal affairs, and economic management. Again seeking to correct a perceived lacuna of security-oriented US approaches, the UK launched a range of training programs with central government ministries. Support was gradually ratcheted up to public service reform initiatives, especially those involving the finance, planning and development cooperation, and municipalities and public works ministries. The efficient and transparent management of public budgets was a thematic priority. Judicial reform was prioritized as an area that other donors had declined to target. The justice sector was the primary beneficiary of UK funds under the Emergency Public Administration Program and was identified for an additional £2 million program under the February 2004 Iraq strategy. Funding included training on human rights law, channeled through a number of international NGOs—despite which

Amnesty International was critical of the UK role in designing Iraq's new legal system.[56] A program for strengthening trade union capacity was also initiated. The new Iraq strategy also committed an additional £20 million for strengthening the institutional capacities of the four southern governorate teams.

UK initiatives were seen as engaging more positively than the United States with tribal structures, and as often usefully cutting across the Sunni-Shia divide and doing more to foster local bodies than the United States. This appeared to chime well with experts' recommendations that interim governance structures should be built around local leaders selected by their own immediate communities.[57] On the other hand, the UK was accused by some experts of repeating the mistakes of its occupation in the 1920s–1930s in depending too much on local notables to establish order and deliver services, invariably overestimating the legitimacy of local tribal leaders in an already fast-urbanizing society; this approach, it was argued, risked further entrenching the structures of premodern ethnicity and making the creation of a modern state more difficult.[58] Indeed, US officials accused the UK of being "too Orientalist" in its approach; some divergence also appeared on this question between UK officials based in the Green Zone in Baghdad and those "on the ground" in the south. The impact of these disconnects was shown in September 2004 when southern provinces pushed for autonomy. The UK argued for a territorially rather than ethnically based federalism and expressed concern that Iraq was moving toward an overarching framework based on democracy between entities, without democratic politics emerging within each entity. In practice, however, British officials acknowledged that they were finding it difficult to move away from working through local religious notables to identify credible national secular alternatives; such a strategy would, they admitted, develop only over the "very long term."

Indeed, most UK initiatives were, in the words of one official, "one step back" from direct involvement in political process, in contrast to US approaches. Media programs benefited from a £6 million injection of funding during 2004 but tended to eschew the kind of direct funding of pro-CPA newspaper and satellite channels that the United States had strongly backed—although the United Kingdom was involved with the United States in supporting "Toward Freedom" Arabic-language TV bulletins immediately after the fall of Baghdad. While DfID managed the UK's institution-building aid budget, its officials acknowledged that they were "not . . . part of the debate" over macrolevel political models; indeed, these debates were seen as being "too big a jump" away from the factors that determined whether development projects could work effectively in the short term. Well into 2004, the UK remained cautious in its support for political party development; the Westminster Foundation for Democracy was significantly more hesitant to launch projects in Iraq than the National Endowment for Democracy. British, Danish, and Italian NGOs started work on strengthening traditional forms of civic culture, but wound down these projects as security deteriorated.[59] Very limited amounts of money were given for directly building up national level, cross-cutting secular organizations. Recognizing the limits of its own possibilities, the UK devoted much of its energy to ensuring the primacy of multilateral funds such as the UN and World Bank trust funds, so as to encourage further contributions from other donors. Certainly, alongside the UK's $4 billion spending on the military and security issues in Iraq, the investment in building democratic institutions remained modest.[60]

The program guiding UK aid in Iraq for 2005–2006 exhibited considerable continuity in terms of thematic priorities. General aid priorities included technical advice to the Iraqi finance ministry; the design of "pro-poor" economic measures; removing institutional barriers to private sector growth; a £20 million "Governorates Capacity-Building" program; a £24 million "Employment and Services" program for southern Iraq; and increasing the role of women in enterprise. The largest share of UK aid continued to be channeled through international institutions, mainly the UN, the World Bank–managed International Reconstruction Fund Facility for Iraq, and the International Monetary Fund (IMF). More politically oriented funding was still relatively limited. A £6.7 million project aimed at developing a free media in the south, and £2.2 million was allocated for the judicial sector. A £5 million Civil Society Support Fund targeted small Iraqi organizations working on poverty, with the aim of helping give "a voice to the poorest." A key issue in this sphere over which UK officials remained ambivalent was the funding of religious-ethnic civil society groups. A parallel £6.25 million Political Participation Fund was more specifically oriented toward boosting participation in elections, in particular among women.[61] Like other donors, the UK claimed to be alive to the need to reorient funds away from prominent exiles' one-man-band NGOs that lacked roots in civil society.

Very gradually, other European states moved to consider for-
warding more assistance after the June 2004 transfer of power. The
EU scoping mission at the end of September recommended initiatives in the field of civil administration and the rule of law, in addition to police training and electoral support. Once again, however,
progress was limited by the caution bred by the deteriorating security
situation. The limits to European deliberations in the wake of the
new strategy continued to reveal extreme caution and hesitancy. The
strategy did not encourage firm commitments to significant amounts
of new aid for democracy building. Practical cooperation on security
sector reform in Iraq remained too controversial for many states. Few
European governments were keen on increasing aid resources while
most of the commitments made at the Madrid donors conference
remained unspent—particularly those of the United States. Southern
European states, and in particular the new Spanish government, were
adamantly opposed to proposals made by some coalition members
that funds from MEDA (Mesures d'Accompagnement), the principal
financial instrument of the European Union for the implementation
of the EMP, be made available to Iraq. This mirrored a broader concern that new possibilities for aid work in Iraq not divert resources
away from other aid recipients. Iraqis were critical of the extent to
which European donors made aid conditional on money not being
spent with US contractors or programs, and also questioned the value
of training and other activities provided from Amman, which they
saw as continually drawing away resources from Iraq to provide
skills with little practical relevance.[62] Only in the summer of 2005
did the Spanish government move toward releasing the $300 million
aid allocation agreed by the previous administration; by the end of
2005 only half of this total allocation had been spent, with the Spanish development ministry channeling funds through the UN and
remaining averse to funding any Spanish organizations to work inside
Iraq. Danish funds declined sharply to €20 million for 2005–2006.

German aid experts lamented the way that German contributions
on the ground had been "infected" by the diplomatic axis between
Berlin and Paris, and they sought to develop a more proactive and
distinctive contribution. They were still reluctant, however, to engage
in politically related work, including in the fields of good governance
and the rule of law. New German projects that began to draw from
the country's €200 million commitment were concentrated in the
areas of water provision, agriculture, and vocational training, along

with cultural initiatives providing support for museums, language training, and sports teams. In terms of civil society engagement, German contact was limited to the two main Kurdish groups and did not include Sunni partners. European donors recoiled in particular as US officials suggested that the European role should be to fund economic and social reparations after US operations had "flattened" places like Fallujah and Mosul.

Incremental advances were not completely absent from EU policies, however. Concern that the UN's focus had remained overly technical—in its role designing formal electoral rules, for instance—encouraged EU aid officials to shift some funds into civil society organizations. The Commission's 2005 aid program for Iraq was notable in introducing a small amount of bilateral funding activity. Of the Commission's €200 million allocation, €130 million was destined for the International Reconstruction Fund Facility for Iraq; €15 million was made available for programs on energy, trade, and investment; €45 million went to a more flexible fund for institution building, with a focus on technocratic organizations such as Iraq's customs agency; and €10 million was forthcoming from the EIDHR—although there was some doubt among officials that Iraqi NGOs would have the requisite capacity for successful fulfillment of the EU's application criteria for this fund. The bilateral aspects of the program were made conditional on Iraq's security situation, with an indication that if this complicated operations, all funds would be sent through the World Bank facility.[63] Commission officials judged their approach to be a counterbalance to the US focus on particular political elite figures, with an aim to prioritize projects designed around themes—such as media freedoms or women's rights—that could cut across and bridge ethnic divisions. Separately, in the summer of 2005 the new EU rule of law mission was mobilized from the ESDP, and aimed to strengthen Iraq's criminal investigation capacity. This incipient aid program was a key aspect of EU policy: divided in the European Council, member states had in effect delegated a growing role to the European Commission through such aid programs.[64] The focus on civic capacity building was seen as crucial as increasing amounts of US reconstruction funds were diverted to cover basic security provision; by 2006 half of the aid allocated by the United States was being spent on security.[65] As it became clear that the United States would plan to wind down its $18 billion reconstruction fund in 2007, the scale of possible increases to European assistance looked set to become a more significant issue.

Conclusion

This account shows that, at one level, European policy toward Iraq divided into two groups, coalition members and noncoalition states. The latter were at most unenthusiastic in contemplating significant postinvasion engagement, both for security reasons and reluctance to bail out the United States and the United Kingdom. Such ambivalence was still evident, and only slightly less acute, nearly three years on from the invasion. While coalition members obviously contributed in various ways to the postinvasion phase, their positions on political and security strategies differed in important ways from those of the United States—without these states gaining any tangible influence over US policy choices. Especially salutary in this regard was the UK's limited impact on overall coalition strategy. By the beginning of 2006 the gap between these two groups of European states had narrowed slightly on some questions—with Germany having, to some degree, emerged as a potential bridge between London and Paris—but still existed.

The scale of the US commitment meant that neither of the two European approaches could be judged a success: significant influence was wielded neither through the French-led option of standing aside nor through the UK-led route of seeking to condition policy from within the coalition. If both models of seeking to influence the United States could be credited with some limited success, neither had any major bearing on Iraq's political developments. To suggest that they could have done so—or even that they should have attempted to do so, given Iraq's increasing tumult—might be seen as setting an unrealistic benchmark. But it might also reasonably be asked whether European governments, and the EU collectively, could not have played a more valuable role at the margins in softening Iraq's unenviable plight. Arguably, some of the areas of engagement that the EU largely eschewed—disarmament, the integration of former regime sympathizers, the development of social market structures, the building of national civic organizations, the strengthening of local representative bodies[66]—were those both of traditional European expertise and those where correction to US strategies was most imperative. Nearly three years after the invasion, the EU—including coalition members, to varying degrees—had failed to delineate in-depth approaches to Iraq's very specific institution-building challenges, but rather remained focused on the more broad-brush strategic question of whether or not to offer greater backing to the United States.

Positions on the range of postinvasion dilemmas—such as whether to move toward elections more quickly or more slowly, whether to encourage a balancing of power between sectarian groups or push for less guided political competition, or what kind of approach to adopt toward security issues—were in significant measure offshoots of states' differing positions toward the United States, broadly speaking. Because of this—Iraq being conceived as a transatlantic issue more than a postconflict challenge in its own right—the debates witnessed in the United States between different departments and agencies on the finer points of political reconstruction strategies found less resonance in Europe. European policies toward Iraq in the period assessed here tell us little about EU approaches to postconflict scenarios in general; indeed, some of the positions adopted by the French and other governments were the precise opposite of those they most commonly pursued in conflict resolution policies. For coalition members, Iraq's democratization—or at least something that could be presented as such—was increasingly seen as an exit strategy. For noncoalition states, the coalition's exit was pressed as a step toward democratization and the development of a more inclusive international strategy to aid that process. By 2005 there was rhetorical commitment on the part of the EU in general to move beyond the rifts with the United States. But a "wait and see" caution still prevailed in the concrete expression of such sentiment.

Notes

1. Niblock, *Pariah States,* pp. 190–191.
2. Litwak, *Rogue States,* p. 137.
3. Crowe, "A Common European Foreign Policy," pp. 533–546.
4. Piccone, *Defending Democracy,* p. 78.
5. Kampfner, *Blair's Wars,* pp. 155–156.
6. Kampfner, *Blair's Wars,* p. 315.
7. *Financial Times,* 15 July 2002, p. 3.
8. Patten, *Not Quite the Diplomat,* p. 190.
9. Transcript of BBC interview, 27 July 2003.
10. Greenstock, "What Must Be Done Now?"
11. Sawers, "Transforming Iraq."
12. It was widely perceived that this strategy prevailed over any fundamental political restructuring of Iraq. See Hollis, "Iraq: The Regional Fallout," pp. 6–7.
13. *The Economist,* 7 June 2003, p. 56.

14. On this tendency in previous US interventions, see Pei and Kasper, "Lessons from the Past," p. 7.

15. *Le Monde,* 30 August 2003.

16. *New York Times,* 23 September 2003.

17. International Crisis Group, *Governing Iraq.*

18. Greenstock, "What Must Be Done Now?" p. 25.

19. *Le Figaro,* 19 February 2004 and 19 March 2004.

20. *Le Monde,* 18 March 2004.

21. Diamond, "What Went Wrong in Iraq?" p. 50.

22. International Crisis Group, *Iraq's Transition,* p. 30.

23. Commission of the European Communities, *The European Union and Iraq.*

24. Speech to the European Parliament, 15 September 2004, www.europa.eu.int/comm/external_relations/news/patten/sp04_399.htm.

25. This regional approach was often seen as a natural comparative advantage for the EU's focus. For example, see Luciani and Neugart, *Toward a European Strategy.*

26. BBC Monitoring Service, 15 September 2004.

27. See Ridolfo, "Assessing Iraq's National Conference," pp. 3–5.

28. *Daily Star,* 29 September 2004.

29. *Middle East International,* no. 751, 27 May 2005, p. 15.

30. *El País,* 24 August 2005, p. 2.

31. Quotes on European positions in this paragraph are taken from Javier Solana, "Helping Iraq," www.consilium.eu.int, June 2005; European Council Secretariat, General Affairs and External Relations Council: Press Statement, 25 April 2005; European Council Secretariat, Iraq International Conference: Conference Statement, 22 June 2005; European Council Secretariat, Council Conclusions, 21 February 2005.

32. *New Yorker,* 5 December 2005, p. 54.

33. On the dangers of which, see Dawisha and Dawisha, "How to Build a Democratic Iraq," pp. 36–55; A. Dawisha, "Iraq: Setbacks, Advances, Prospects."

34. Byman, "Constructing a Democratic Iraq," pp. 47–78; Zakaria, "No Security, No Democracy."

35. For French positions, see http://special.diplomatie.fr, from April 2003.

36. *Le Monde,* 29 April 2003.

37. *Le Monde,* 28 May 2003.

38. Greenstock, "What Must Be Done Now?" p. 26.

39. *The Economist,* 19 June 2004, p. 61.

40. *Financial Times,* 23 July 2003.

41. Dodge, "A Sovereign Iraq?" pp. 39–58.

42. A critique also picked up by Dodge, "A Sovereign Iraq?" p. 54, from contacts with Iraqi officials.

43. *New York Times,* June 2004.

44. *Financial Times,* 22 September 2004.

45. *The Economist,* 13 September 2003, p. 21.

46. MacGinty, "The Pre-War Reconstruction of Post-War Iraq," pp. 601–617.

47. *Financial Times,* 31 March 2003.

48. *Financial Times,* 28 April 2003.

49. *Le Monde,* 24 June 2003.

50. Communication from the Commission to the Council and the European Parliament, "The Madrid Conference."

51. Diamond, "What Went Wrong in Iraq?" p. 55.

52. For these figures, see Commission of the European Communities, *Iraq: Assistance Programme 2005,* pp. 14, 18, 23, and 25.

53. Dodge, Luciani, and Neugart, *The European Union and Iraq,* p. 10.

54. Department for International Development, *Iraq Update,* no. 48.

55. Diamond, "What Went Wrong in Iraq?" p. 45.

56. Amnesty International press releases, from April 2003.

57. L. Kubba, "Iraq's Interim Government Must Be Democratic," *Financial Times,* 7 May 2003.

58. Dodge, "US Intervention and Possible Iraqi Futures," pp. 103–122; Byman and Pollack, "Democracy in Iraq?"

59. Jennings, "The Ghosts of Baathists Past."

60. Information on UK funding from weekly Department for International Development Iraq updates, and Department for International Development, *Iraq Country Strategy Paper,* February 2004.

61. Department for International Development, *Iraq Update,* no. 8, June 2005.

62. International Crisis Group, *Reconstructing Iraq.*

63. Commission of the European Communities, *Iraq: Assistance Programme 2005.*

64. Vasconselos, "The EU and Iraq," p. 90.

65. *The Guardian,* 3 January 2006.

66. For accounts of some of the trade-offs involved in these dilemmas, see Royal Institute of International Affairs, "Iraq in Transition"; and Ottaway, "Iraq: Without Consensus."

3

Iran: The End of the Affair

As debates over Middle East reform gathered pace, Iran took what appeared to represent a significant step back from democratization. In June 2005 Mohammed Khatami's reformist presidency gave way to a government presided over by the conservative Mahmoud Ahmadinejad, after hard-line clerics had succeeded in gradually stifling political reforms. At the same time, Iranian efforts to develop a nuclear capacity progressed, reaching what many international observers judged to be a pivotal juncture when, in January 2006, Iran's recommencement of uranium enrichment-related activities triggered an International Atomic Energy Agency (IAEA) vote to refer the country to the UN Security Council (UNSC). This chapter charts the EU's efforts to strengthen its engagement with Iran, in particular after Khatami's 1997 electoral victory and again after 9/11. While this engagement enabled the EU—most notably through the diplomacy of a British-French-German triumvirate—to retain purchase over Iran's nuclear-related activities, by early 2006 the apparent achievement of having encouraged Iran to suspend uranium enrichment in return for a package of European incentives appeared to have been nullified. Even more clearly unsuccessful had been the EU's efforts to work in partnership with Khatami to support liberalizing reforms. The European rapprochement with Iran was justified on two grounds. First, Iran was a case where a clear, homegrown momentum of reform had emerged, around which international efforts could be molded. And second, it appeared to be the case par excellence of a promising European engagement contrasting with a self-defeating US strategy of ostracism. This chapter demonstrates how in practice the EU equivocated over issues of democratic reform and prioritized a counterbalancing stance toward US strategy on Iran, failing to react adequately as the window of opportunity that had opened in 1997 gradually closed.

From Critical Engagement to Rapprochement with the Reformists

After the 1979 revolution European engagement with Iran was relatively modest. Of course, the 1953 military coup against the government of Mohammed Mossadeq and the subsequent installation of the shah, orchestrated by the US Central Intelligence Agency (CIA), came to taint US credibility in a way that did not affect European governments. After the 1979 revolution it was the United States more than the West in general that was subject to Iranian ire. Iran's desire to develop relations with Europe to offset tensions with Washington, and its ploy of often seeking to play Europe and the United States off against each other, date back to this period. Yet European relations with Tehran were themselves limited in substance. Britain was a partial exception to the generally smoother relations with Europe, the UK having been associated with the CIA's role in the overthrow of Mossadeq. While the French tried to remain relatively equidistant between the shah and the ayatollahs, France favored Iraq strongly in the Iran-Iraq war in terms of weapons sales and became increasingly critical of Iranian terrorism affecting French citizens and interests. Paris consequently broke off relations with Tehran in 1987, and Franco-Iranian relations did not improve until Iranian-backed international hostage taking abated in the early 1990s.[1]

Until 1997 the development of the EU's "critical dialogue" with Iran accorded primary importance to the question of the fatwa issued against British author Salman Rushdie. Alongside the UK, Denmark was the most hard-line of the European states, its frustration with Iran's political stagnation and human rights conditions leading it to withdraw for a time from the EU's critical dialogue in 1996. European policies during this period could be categorized as a "neither-nor" strategy: neither was any significant degree of positive engagement developed, nor was there support for the kind of ostracism—and covert operations—pursued by the United States.

Khatami's election victory in 1997 triggered a significant policy shift from the EU. An agreement on the Rushdie affair was reached shortly after Khatami's election, based on the Iranian government agreeing to clarify that it did not seek the implementation of the fatwa. This opened the way for an improvement in relations, and crucially to Britain reestablishing full diplomatic relations with Iran. Shortly before the Iranian elections, relations had hit a new low after a German court's judgment that the Iranian leadership had been involved in the 1992 murder of Kurdish leaders in Berlin. European ambassadors had been withdrawn from Tehran and dialogue suspended. However, this issue was also quickly resolved and ambassadors were back in Tehran by November 1997. With Iran insisting that the German ambassador return last, and not with the group of EU ambassadors, an agreement was reached to have the former return a few days after other European ambassadors but with his French counterpart. In both cases, some creative diplomacy enabled both sides to save face and position themselves for a new rapprochement. All parties were openly keen not to let these specific issues scuttle the opportunity presented—it was judged—by Khatami's election.

President Khatami made historic visits to Rome, Paris, and Berlin shortly after taking office. In 2000, Foreign Minister Kamal Kharrazi made a visit to the UK. The visit to Iran by French foreign minister Hubert Vedrine in 1998 was seen as being in the vanguard of pressing a more positive and committed EU policy. Senior official exchanges between Iran and the EU resumed in early 1998, and two troika meetings were henceforth to be organized each year at deputy minister level. The "critical dialogue" morphed into a "comprehensive dialogue." A Commission communication of February 2001 forwarded a package of proposals for developing closer relations with Iran, which was approved by member state governments in May 2001. The Council had instructed the Commission to work up such ideas specifically as a response to reformists' victory in the parliamentary elections of February 2000. The trend toward rapprochement was given further impulse when Khatami was elected for a second term in June 2001. Jack Straw traveled to Iran in September 2001—the first visit by a British foreign secretary since the revolution—and again in November 2001 and October 2002.

The improvement in diplomatic relations was underpinned by trends in trade and investment. With a strong US security presence in Saudi Arabia and the smaller Gulf states, Europeans saw Iran as a strategic foothold and important source of Middle Eastern oil and gas, from which the United States had excluded itself. The EU consolidated itself as Iran's main trading partner, running a growing trade deficit with Iran. Oil products accounted for nearly 80 percent of European imports from Iran. EU-Iranian working groups on energy and on trade and investment were established in 1999 and 2000, respectively. During this period, European governments expressed an optimism regarding the commitment of Khatami's government to push ahead with economic liberalization. Iran's long-standing special relationship with Germany deepened on the back of increasing trade flows between the two countries and Germany's provision of extensive debt relief to Iran. French multinational Total agreed to a large new venture with the National Iranian Oil Company in 1997, focusing on the development of Iran's offshore gas field—sufficient to supply two-thirds of France's domestic requirements.[2] It was this investment deal in particular that fed into the promulgation of the D'Amato bill, under which the United States threatened to impose extraterritorial sanctions on companies doing business in Iran. It was significant that the United Kingdom sided firmly with European governments against the United States on this issue—although London sought to mediate on the details of the deal eventually struck with President Clinton, under which the United States would refrain from imposing sanctions against European firms in return for the EU agreeing (in relatively noncommittal fashion) to delineate rules for applying sanctions against nondemocratic regimes.

In terms of Iran's political development, Europeans backed Khatami's efforts at very gradual reform. Europeans did not back the kind of opposition groups, including some linked to the former regime, which did occasionally seem to be securing a hearing in Washington. Even the European governments most critical of Iran declined to support exiled opposition groups, professing a difficulty in finding among such organizations what could be deemed credible interlocutors. The UK banned the People's Mujahideen (MKO) in 2000. At most, a small number of Members of Parliament (MPs) in some northern member states expressed a degree of sympathy for the National Council of the Iranian Resistance (NCIR), an organization seen as close to the MKO. One key diplomat suggested that the European aim was conceived not so much in terms of "trying to change the system from within" as trying to help function better the elements of pluralism already existing in Iran's political system. Those involved in the 1999 student-led protests lamented the timidity of European support. European backing for Khatami began to confront some uncomfortable facts: that Khatami's presentation of his reforms as being in defense of the revolution had increasingly little resonance among the younger generation; that there was some division between those pushing for political liberalization and those advocating economic reform; and that the Iran Freedom Movement actually suffered increased harassment in the late 1990s. Despite the increasingly patent difficulties facing the reform process, European diplomats remained comforted by an apparent congruence between Khatami's formal commitment to reform and an apparent moderation of Iranian foreign policy.

Specific human rights issues, such as the use of stoning as judicial punishment and the arrest of Iranian Jews in 2000, did elicit strong European reaction—and on both counts the Iranian government did bend. Tensions resulted in 1998 when Iranian judicial authorities imposed sentences against a number of Iranian intellectuals and civil society experts attending a conference in Germany. The UK launched a small number of judicial reform projects, but acknowledged that these had to be kept ostensibly apolitical. No significant aid cooperation emerged, with only small amounts of assistance offered to relatively rich Iran primarily for narcotics control and help for Afghani refugees in Iran. Iran's total aid receipts for 2001 amounted to only $115 million, 0.1 percent of GDP; five EU donors were among Iran's ten largest aid contributors (Germany, followed at some distance by France, Austria, the UK, and the Netherlands).[3] Notwithstanding European pressure on select human rights concerns, the expressed desire to assist Khatami in furthering the process of political liberalization did not translate into a proactive program of reform-oriented assistance.

Post–September 11 Partnership

If the period after 9/11 saw a tightening of US policy toward Iran, the attacks appeared to reinforce the European determination to embed more systematic engagement with President Khatami. The interplay between Iran's relations with the EU and the country's domestic political debates became increasingly complex. As tensions grew between Iran's competing power centers, positions toward the EU became even more notably the product of such intra-Iranian dissension. As Khatami and the nonelected religious elite joined battle, the common ground between these two camps appeared to diminish, so that a single Iranian approach to the EU became more difficult to discern. This evolution impacted crucially upon both European objectives and the receptiveness of the Iranian political context within which they were articulated.[4]

European governments rejected the "axis of evil" denomination accorded Iran by the Bush administration—expressing particular anger they had not even been consulted by Washington on what was clearly going to be an inflammatory move. The interruption of an arms shipment from Iran to Palestine in early 2002 was the crucial event that intensified concerns in Washington. Washington increasingly cast doubt on the supposed distinction between reformists and hardliners. Bush adviser Zalmay Khalilzad declared, "Our policy is not about Khatami or Khamenei, reformers or hardliners, it is about those who want freedom, human rights, democracy."[5] In direct contrast, the EU placed greater stress on the potential value of working through Khatami. The whole European strategy was predicated on a split between reformists and hardliners, the significance of which the United States had come to question.

Negotiations for a new trade and cooperation agreement between the EU and Iran were launched in December 2002. The proposal to open such talks was forwarded a few days after the 9/11 attacks; the UK and Denmark, with modest support from a small number of other member states, held the process back to ensure, among other things, that trade negotiations were linked to political dialogue and cooperation on counterterrorism. Trade talks did not proceed without difficulty. By the second round of negotiations in spring 2003, conservatives had blocked many proposals for increasing access for foreign direct investment (FDI); the left-wing Islamists backing Khatami were also unhappy with the degree of economic liberalization involved in reaching a trade and cooperation agreement with the EU—this latter dimension seen as developing into a crucial obstacle to Europe's ability to deepen its partnership with the reformist camp. It became clear that negotiations with Iran would for some time not approximate to anything resembling free trade, but would rather take the form of the EU making additional offers of access to Iran under the latter's Most Favored Nation status. The key stated aim was to use a trade and cooperation agreement as a stepping-stone toward preparing Iran for World Trade Organization (WTO) membership— this being another important difference with the United States, which at this stage remained determined to block Iran's accession to the trade organization.

By the end of the summer of 2003, after four rounds of meetings, talks were still largely exploratory, with EU officials stipulating the economic reforms they thought necessary for Iran to implement. No detailed negotiations had progressed on precise access conditions for specific products. Acknowledging the level of economic engagement to be relatively limited, primary importance was deemed to lie not so much in pushing the overall level of market opening in Iran as locking the latter into a legal, contractual framework. Iranian authorities were themselves nervous about precisely this aspect of restraint over the country's future actions. European officials acknowledged that there was not the same degree of interest from multinationals that had facilitated and driven the WTO-inspired traction on governance issues in negotiations with China; indeed, European companies such as Shell, Airbus, Rolls Royce, and British Petroleum held back new investment plans in Iran as the Bush administration hinted once again at the possible imposition of extraterritorial sanctions. Even at the relatively technical level, moreover, there were significant differences between member states over how far to push governance reforms in Iran as a precondition to WTO accession.

While the original proposal was to focus on trade, political dialogue gradually developed into a central element of European relations with Iran. The partnership sought by the EU after 9/11 included a tighter focus on human rights than had existed prior to the attacks. This was presented as building on Khatami's advocacy of a dialogue on convergence between different cultural values. The leverage of the Trade and Cooperation Agreement (TCA) offer was seen by diplomats as the factor that succeeded in enabling the beginning of a formal human rights dialogue. This dialogue in turn led to Iran opening up to UN human rights inspections, declaring a moratorium on stoning, and releasing a number of dissidents. Seeking to boost its own reformist credentials, Tehran regularly reminded EU negotiators that its willingness to engage in political dialogue and accept the EU's democracy clause had taken Iran beyond the nature of EU political relations with China. Unlike the human rights dialogue with China, the talks with Iran included the notion of concrete benchmarks, with the EU linking progress on trade to specific measures, such as Iran agreeing to the visit of the UN rapporteur to inspect prison conditions. A declared priority for the EU was to use the dialogue as a means of holding Iran to its moratorium on stoning. In addition, the EU's focus on judicial reform opened the way for engagement between experts from the two sides on the structure of the procurator's office in Iran. These were areas where Iran reacted specifically to EU pressure through the new human rights dialogue. Increasingly, the view held that, in the words of one European diplomat, Iran was willing to "play the game," making just enough compromise on human rights to maintain a forward momentum in negotiations with the EU. Indeed, some officials judged that Iran was more willing to do this than most of the EU's other Middle Eastern partners.

A relatively sanguine pragmatism prevailed in European reasoning. A judgment common to all member states was that the Bush administration's hard-line approach had fanned the flames of the conservatives' gradual reassertion in Iran. A diplomat of one large member state revealed that European support for reform efforts was conceived in terms of encouraging and assisting Iran to implement international human rights covenants and standards, and was "not crystallized in terms of democracy." The aim was to progress with immediate human rights changes, which did "not commit us very far to what this means in the longer term." Officials admitted to a lack of debate on the broader relationship between theocracy and democracy in the Islamic republic. The senior official of another large member state asserted that in some measure Iran was "already democratic," and dismissed the US view that the country was an autocracy in need of fundamental regime change. Indeed, many European officials declared themselves sympathetic to the view that Iran's hybrid system had succeeded in stabilizing the country. By 2003, the EU was of the view that Iran was genuinely trying to restrain Hizbollah and welcomed the fact that Tehran was declaring more clearly that it would support any peace process settlement accepted by the Palestinians.

While Iran was a country in relation to which some of the clearest blue water separated US and European strategic thinking, it was at the same time one that elicited some significant differences *within* the EU. In debates over how hard the EU should insist on specific reforms, familiar differences existed between the French, Italians, and Greeks on the one hand, and Denmark, the Netherlands, and the UK, on the other hand. While the former insisted on concerns being raised and pressure exerted in private, the latter argued that the regime could best be nudged along by more public criticism. Italy enjoyed one of the closest relationships with the Iranian government and appeared the most optimistic over the gains achieved by reformers. Officials at the EU level placed the United Kingdom closer to the United States than its European partners in terms of London and

Washington sharing a "credibility problem" in Iran. Some opined that the UK, Denmark, and other "toughs" were "hiding behind" the French and Italians, protesting about Iran in part to placate the United States, while actually being wedded to the utility of the engagement they attained through EU policy. One senior Common Foreign and Security Policy official lamented that there was virtue in both the hard and softer approaches, but that the EU needed to pursue at least one of these with clarity. According to one source, if there was a minimum common core between different European governments and Brussels institutions, it was that the European Union, unlike the United States, "ha[d] not given up on the reformers"—despite increasing disappointment with the pace of change.

European policymakers acknowledged that policy toward Iran was one of the cases where EU strategy was most reactive to US policy. Some diplomats recognized that the EU had begun to exert a degree of pressure on human rights issues in part to "demonstrate progress" to the United States, not due to particularly extensive strategic deliberations on internal Iranian developments themselves. Counterbalancing this concern to "keep the United States on board," the EU was driven by the desire to maintain a distinct approach from Washington, without which the Iranian government was unlikely to treat the EU as a serious interlocutor. What was widely seen in Europe as the Iranian fixation with the United States worked as a double-edged sword: on the one hand, some EU policymakers lamented that it made Iran "completely blind" to European initiatives; on the other hand, other diplomats insisted that it was precisely the uniquely disengaged nature of US strategy toward Iran that accorded the EU greater scope for raising a range of political concerns without squandering access to the regime. Many in the EU suggested that Europe's principal role was to mediate between the United States and Iran, seeking to change the frozen image each had of the other. This explained the primary concern over the deepening impatience within the US administration with what were judged to be the increasingly meager fruits of engagement, a stance that was seen as undermining European policy rather than harnessing EU access to Iran for supposedly common transatlantic objectives.

Relative to many other countries in the Middle East, in Iran the scale of European reform assistance remained negligible. The UK supported very small-scale work assisting civil society organizations with seminars, visits, and publications. By 2002 there were moves to coalesce this work into larger and more visible projects, but with only a small embassy in Tehran, diplomats alluded to a lack of capacity to identify and develop good quality grassroots reform-oriented projects. Indeed, even as the EU sought to stress its efforts at engagement, in February 2002 Iran refused to accept the new UK ambassador, requiring an alternative appointment to be made. Moreover, these small-scale projects funded at the discretion of the UK embassy were not backed by a mainstream bilateral aid program. The German government began to focus on Iran's legal system, establishing a program for the training of judges. Working to a relatively apolitical definition of the "rule of law," German funding sought to help strengthen judicial capacity, in particular in relation to the area of family law. The German development ministry supported small-scale projects relating to the possible reform of family codes and provisions for family planning. German diplomats suggested that these projects were able to encroach on slightly more sensitive issues than were UK-backed initiatives. New funding for Iran was also forthcoming from the French government for a series of activities related to a "dialogue of cultures."[6] Funds from the European Initiative on Democracy and Human Rights were made available to help disseminate information on the EU-Iran Human Rights Dialogue and to facilitate civil society involvement in this forum. Apart from this support, only one EIDHR project was funded in Iran, financing the production of a series of TV documentaries on human rights. Khatami's brother, a key reformer in parliament, spoke of the "Spanish model" of transition as a desirable path for Iran, but this elicited little concrete response from Madrid in terms of democracy assistance initiatives. European donors suggested that funding genuinely reform-minded civil society organizations had become increasingly difficult due to conservatives' influence within associations and societies. While European diplomats commonly insisted that their presence gave the EU a better feeling than the United States for what was happening on the ground in Iran, Iranian reformists did not always concur that in practice they were receiving locally attuned reform-focused support from European sources.

While the EU sought to develop a new partnership, in Iran conservatives reasserted themselves. Ayatollah Khamenei, having subjected the post of Supreme Leader to some accountability through debate in the Assembly of Experts, switched back to supporting the conservatives from 2001. A similar move was made by Ali Akbar

Hashemi Rafsanjani, who as head of the Expediency Council was mandated to mediate between Khatami and the clerics. Both the Revolutionary Guard and key sections of the judiciary moved against the reformists. In the February 2003 municipal elections, conservatives gained on reformists, with a very low turnout. The Iranian Freedom Movement was shut down in 2002, and new restrictions were imposed on the media. Analysts pointed to a fracturing of the alliance between Islamic clerics and nationalists, which had underpinned the 1979 revolution, as the latter became increasingly frustrated with the clerics' failure to adapt and evolve.[7] At the same time, tensions surfaced over reform questions between liberal technocrats and left-wing Islamists, the two constituencies whose support had helped bring Khatami to power.[8] These trends provoked the emergence of a more radical reformist strand. Despairing of Khatami's gradualism, a group of parliamentarians threatened to boycott their seats if conservatives blocked key reforms. More clerics broke ranks, revealing further opposition to conservatives from within the religious establishment. Crucially, the security services also began to show signs of fracturing. Most prominently, a series of further student demonstrations erupted. By working essentially with and through Khatami, the EU earned the opprobrium of the more impatient and ambitious reformists, who likened EU policy, in the words of one intellectual, to "giving medicine to a patient who is already dead." Reflecting the frequency of his talks with the regime, "Mullah Straw" became a familiar epithet among Iranians for the UK foreign secretary.

Iran's Nuclear Program and Post-Iraq Dilemmas

Increasingly, Western relations with Tehran came to be dominated by Iran's incipient nuclear technology program. Iran's Russian-built nuclear reactor was soon to come online, and there was a common judgment among European governments that Iran could be two to four years away from possessing a nuclear weapons capability. The concern was that Iran's membership in the international regime governed by the Treaty on the Non-Proliferation of Nuclear Weapons (NPT) was enabling it to engage, legitimately, in some IAEA-monitored, nuclear-related activities that would suffice to take it to the brink of developing nuclear weapons capability, and that at this point Tehran would—it was feared—withdraw from the NPT and thus be beyond restriction. The regime insisted that its activities were aimed at the peaceful, civilian use of nuclear capability. At the same time, conservatives in particular argued for a stronger focus on security capacities, pointing to the instability of Iran's neighborhood; its encirclement by the US military presence in Iraq, Afghanistan, and the Gulf; its general fear of a Western-backed Iraq coming to out-compete Iran; Israeli actions in the Occupied Territories; and Israel's possession of nuclear weapons. A common official refrain from hard-line Iranian politicians and clerics was that Iran needed a nuclear weapons capability because of the existence of the "artificial country of Israel." The fact that Iran possessed plentiful supplies of oil and gas for power generation made some doubt that it genuinely needed heavy-water reactors and uranium enrichment facilities for civilian use.

From 2002, European focus and pressure in relation to the nuclear issue became more notable. As more evidence emerged that Iran was developing nuclear weapons, the key demand was that Iran commit itself to allowing further inspections by the IAEA, in particular by signing an additional IAEA protocol providing for reinforced and random visits by international inspectors. It was in part reflective of growing tensions with Iran that the EU drew up its Action Plan for WMD. The increased attention was inextricably linked to changes in the regional environment and in US strategies. Diverse logics were present in European calculations. On the one hand, a tougher line on Iran's apparent desire to develop a nuclear weapons capability was valued as a means of demonstrating resolve to the United States in a way that might keep Washington to a multilateral track on issues of proliferation. On the other hand, the counterbalancing dynamic clearly intensified during this period. European governments argued that in the wake of 9/11 the United States had erred in presenting Iran as a general sponsor of global terrorism and that Washington's demonizing of the Iranian regime would simply strengthen its desire to acquire WMD as protection. Some diplomats detected that Iran might be close to the point that Saddam Hussein reached—of judging that whatever cooperation was offered, this would not be enough to placate the United States; and that therefore escalation became a rationalized strategic response. One senior official from one of the big three EU governments encapsulated what he saw to be the essential difference with the Bush administration: while 9/11 and the prospect of Iran meddling in post-Saddam Iraqi politics had made the United States more hostile to Tehran, these new contextual uncertainties had obliged Europeans to be more understanding of Iran's strategic preoccupations.

The apparent European breakthrough came on 20 October 2003, when Iran agreed to a deal with the British, French, and German foreign ministers, Jack Straw, Dominique de Villepin, and Joschka Fischer, respectively. The agreement was based on Iran's acquiescence to a strengthened inspections regime in return for European assistance in developing a civilian nuclear energy program. The EU3 (France, Germany, and the UK) position was predicated on the notion of European governments supplying sufficient low-enriched uranium for Iran to develop a civilian energy program, while closing off the perceived danger of Iran producing such material in a way that it could then be enhanced into weapons-grade enriched uranium. The deal included commitments from Iran to publish a list of where its materials were being supplied from; to accept a more intrusive inspections protocol; and to suspend uranium enrichment. Crucially, the EU3 accepted a commitment on Iran's part to "suspend" rather than "cease" nuclear activities. Some other European governments, particularly the Spanish Partido Popular administration, were angered, both at being excluded from the negotiations and at the dilution in wording that was accepted by the three European ministers without consulting their EU counterparts. Reputedly, the three governments had suggested including Javier Solana in their delegation but could not do this without inviting the Italian presidency—which, given Rome's traditional line toward Iran, they strenuously wanted to avoid being obliged to do. President Bush reportedly made a personal plea to Tony Blair not to sign the deal.[9] The main US complaint was that the EU3 had resisted the notion of an automatic trigger clause that, in the event of Iran's noncompliance, would refer Iran to the United Nations Security Council for sanctions; a clause in the agreement stipulated that further concealment on Iran's part would trigger action, but of an unspecified type.[10] The reopening of negotiations for an EU-Iran trade and cooperation agreement was made conditional upon Iran's full compliance with the agreement. The agreement was accompanied by positive-sounding sympathy from European governments for Iran's security concerns and intimation that the EU might consider sponsoring a regional security body, along the lines of the Organization for Security and Cooperation in Europe (OSCE).[11]

In February 2004 the EU3 tightened their agreement with Iran, extending the accord to cover preenrichment preparatory activities. In March the IAEA censured Iran, having found traces of enriched uranium omitted from its declarations. Apparently with some reluctance and after much debate, France, Germany, and the UK did back a toughly worded UN resolution criticizing Iran in relation to this—although still without agreeing to a trigger for UNSC sanctions.[12] In response, Iran cheekily warned that if European governments maintained their pressure on WMD *it* would press charges against *them* for providing Saddam with the materials that helped him develop the chemical weapons used in the Iran-Iraq war.[13] In July Iran announced that it would cease to respect the extended February deal and thereafter began to prepare material for the centrifuges that enrich uranium. As European pressure mounted, an increasingly hard-line reaction was witnessed from the *majlis:* "The Europeans will not decide for us" became a frequent protestation. At an EU-Iran meeting at the end of July the EU pushed Iran for a commitment not to withdraw from the NPT in the future. With Iran revitalizing preenrichment activity and threatening to stop selling crude oil to the UK, France, and Germany, the EU kept in abeyance talks over a trade and cooperation agreement. European authorities did not, however, contemplate extending bilateral sanctions, beyond the few ad hoc measures in place, such as a number of embargos on the sale of some aircraft parts. Indeed, this juncture witnessed the signing of a new Italian-Iranian cooperation agreement, in labor and social affairs.

A further IAEA report in September 2004 asserted that progress had been made but that Iran was still resisting full cooperation and transparency. This report triggered renewed European effort and debate. By the early autumn of 2004 European governments were deliberating on a package of new inducements that might be offered to Iran, including the provision of light water nuclear reactor technology and an undertaking by the EU of responsibility for the transport of (and thus control over) fuel for the Russian reactor. The United States explicitly declined to support these inducements. The EU's offer of a trade and cooperation agreement contrasted with Iran's exclusion from the scope of the United States' proposed Middle East Free Trade Zone. Reports surfaced at this stage that the EU might support a decision in the UN to impose sanctions, but with no internal agreement on what precise kind of punitive measures would be appropriate and legitimate.[14] Some diplomats reported an incipient split between the UK, on the one hand, and France and Germany, on the other hand, on the question of UNSC referral.

With European governments ratcheting up the degree of diplomatic pressure, intimating at a possible reining back of engagement with Iran if the latter did not demonstrate progress on WMD cooperation by the end of November, an agreement was struck between Iran and the EU3 under which the latter formally committed themselves to the firmer and more far-reaching set of inducements that had been discussed with Tehran: a reopening of negotiations for a prospective EU trade and cooperation agreement; a broad range of political, economic, and security cooperation; and an undertaking to provide Iran with uranium enriched for civilian use. Despite reacting initially to the two-month deadline set by the Europeans by reinvoking the threat to withdraw from the NPT, Iran agreed to suspend enrichment until talks in relation to this package of benefits were successfully concluded—or, in the words of the official agreement, "while negotiations proceed on a mutually acceptable agreement on long-term arrangements." Crucially, the deal focused on tightening provisions relating to the preenrichment phases of the nuclear cycle. Negotiations regarding a trade and cooperation agreement were to resume immediately, and the EU undertook to push actively for Iran's entry into the WTO. When the IAEA reported at the end of November, the EU response was positive; Javier Solana stated that he was "pleased that the IAEA has been able to verify Iran's full and complete suspension of uranium enrichment activities"[15]—a very different reaction from that of the US administration. Trade and cooperation agreement talks were duly reopened on 12 January 2005. These were structured around three baskets, on economics, politics, and nuclear issues, and were chaired on the European side by the UK, Germany, and France, respectively—the lead role of the "big three" thus being reflected and enshrined in the renewal of talks at the EU level.

It was not long, however, before tensions resurfaced. Chief negotiator and Khamenei confidante Hassan Rowhani stressed Iran's success in resisting the EU3's pressure for a permanent "halting"—rather than temporary suspension—of enrichment activities.[16] Domestically, Rowhani's role was indicative of an attempt to circumvent reformists in the formal government. On February 9 Khatami himself warned the EU of "massive consequences" if the negotiations did not prosper. At this juncture the United States intimated that it was searching for select bombing targets in Iran, leaving some European diplomats irate that their efforts should be undercut at such a delicate moment. Jack Straw returned from a visit to Washington at the end of January asserting that for the UK government the use of force against Iran was "inconceivable"—although the wording chosen by his prime minister was not quite as unequivocal.[17] Quite apart from doubts over its wisdom, the military option, in the judgment of EU officials, lacked practical feasibility.

During the early part of 2005 talks did indeed gradually grind to a halt. Iran threatened to end its suspension of uranium enrichment. In response, the UK, France, and Germany agreed to back the US position that Iran should be referred to the UNSC if it restarted enrichment activity. As quid pro quo, the Bush administration offered firmer support for the EU incentives-based approach, holding out the prospect of backing Iran's accession to the WTO as a potential reward for a nuclear deal and giving clearer rhetorical support for the EU3's negotiations. European governments rejected Iran's proposal that it retain a number of centrifuges for uranium enrichment under the supervision of the IAEA. Another Iranian proposal was that it would transfer enriched uranium to Russia to be pumped into centrifuges before being returned to Iran; this elicited an unambiguous US rejection but a studied silence from the EU. Debate ensued among European states over the acceptability of an arrangement short of full cessation of enrichment; but no state advocated pulling back a significant distance from this being the essential bottom line of EU demands.

On 25 May in Geneva the two sides agreed to a pause in negotiations until after Iran's June 17 elections, and Iran agreed not to move to restart enrichment until new talks were held in July. The European hope was that a new president would emerge capable of renewing Iran's commitment to reach a deal. With Rafsanjani favoring "more patience" in talks with the EU3, his candidature was reported to have received tacit, behind-the-scenes (although obviously not officially acknowledged) European backing.[18] After Ahmadinejad's victory, Javier Solana's reaction was tougher than hitherto, suggesting that for the EU, "nothing outside the Paris agreement terms [on full cessation of enrichment] will be acceptable."[19] Arguably, the high representative was undercut by Gerhard Schröder, who, when questioned about how Europe would respond if Iran resumed enrichment, equivocated that "When we talk about sanctions it should be sanctions that do not hurt us more than the Iranians."[20]

European unity tightened as Iran inched toward resuming uranium conversion activity during the final months of 2005. Of the UK-German-French triumvirate, the language emanating from Paris was toughest. French foreign minister Philippe Douste-Blazy warned Iran it would face a "major international crisis" if it chose not to accept the EU's package of incentives.[21] Senior Iranian officials claimed that they had all along used talks with European governments as a means of buying additional time to complete the nuclear facility at Isfahan.[22] The EU did not offer additional incentives at this stage, perceiving little scope for productive bargaining and with any resumption of TCA talks now an increasingly remote possibility. When Iran restarted the enrichment plant at Isfahan in August 2005, European governments continued to decline to support unequivocally an immediate referral of Iran to the UNSC. However, when in January 2006 the seals were broken to restart experiments at the Natanz plant and both China and Russia expressed new concern, EU states did vote for Iran's referral to the Security Council—an apparently significant turning point in light of European efforts since 2001–2002 to avoid precisely this course of action. It remained to be seen at this stage what forms of sanctions would actually be contemplated by the European Union; officials acknowledged that debate was only just starting on this question in early 2006. This issue was set to dominate discussions thereafter.

Political Reform: A Mistaken Trade-Off?

As tension increased on the nuclear issue, the focus on Iran's internal political development became more circumspect. The assumption most commonly made was that efforts to contain Iran's nuclear activities required greater caution in relation to Iran's domestic politics. This was the essence of the conservatives' negotiating pitch: cooperation with the IAEA in return for less interference in Iran's domestic politics. Iran's conservatives had sought to convince European governments that they were the essential players the EU must court to secure progress in nonproliferation negotiations. It was acknowledged that the October 2003 nuclear deal had indeed depended on a group of "pragmatic conservatives," led by Hassan Rowhani, who had been able to deliver the commitments that reformers had not been in a position to guarantee; this group was consequently judged to have been strengthened by the process of negotiations with the EU3. The direction of EU policy suggested that European governments had largely accepted the conservatives' arguments.

A widespread European conviction was that reformists tended to be central figures in the more "Persian nationalist" strand of Iranian politics, and thus not necessarily more amenable to cooperating on the nuclear issue. One prime-ministerial aide, in one of the most critical European states, suggested that the EU had "two and a half issues" at stake with Iran: WMD and terrorism, with human rights as the "half" issue. Considerable advantage was, he suggested, to be found in a balance between reformists able to keep basic human rights issues alive and the pragmatic conservatives able to deliver on the nuclear issue. Many in the Bush administration reached exactly the opposite conclusion: for the neocons it was precisely because the reformists supported the nuclear program that root and branch regime change should be pressed. Indeed, US officials professed that the order of their priorities was the inverse, with the need to reduce Iran's "freedom deficit" at the top of the list.[23]

If it was undeniably the case that systemic political change in Iran would not immediately solve the nuclear issue, neither was it clear that it would make negotiations significantly more difficult. Indeed, a defining aim adopted by the new conservative-dominated *majlis* in 2004 was to push the Khatami government for a less cooperative attitude toward the IAEA. The same conservative politicians prominent in frustrating internal reform were those who took the lead in pressing the government into a tougher line on the question of nuclear inspections and in negotiations with the UK, France, and Germany. Reformers were critical of conservatives for pushing the EU into a harder stance by vigorously advocating that Iran move ahead with the development of a nuclear program and refusing to offer clear guarantees that the nuclear technology program would be for peaceful, civilian use.[24]

By the middle of 2003 European diplomats were freely acknowledging that the Human Rights Dialogue was having little tangible impact. Ministers had, it was admitted, expected relatively quick and smooth progress under the Dialogue, sufficient to demonstrate that engagement was a fruitful approach, and had soon become frustrated with the lack of even modest cooperation on political reforms. Iranian exile and opposition groups that had initially accepted the Dialogue as a promising way forward were soon berating the EU for having been duped by the Iranian regime. Despite the existence of the Dialogue and a supposedly shared agreement to cooperate on human rights, observers from the UK, the Netherlands, and France were barred from the trial covering the murder of Zara Kazemi, an Iranian-Canadian photographer.[25] Diplomats lamented that the Human Rights Dialogue had turned into a series of predictable, set-piece occasions, too cumbersome and formalistic to provide a "nimble, effective way of engaging" Iran on political reform issues. Dissatisfied with the EU Dialogue, Denmark developed its own human rights forum with Iran and funded reformist lawyers to follow human rights debates in the UN.

Despite their growing disillusion, member states resisted suggestions that the Dialogue and other areas of cooperation should be completely broken off. It was argued that the EU had at least won useful access to senior reformers, as when Chris Patten was able to discuss potential cooperation with the head of the Iranian judiciary during a visit to Tehran in February 2003. The Dialogue was felt to at least help keep the EU better informed of human rights issues in Iran. Trade negotiations had, of course, been broken off because of nuclear proliferation concerns, not in response to already worsening internal political developments. Some diplomats confidently predicted that prevailing difficulties would, in the words of one senior negotiator, be no more than a "speed bump" along the path toward deeper cooperation with Iran. In October 2003 Britain, the Netherlands, Sweden, and Ireland advocated EU sponsorship of a resolution in the United Nations Commission on Human Rights criticizing Iran for human rights abuses; a majority of member states opposed this, in large part because of the likelihood that Iran would withdraw from the Human Rights Dialogue in retaliation.

Most diplomats acknowledged that the increasing pressure exerted on Iran's nuclear activities was working to the detriment of gaining purchase over political reform. WMD concerns were, in the words of one EU policymaker, "getting in the way" of the human rights dimension. Reporting on the nature of discussions within political dialogue forums, one diplomat lamented, "It is all WMD." Indeed, much European effort was invested in trying to convince Iranian interlocutors that proliferation concerns were genuine and not merely an instrument in a campaign aimed at regime change. Europeans admonished the US administration for unhelpfully conflating these two dimensions. The greater prominence this tenor assumed in US discourse, the more strenuously European governments sought to *de*link the issues of nonproliferation and Iranian political reform. Convincing President Khatami to cooperate on WMD was indeed seen by European governments as a means of staving off the prospect of violent and destabilizing regime change. One argument common in European chancelleries was that pushing Iran on too many fronts would drive Tehran into cooperation with Russia and China on the development of nuclear technology.

Dealings with the People's Mujahideen became an increasingly conflictive issue. UK and US forces committed themselves to suppressing the MKO, a listed terrorist group in both countries, as the organization developed its activities in postinvasion Iraq. Iran accused the United States of in reality engaging with the MKO, however, as a possible ally against the Iranian regime. A ceasefire between coalition forces and the MKO in Iraq caused considerable tension with Iran. The MKO had been placed on the European Union's list of terrorist organizations in 2002, bringing Europe into line with the United Kingdom and the United States. There was no systematic European contact with or support for opposition groups—although Tehran accused the British government of meeting covertly with MKO representatives. Some member states raised the possibility of dropping the ban on formal contacts with the National Council of the Iranian Resistance, the de facto political branch of the MKO, but no consensus formed in favor of this. Nonetheless, a constant Iranian criticism was that European governments had failed to be tough enough in curtailing MKO activities in Europe.

Street protests erupted in Tehran in the summer of 2003, in the wake of which 135 parliamentarians wrote to Ayatollah Khamenei urging democratic reforms. The EU urged the regime not to clamp down in heavy-handed fashion, but was less explicit in its support for the protestors than was the US administration. The French foreign affairs spokesman was even implicitly critical of the protestors, opining that they had the "occasion to express a desire for change through municipal, legislative, and presidential elections"; invited repeatedly to support US concerns, he refused to do so.[26] Most European diplomats did not see the protests as a first step to full democratization or as signaling that the time was now ripe for external intervention, but rather as evidence that political space was gradually widening in Iran. Many protestors themselves complained that US pressure had enabled the regime to claim "external incitement" as grounds for a subsequent clampdown. In the wake of the student protests, Republicans in the US Congress stepped up their efforts for US support to be channeled to Iranian opposition groups, with some hawks suggesting that the MKO be declassified to qualify it for US funding to campaign against the regime. A proposed Iran Democracy Act, which attracted backing from some Democrats, suggested a $50 million fund to support reformists and a complete suspension of trade. Not entirely coincidentally, France moved at exactly this time—June 2003—to close parts of the MKO network in France.

After the summer protests hardliners reasserted themselves, while divisions grew between reformists in parliament and students urging a more radical approach. In the run-up to the February 2004 legislative elections the regime banned nearly four thousand reformist candidates, many currently sitting MPs. After protests and the resignation of over one hundred MPs, only a small proportion of the barred candidates were reinstated. Palpable disillusion was evident in European chancelleries in reaction to this blatant electoral manipulation and the consequent commanding victory secured by conservatives. One diplomat acknowledged that the elections had "taken the wind out of the sails" of European engagement. It was significant that European criticism of the elections was as strong as US criticism.[27] Even the French and Italian governments professed to be increasingly "glum" about Iran. Senior officials reported that the sheer degree of manipulation had come as a surprise to the EU. Far from the gradual process of change since 1997 having generated an incremental momentum of deepening reform, it was increasingly clear that in the face of growing frustration among the Iranian population autocratic control was gradually being reasserted.

Despite these concerns, European intentions remained vague. National and EU statements warned that the nature of the elections would "be taken into account," that the EU would have to "wait and see" how the prospects for future cooperation would be affected. British foreign secretary Jack Straw admitted to being "disappointed with the elections" and to having "to think about our engagement." Officials indicated that dialogue would not be broken off, but that efforts at rapprochement would slow down. Positioning itself in the "middle of the European pack" on Iran, Spain argued that the EU could not insist on more rigorous conditions than those imposed toward other Middle Eastern states.

The feasibility of running productive aid projects was also increasingly questioned. Commission plans for new projects on penal and judicial reform were "put on the back burner." The UK had already started projects on judicial reform, the training of judges, reform of the prison system, and parliamentary exchanges. But it now commenced an analysis of where rule of law and other aid projects might in practice be helping conservatives more than reformers;

pulled out of a joint project with Denmark on torture; and abandoned plans for two further reform projects due to worsening conditions on the ground in Iran. An EU official admitted that the June 2004 round of the Human Rights Dialogue was the least productive so far, with reformers' places in the forum having been taken by new conservative deputies, many under the tutelage of the Iranian Revolutionary Guard Corps. This contrasted with the claim made by officials running the European Initiative on Democracy and Human Rights that Iran had signaled an increased willingness to permit human rights projects, with the Initiative identifying support for women's rights, human rights advocacy networks, and Iran's adherence to international human rights standards as new EIHDR priorities for 2005.[28] A Commission-funded project run by the British Institute of International and Comparative Law, comprising biannual roundtables with European and Iranian legal experts to engage in dialogue on the ratification of UN human rights instruments, commenced but soon stalled as tensions deepened on the nuclear issue. A principal EU focus was the extension of university exchanges as an indirect means of assisting and engaging with student reformers.

Offsetting concerns over internal political trends within Iran, and quite apart from the nuclear issue, some European states concluded that growing instability in Iraq required stronger engagement with Iran. This was the line pursued in particular by the French government; a new Franco-Iranian investment treaty was signed in May 2005, just as a swath of candidates was being barred from standing in the June elections. A view expressed in some member state governments was that the United States' travails in Iraq were handing the lead role to the EU in Iran. In July 2004 Italian ministers visited Tehran to prepare for a joint Iran-Italy cooperation meeting, and agreed to new FDI incentives.[29] Italian energy giant ENI had already begun to develop new investment projects in Iran—attracting veiled threats from the United States. Some in Europe were candid enough to acknowledge that the hardening of US policy that they bemoaned actually suited European investors, giving them a freer field in the Iranian market. (However, the conservative *majlis* was by now trying to take over control of FDI contracts, to exert more restrictive conditions; these were the same conservative clerics, of course, who retained control of large parts of the Iranian economy through numerous foundations and other organizations.) Spain defined itself as shifting under its new Socialist government toward a more engagement-based approach. Reacting to such EU caution, in September 2004 a large demonstration was organized by the NCIR in Brussels to urge the EU to adopt a tougher policy toward the regime. This represented a potential change: the influence of exiles had always been felt in the United States but had been relatively absent in the EU and their influence over European policymaking negligible. Indeed, in December 2004 the European Parliament invited the MKO leader to speak, causing an angry reaction from Tehran and consternation in a number of European capitals.

Diverse trends emerged in European policies. As talks between the EU and Iran (briefly) reopened on 12 January, Jack Straw claimed that the progress of negotiations on the nuclear issue was precisely what would enable human rights to be raised in systematic fashion again.[30] In Denmark, long the most outspokenly critical member state on human rights, there was some optimism that the nuclear deal would unblock the human rights initiatives that had been hindered by Iran, including Denmark's own bilateral human rights dialogue. The Danish government backed the nuclear focus, albeit with some doubt, on these grounds. Iran did, indeed, begin cooperation with Denmark and the Netherlands on a project relating to the UN antitorture convention run through Tehran University. The European Parliament used the reopening of TCA talks to press the Iranian government on its repression of journalists and homosexuals. Within the renewed trade negotiations, the EU insisted that the standard democracy clause would have to be accepted by Iran; Iranian officials then stated they would not be willing to sign this. It was reported by some diplomats that the sclerotic Human Rights Dialogue might be folded into more general and broader political dialogue. Ironically, Italy expressed a desire to see a renewal of the Human Rights Dialogue in part so as to rein the focus back to the EU level away from the diplomacy of the "big three" member states.

Even the more critical European states emphasized the need to pursue any governance initiatives through the United Nations Development Programme, so as not to complicate EU advances on the nuclear dossier. There was no intimation that the EU would consider large-scale, reform-oriented funding, beyond the small-scale EIDHR projects underway. This contrasted with US policy: in her first address as secretary of state, Condoleezza Rice listed Iran (along with Burma, Belarus, Cuba, North Korea, and Zimbabwe) as one of the world's "outposts of tyranny," and in May 2005 the State Department launched a $3 million program for democracy and human rights projects related to Iran—this after a first set of limited projects had been funded at the beginning of the year for NGOs aimed at documenting abuses occurring in Iran.[31] (The administration did not pronounce on the growing pressure emanating from some Republican congressmen for the MKO to be taken off the list of terrorist organizations.)[32] EU officials questioned the legitimacy of funding European NGOs headed by secular Iranians, while also lamenting the difficulty in finding local partners for projects in the health, education, and environmental sectors.

In the run-up to the June 2005 elections it was Iran's conservatives who most clearly sought to use a hardening of positions on the nuclear negotiations for domestic political advantage. European diplomats expressed disappointment that reformists had failed to temper the toughening of nationalist sentiment. As earlier noted, it was reported from the ground that prior to the elections Western diplomats were quietly favoring Ali Akbar Hashemi Rafsanjani. European ambassadors incurred the regime's wrath when they also met publicly with (later banned) reformist candidate Mostafa Mo'in.[33] European officials referred to the barring of reformist candidates as a turning point in their perspectives on Iran. Notwithstanding this, some of Iran's most prominent human rights activists berated the weakness of European reaction to the barring of a large number of reformist candidates.[34] European statements after the elections were strongly critical of the manipulation undertaken by conservative forces. A declaration professed that the EU "regrets the fact that a very large majority of candidates, including many reformists and all the women, were excluded from this election."[35] Joschka Fischer lamented the "considerable deficiencies in the electoral process" and promised Iranian civil society Germany's "full support . . . in the future."[36] Jack Straw also condemned these "serious deficiencies," while the French foreign ministry criticized press and other restrictions and stressed the need for "positive steps" on human rights from the new Iranian government.[37] EU commissioner for justice and security Franco Frattini suggested that if the EU did not receive "clear words on human rights" it should "freeze dialogue with Iran."[38] Officials pointed to concerns not only in the political sphere but also over Ahmadinejad's apparent coolness to deepening economic cooperation in relation to WTO-linked reforms. However, by the end of

2005 it remained unclear whether such concerns and strictures would in fact translate into qualitatively different policies. Diplomats acknowledged that a decision remained outstanding on whether the EU should "insulate" the Human Rights Dialogue from the nuclear dossier or accept that the latter would become a casualty of the nuclear impasse, as increasingly was the case.

The EU reaction to the new government was notably more measured that that of the United States, with Washington revealing Ahmadinejad's participation in the US hostages siege that formed the backdrop to Iran's 1979 revolution. European governments expressed concern when the Bush administration (briefly) threatened to deny the new president a visa to attend the United Nations General Assembly.[39] Responding to the new president's suggestion that Israel should be "wiped from the map," Tony Blair was notably more critical than his EU counterparts. Iran "informally" imposed sanctions against the UK, accusing London of fostering disturbances in the south of Iran, as the UK accused Tehran of destabilizing the south of Iraq. The Swedish parliament later cut ties with Iran's national assembly. Despite the initial "wait and see" posture of most member states, Ahmadinejad's broadsides against European governments became as vitriolic as those aimed at the United States. By the start of 2006, the EU Human Rights Dialogue and incipient rule of law projects remained firmly frozen; this was due mainly to the nuclear impasse but was also indicative of Iran's internal political development.

Conclusion

Iran might be classed as one of European foreign policy's most notable successes, or equally as one of its biggest disappointments. European governments kept Iran talking on nonproliferation, and at least in the short term reined back its nuclear activities; the deals struck on Iran's nuclear program in October 2003 and again in November 2004 were certainly widely lauded as among the most significant vindications of a European approach to international challenges. But the EU was also unable to prevent reversals to Iran's internal political reform momentum and the return to power—at both the presidential and parliamentary level—of conservative forces opposed to democratic change. With Iran moving to resume enrichment-related activity, the EU3's achievements on the nuclear dossier were themselves also seriously at risk by the beginning of 2006. It was by this stage patently clear that the EU had not been able to fashion the kind of broad-ranging package of trade-offs requisite to striking a firm and sustainable deal covering Iran's nuclear activities. Arguably, the key European shortfall was to have failed to convince the United States to join in a coordinated offer to Tehran of some alternative form of security guarantee in return for the relinquishing of a nuclear program; European efforts were probably doomed all along to insufficiency without engagement from Washington.

Europe's strategy was predicated on the hope that, subjected to US pressure in relation to domestic politics and general international pressure for a commitment to nonproliferation, Iran would acquiesce to human rights improvements to keep Europe on board and positively engaged. A uniquely favorable set of conditions appeared to exist for positive European influence: an increasingly popular internal reform movement coupled with an especially hard-line US strategy that increased the need for Iran to secure other international alliances. By 2004 this dynamic was not taking root to the extent expected. The EU reacted late in trying to articulate some kind of effective linkage between its nuclear negotiations and Iran's backsliding on democratic and human rights. An increased European focus on human rights after 9/11 soon dissipated, colliding with both the priority attached to securing a deal on the nuclear issue and the reluctance to look beyond Khatami as the principal source of reformism even as the president's standing so evidently began to wane.

As in Iraq, this was a case where the EU "as the EU" was not the primary protagonist within overall European strategies. A complex relationship developed between the national interests and initiatives of the most powerful member states, on the one hand, and the instruments deployed at the EU level, on the other hand. Tension, perhaps unsurprisingly, arose between the EU3 and other member states; but there was also more positive linkage, with the UK, France, and Germany keen to harness EU initiatives to their own diplomacy and other member states gradually dovetailing much of their economic and political efforts with those of the triumvirate. This was a mix that might be classified as an appositely flexible model of European actorness. In the aftermath of the 2005 elections it remained to be seen whether this had indeed created the foundations for managing a more difficult period in relations with Tehran.

Notes

1. Tarock, "Iran–Western Europe Relations," pp. 41–61.
2. Tarock, "Iran–Western Europe Relations," p. 48.
3. www.oecd.org.
4. Moshaver, "Revolution," pp. 190–191.
5. Quoted in Takeyh, "Iran at a Crossroads," pp. 42–56.
6. www.diplomatie.gouv.fr/act/article.asp?ARF=49383.
7. Takeyh, "Iran at a Crossroads."
8. International Crisis Group, *Iran: Discontent and Disarray,* p. 12.
9. Everts, "Iran: The Next Big Crisis," pp. 46–49.
10. Everts, *Engaging Iran,* p. 14.
11. Everts, "Iran: The Next Big Crisis," p. 47.
12. *The Economist,* 19 June 2004, p. 62.
13. *Daily Star,* 9 July 2004.
14. *Financial Times,* 21 October 2004.
15. Statement by Javier Solana, 29 November 2004, www.consilium
.eu.int.
16. BBC Monitoring Service, 2 January 2005.
17. *The Economist,* 29 January 2005, p. 38.
18. *Middle East International,* no. 752, 10 June 2005, p. 13.
19. Javier Solana, press statement, 27 June 2005, www.consilium.eu.int.
20. Interview, 27 June 2005, in www.euobserver.com.
21. www.euobserver.com, 8 August 2005.
22. BBC Monitoring Service, 19 August 2005.
23. Undersecretary of State for Political Affairs Nicolas Burns, quoted in Heisbourg, "Iran: The Moment of Truth."
24. BBC Monitoring Service, 18 October 2004.
25. *Financial Times,* 19 July 2004, p. 4.
26. www.diplomatie.gouv.fr/actu.
27. *Le Monde,* 26 February 2004.
28. Commission of the European Communities, *EIDHR Programming Document 2005–2006,* p. 22.
29. BBC Monitoring Service, 21 July 2004.
30. BBC Monitoring Service, 18 January 2005.
31. US Department of State, *Supporting Human Rights and Democracy.*
32. *Middle East International,* no. 750, 13 May 2005, p. 14.
33. BBC Monitoring Service, 17 June 2005.
34. S. Ebadi and M. Sahemi, "In the Mullahs' Shadow," *Wall Street Journal,* 15 June 2005.
35. EU declaration on the Iranian elections, 28 June 2005, www.consilium
.eu.int.
36. BBC Monitoring Service, 27 June 2005.
37. *Financial Times,* 27 June 2005; www.diplomatie.gouv.fr/actu.
38. www.euobserver.com, 27 June 2005.
39. *Financial Times,* 8 August 2005.

4

The Maghreb and Mashreq: New Directions

If, as demonstrated in the preceding two chapters, Iraq and Iran represented two of the most conflictive challenges for European diplomacy, relations with the Maghreb and Mashreq could count on one of the EU's most institutionalized frameworks of positive engagement. The Euro-Mediterranean Partnership (EMP), established in 1995, included Morocco, Algeria, Tunisia, Egypt, Jordan, Syria, and Lebanon. (Palestine and Turkey, also partners, are covered in separate chapters of this book.) This produced a distinctive feature of the EU's incipient foreign policy: the choice initially to construct a "Mediterranean" rather than a broader Middle East policy, as the primary lens through which strategic and political issues were approached. It was this forum that initiated and crystallized many of the most significant European policies on security, counterterrorism, and support for political reform after 9/11.

This chapter assesses the new initiatives developed through the EMP with Arab states in the Maghreb and Mashreq in response to the changed post-9/11 international security environment. At the Mediterranean, regional level significant new strategies were introduced as the EU sought a more operational, multifaceted, and targeted approach to supporting political reform, in particular, by 2004, through the European Neighbourhood Policy (ENP). In overall terms, policy evolved incrementally after 9/11 and was bereft of any dramatic rupture or fundamental reassessment. Policies directly aimed at promoting democratic change were enhanced, but to a lesser degree than other areas of the EMP; these latter were presented as indirectly contributing to political reform in the Maghreb and Mashreq, but not always convincingly so. The chapter finds that the EU supported "elite-bounded" reform in Morocco, Algeria, Egypt, and Jordan, backing genuine reform dynamics but also doing much to legitimize the limitations to these incipient processes of change. Criticism toward the Tunisian regime in fact subsided after 9/11, while changing relations toward Syria and Libya were dominated by direct security issues, and in particular the proliferation of weapons of mass destruction, rather than these countries' internal politics. Debates at the EMP's tenth anniversary summit in November 2005 exhibited an uneasy balance between the political reform and traditional security agendas.

Barcelona and the Tentative Steps to a New Policy

The Euro-Mediterranean Partnership seemed to herald a new direction in European strategy. The EMP enshrined one of the EU's most high-profile commitments to democracy promotion, incorporated within one of its most far-reaching and deeply institutionalized external policy frameworks. Six years before the attacks of 9/11, the Barcelona Process was predicated on a declared need to encourage political reform as a means of mitigating "soft security" challenges: rising migratory flows from North Africa, the region's economic weakness, the security of energy supplies, as well as the buildup of arms in the Maghreb and Mashreq. The official philosophy was that progress on economic liberalization, political-security issues, and cultural cooperation—the respective themes of Barcelona's three OSCE-like baskets—would combine to produce a holistic strategic framework. The focus on democracy and human rights in the southern Mediterranean had lagged behind the incorporation of political reform commitments into EU agreements with Eastern Europe, sub-Saharan African states, and Latin America during the early 1990s. After the Gulf War, states supporting the coalition, and in particular Egypt, had won significant increases in aid from the European Union. The creation of the EMP brought Mediterranean relations into line with other areas, through a formal commitment to support political liberalization, the inclusion of standard democracy and human rights clauses within the new association agreements offered to Maghreb and Mashreq countries, and new democracy and civil society funding for this region.

The EMP initiated plans for a Euro-Mediterranean free trade area (FTA); increased geopolitical efforts through proposals for a trans-Mediterranean "zone of peace and security"; and made available a

4.6 billion ecu (European currency units) MEDA aid package for the 1995–1999 period. In the Mediterranean after 1995, a larger share of overall European aid was accounted for by Commission aid than in any other area. In 2001 no Mediterranean state appeared among the ten largest recipients of Dutch, Swedish, or British aid; Germany registered only Egypt and Jordan, and Spain only Morocco, among their ten main recipients. Egypt, Morocco, and Tunisia all appeared among the ten main destinations for French aid, while the Commission counted four Mediterranean states among its ten highest recipients. The Commission and France were the two largest donors in Tunisia and Morocco. No European donor gave significant aid to Syria.

The vast majority of observers judged the EMP's record up to 2001 to have fallen short of initial expectations. In practice, a significant strand of European strategy continued to prioritize engagement with incumbent regimes in the Maghreb and Mashreq. Such engagement was pursued in response to weakening trade relations and, by southern member states, in order to offset new funding for Eastern Europe. Cooperation with autocratic governments was seen as necessary to shore up the Middle East peace process—most southern Mediterranean regimes supported the Oslo accords against more skeptical domestic opinion—and to progress with ongoing arms control negotiations. Security approaches contained many initiatives that clearly reflected a defensive-containment logic: the creation of the Eurofor and Euromarfor forces; the development of new missile defense systems specifically designed to rebuff threats from the Mediterranean; the large amounts spent by southern European states in particular on new border control systems. Indeed, despite signing up to the EMP commitment to pressing "political pluralism," in private, southern EU states at this stage still expressed reservations over the ostensible strategic logic behind support for democratic change. During the late 1990s these states diluted statements and initiatives on political reform, and their bilateral actions were less than fully consistent with EU-level strictures on democracy. After some internal EU debate, the Common Foreign and Security Policy Common Strategy for the Mediterranean, adopted in 2000, did not adopt any new concrete democracy promotion initiatives—such efforts were overshadowed again by a focus on the peace process. Critics maintained that the stated intent to encourage political liberalization in the Maghreb and Mashreq had remained empty rhetoric.[1]

Trade relations did not become less imbalanced under the EMP. The Euro-Mediterranean FTA declined to offer free trade in agriculture, and quotas agreed upon in this sector remained restrictive. Differences on agriculture also delayed conclusion of association agreement negotiations. Agricultural and textile quotas were increased slightly in 2000, but well below southern Mediterranean demands. Moreover, preparations for free trade soon fell significantly behind schedule and failed to begin at all in earnest in the services sector. Notwithstanding this, MEDA funds were gradually diverted toward forms of stop-gap protection to assuage the effects of restructuring. Serious friction was provoked by the fact that only a quarter of the first MEDA protocol had actually been spent by 2000. At the end of 2000 the budget for MEDAII, covering the period between 2000–2006, was set at €5.3 billion, a small decrease in real terms. The share of European foreign direct investment going to the Mediterranean did not increase above 2 percent in the latter half of the decade.[2]

In overall strategic terms, the overwhelming and prejudicial influence on the EMP was the gradual collapse of the Arab-Israeli peace process. If the underlying rationale of the EMP had been to harness the progress of the Oslo accords by incorporating Israel and Arab states in the same framework of broad security and low-politics cooperation, the decision to link relations with Arab states to Israel soon became a millstone weighing down the EMP: the latter's "infection" by the peace process's waning momentum became the central issue of the late 1990s and into the new century. This caused a range of security cooperation proposals to be blocked or diluted, including proposals for a Charter for Peace and Stability; conflict prevention networks and initiatives; military confidence-building measures; the incorporation of a strengthened version of the UN Register of Conventional Armaments; and Mediterranean-wide mediation mechanisms and joint peacekeeping operations.

A modest investment was forthcoming in support of democracy and human rights. The EU eschewed coercive pressure against the nondemocratic regimes of the Maghreb and Mashreq. The EU's democracy clause was not operationalized, and notable increases in MEDA aid were granted to states such as Egypt and Tunisia acknowledged to be in the process of further tightening authoritarian control. National governments' bilateral aid flows to the region also remained skewed heavily and disproportionately toward Egypt. French aid tilted in favor of francophone states, and away, for example, from relatively reformist Jordan. European arms sales to the region also increased. Diplomats acknowledged that new, formal political dialogue consisted of little more than "woolly" presentations by national delegations on their adherence to international human rights instruments. Significantly, no systematic dialogue on democracy with Islamist opposition forces was developed; and no common EU line emerged on whether this was desirable. In short, democracy appeared in practice to fall well down the list of priorities, with more support for and pressure on economic reform, mitigating drugs trafficking, environmental protection, and population control.

At most, although arguably not without significance, the EMP began to force governments in the Maghreb and Mashreq to adopt a new discourse on political reform. European diplomats pointed to the importance of being able to refer to the reform commitments that Arab regimes had themselves agreed to in the Barcelona Declaration. If issues of systemic political change did not appear at the forefront of political dialogue, individual cases of human rights abuses were raised more regularly and with greater force. A more optimistic assessment of the EMP's early years might suggest that Barcelona had slowly begun to remold expectations of the kinds of political values integral to full, long-term partnership with the EU and to assure reformist voices some resonance within Arab societies. The generation of intangible socialization dynamics was often presented as the EMP's main achievement during this period.

Post–September 11 Approaches

The evolution of EU policies in the Maghreb and Mashreq after 11 September 2001 exhibited a mixture of reinforced direct approaches to security, on the one hand, and new initiatives in the area of political reform, on the other.

Two strands of direct approach to security were evident, one aiming at enhanced counterterrorist cooperation with Arab governments, the second tightening immigration controls—with these two strands increasingly merging within EU strategies. From the end of 2001 the EU insisted that antiterrorism cooperation clauses be inserted in all new third country agreements, an obligation applied to Algeria and Lebanon in the concluding stages of their association agreement negotiations. Counterterrorist cooperation was for the first time formally included as part of EMP ministerial meetings, with substantive discussions and experience-sharing underway by 2004. Parallel to this cooperation, member states toughened antiterror legislation domestically: curiously, it was hard-line French provisions on the detention of suspects that most closely resembled those introduced in the United States. A number of states increased the return of suspects to southern Mediterranean states, where previously human rights conditions in the latter had dictated greater caution.

An initiative to intensify security cooperation with southern Mediterranean governments under the rubric of European Security and Defence Policy was launched by the Spanish presidency in 2002. By the autumn of 2004 cooperation on ESDP was regularized, while the EU's new nonproliferation initiative incorporated a regional disarmament and WMD control process to be applied in the Mediterranean. The EU offered Mediterranean states participation in military training, the placement of military liaison officers, and involvement in EU-led crisis management operations; in respect of these ideas it was Arab governments who were the more ambivalent.[3] Simultaneously, NATO's Mediterranean Dialogue was upgraded in 2002 and was then relabeled a Partnership in the summer of 2004, having agreed to some Arab participation in NATO-led operations in the Balkans and Afghanistan.[4] A €2 million MEDA-funded project carried out by the European Police College and police forces from five member states commenced in March 2004 with the aim of enhancing cooperation with southern Mediterranean police forces on "fighting terrorism" and "human trafficking."[5] French diplomats saw one of their principal post-9/11 roles in the EMP as being to convince other EU member states of the merits of Moroccan and Algerian pleas for more robust security assistance. France, Spain, and Morocco joined forces before the EMP's tenth anniversary summit to propose that a formal, new initiative on political and judicial cooperation assume priority in the Barcelona Process. The EMP's tenth anniversary summit was dominated by the failure to reach a commonly accepted definition of terrorism, and by the more successful aim of agreeing upon a new code of conduct for antiterrorist cooperation. Significant developments at the bilateral level included a new €100 million French arms deal with Morocco and German tank sales to Egypt.

At the fifth ministerial meeting of the EMP, held in Valencia in April 2002, a new justice and home affairs pillar was added to the partnership, enshrining commitments further to clamp down on illegal migration. The EU pressed with increased vigor for readmission clauses to be inserted into association agreements. Spain and the UK introduced plans for stiffer controls on migrants at the Seville European Council in 2002. Funding for migration controls was a declared priority under a new Commission strategy for "cooperation in the field of Justice, Freedom and Security." The French, Italian, and Spanish governments were seen as pursuing security policies increasingly concerned with strengthening border controls and monitoring migrant communities internally.[6] The 5+5 Dialogue—grouping France, Spain, Italy, Portugal, and Malta with Algeria, Libya, Morocco, Tunisia, and Mauritania—was relaunched, with each of its three ministerial meetings up to the end of 2004 focusing on the strengthening of controls on illegal migration. The further development of this forum was stated as a French priority for 2005, with Paris introducing a new package of security cooperation at this level. In January 2003, the UK, France, Spain, Portugal, and Italy participated in Operation Ulysses, aimed at enhancing the capacity and effectiveness of border guards and patrol vessels in the Mediterranean. Italy went as far as providing armed patrol boats to Libya to police the Mediterranean. Some of the largest new aid allocations went to projects to reduce migration pressures, with Morocco receiving a €40 million allocation for such a program. In the wake of a series of fatal incidents at the Ceuta and Melilla borders, in December 2005 the Spanish government proposed an €800 million EU program for controlling illegal immigration.

While this emphasis on security cooperation and migration control was increasingly prominent, there were efforts to strengthen the democracy and human rights elements of the Euro-Mediterranean Partnership. One senior national diplomat defined post-9/11 political reform efforts as being important "to prevent revolution in the long term." In 2003 new guidelines were agreed committing the EU to intensifying its strategies aimed at promoting political reform. A key commitment was to offer additional resources to states willing to cooperate on human rights and governance reform. Crucially, this would involve the use of mainstream MEDA funds for democracy and human rights projects, significantly increasing the funds potentially available for such political aims.[7] Political dialogue should, it was argued, be oriented toward more practical impact, in recognition of the fact that such dialogue had so far taken the form of partners' simply giving a general presentation of their supposed human rights improvements, in the words of one diplomat, "as a pretext to avoid serious discussion." To this end, the commitment was subsequently made to establish new subcommittees on democracy and human rights under EMP association agreements.

The new guidelines reflected notable activism on the part of the European Commission. Driven in large part by Chris Patten, the Commission's initiative sought to hold member states to account for their commitment to strengthen democracy promotion efforts. Lamenting the reluctance still expressed by a number of member states, Patten announced the new guidelines prior to consultation with European governments. The initiative garnered strongest support from the Dutch, Danish, Swedish, and British governments; Spain was more amenable than it had traditionally been to a tougher approach toward reform; France was noncommittal but did not actively oppose the proposed measures; geographical desk officers from within both the Commission and some national ministries were more skeptical. It was acknowledged that efforts to invest EMP democracy policies with greater content were driven in part by new US activity in this area. At the inaugural meeting of the G8-inspired Forum on the Future in Rabat in December 2004, Javier Solana insisted that within the Barcelona Process the EU was itself now "talking Politics with a large P."[8] Even traditionally critical civil society actors, such as the Euro-Mediterranean Human Rights Network, welcomed what was judged to be a genuinely upgraded focus on democracy and human rights. Attracting particular attention was an April 2005 EU foreign ministers' call for engagement with faith-based groups in the southern Mediterranean.

A number of new initiatives were supported. The European Commission launched several projects at the regional level, bringing together NGOs, journalists, and women's groups from the various EMP countries—this manifesting a very EU-type conception of democracy dynamics taking root as part of a region-building enterprise. A number of tranches of human rights funding were allocated from the mainstream MEDA budget. In 2004, Egypt, Jordan, Morocco, and Syria were made eligible for EIDHR microprojects, and each allocated between €500,000 and €1 million annually for democracy projects under this facility. Germany set up a regional good governance fund, structured around two reform networks in the Maghreb and Mashreq, respectively; supported a regional colloquium to identify priorities for the protection of press freedoms in North Africa; and coordinated best practice cooperation between southern Mediterranean audit offices. The Commission funded the Friedrich Naumann Stiftung to develop a nine-country reformist network to explore governance reform options in the southern Mediterranean. Spain, still feeling a strong sense of ownership over the Barcelona Process, pressed for new democracy and human rights funds to be channeled through the EMP into the Maghreb in part so as to prevent the Broader Middle East Initiative diverting resources to the Gulf. The Spanish development ministry also began developing a Maghreb-wide governance initiative. Bilaterally, France allocated a significantly increased 10 percent of its aid allocation to democracy and governance projects in the Maghreb and Mashreq. Diplomats acknowledged that new French-funded civil society initiatives were part of Paris's strategy to retain influence in response to a US-led focus on civil society within the Broader Middle East and North Africa Initiative.[9] The British, German, and Danish governments convened roundtables with wide-ranging local representation to discuss the implications of the new UNDP Arab Development Reports.

Overall, funds allocated for political reform efforts remained modest. The overall share of French aid to the Maghreb and Middle East declined to 18 percent for 2002–2003, while the UK wound down its bilateral aid programs in Egypt and Jordan.[10] Mediterranean states did not in practice attract more EIDHR funds after 9/11. The region accounted for only 7 percent of this democracy and human rights budget in 2002–2003, while a revision to the program in 2004 allocated only €3 million to Tunisia and Algeria—the only Arab EMP states identified as target states, outside the Palestinian Territories—along with €2 million for regional projects in the Mediterranean basin.[11] Despite the injunction to dovetail development aid with democracy assistance funds, MEDA desk officers—long enjoined to focus on a small number of poverty-related priorities—remained uncertain over incorporating a rights focus into their projects. Decisionmaking procedures were acknowledged by officials to have remained insufficiently coordinated to give effect to such desired coherence, and the Commission itself acknowledged that MEDA remained "too developmentally oriented."[12] While 40 percent of MEDA funds were being channeled to social actors by 2003, Commission officials lamented that even in relation to nonpolitical projects, southern Mediterranean governments continued to limit NGO participation. Out of €3 billion of MEDA II funds committed by 2002, only €232 million had gone to governance projects; those projects that were funded were relatively technical, focusing on the provision of equipment and professional training, and failed, in the words of one of the principal architects of the MEDA governance program, to act "as a lever on reform."

As a result of the 1999 Commission corruption scandal, EU aid was still oriented more toward big government-linked institutions rather than small grassroots groups lacking the capacity to fulfill the EU's reporting obligations.[13] It was acknowledged that democracy was the issue least addressed in the EU's support for south-to-south cooperation in the Mediterranean. Interestingly, the United States' new Middle East Partnership Initiative also moved away from civil society support to reform projects incorporating governments.[14] EU member states' bilateral initiatives still eschewed, in the words of one diplomat, "hard core" democracy work. Most work defined as political aid continued to be structured around an emphasis on economic and social rights or technical-financial governance issues, rather than political-institutional change. Rule of law programs remained relatively technical in nature and were in fact less ambitious than judiciaries themselves pressing for more political autonomy in countries such as Egypt and Jordan. French aid retained its traditional focus on state reform, with all governance projects having to gain assent from the government of the country in question.

European governments presented their increased security cooperation with southern Mediterranean states as being consistent with the governance reform agenda. The MEDA aid program for 2002–2004 framed a range of programs on migrants, drugs, and counterterrorism as being "in support of" democracy.[15] The guidelines for new counterterrorist cooperation stipulated that this should be developed "without prejudice to respect for human rights and democracy."[16] Ministers suggested that counterterrorist cooperation "should respect and further the rule of law, human rights and political participation."[17] National diplomats insisted that the new antiterrorist clauses were significant for providing a route into dialogue on the principle that effective counterterrorism required a loosening of political repression. The new strategy for cooperation in the areas of justice, freedom, and security balanced funding for security and law enforcement initiatives with support for judicial reform projects and vocational training for legal migrants from the southern Mediterranean.[18] The EuroMeSCo (Euro-Mediterranean Study Commission) network judged that this all represented a genuine and stronger reform-oriented dimension to the EMP's hard security concerns.[19]

However, officials also acknowledged that cooperation with southern Mediterranean security forces in practice struggled to gain any tangible purchase on the stated aim of strengthening civilian oversight of militaries. Diplomats acknowledged that ten years of NATO's Mediterranean Dialogue, with a supposed focus on the reform of civil-military relations, had at best been able to contribute to more transparent security governance only in a very indirect and unquantifiable sense through facilitating the participation of Arab forces in UN peacekeeping missions. It was noted that significant security sector reform work had been supported by the EU only in Turkey and Palestine; that the first attempt to broaden the focus to Jordan at the beginning of 2005 had proven difficult; that Arab governments blocked a proposal from the EU to provide human rights training for Arab forces prior to their participating in ESDP missions; that police support had focused overwhelmingly on helping southern Mediterranean forces document and control migration flows; and that security cooperation and political reform were linked in European policies "only by approximation and not by design."[20] In the autumn of 2004, an enhanced program of "human rights sensitive" training for southern Mediterranean police forces at the EU Police College was presented as aiming to rectify these shortcomings. However, southern Mediterranean states became increasingly determined to use their acquiescence to counterterrorist cooperation to leverage a diluted focus on political reform conditions.[21]

In November 2005 the EMP's tenth anniversary summit agreed on the creation of a new Governance Facility, which would be a "substantial financial facility to support willing Mediterranean partners in carrying out . . . reforms." This was proposed by the Commission as a Democracy Facility, but the term "democracy" was not acceptable to Arab leaders. Decisions were not made on funding levels for the Facility, with new Central and Eastern European member states arguing against significant new injections of money for countries to the south where not accompanied by similar increases to the EU's eastern neighbors. The Governance Facility was not designed to provide democracy-related assistance but rather to let Arab governments decide how to spend additional pots of money given in reward for reforms. In this sense the Governance Facility contrasted with the Foundation for the Future agreed upon at the second summit of the Forum on the Future, held also in November 2005: this foundation was allocated an initial $50 million, mainly from US funds although with some European contributions, specifically to fund civic organizations as decided upon by a board of independent civil society representatives. While EU officials argued that the change of wording from "democracy" to "governance" was inconsequential, it raised the prospect of relatively technical and anodyne change being rewarded. Language on rewards for political reforms remained vague and noncommittal. EU assistance was to be provided to assist Arab states "to go at their own chosen pace," in the words of one official. A new initiative on election monitoring was also agreed upon, although, at the behest of Arab governments, it was limited to exchanges of "experience in the field of elections . . . on a voluntary basis and upon request of the country concerned." Despite the restrictions to these new initiatives, all Arab leaders except Mahmoud Abbas declined to attend the summit in part because of the focus on political reform. Recriminations followed between the European co-organizers: the Spanish and many other member states admonished the British presidency for "breaking the spirit of partnership" by being too forceful on political reform issues, while being ready to sell out to Israel's resistance on peace process issues; the British berated the Spanish chair for being willing to sell out on political reform issues in order to patch together a bad-tempered summit.

More vigorously strengthened as a response to 9/11 was the plethora of less directly political EMP initiatives aimed at shaping underlying social and cultural attitudes in the southern Mediterranean. These approaches were conceived to constitute the basic groundwork for eventual political change; southern European states advocated a priority emphasis on this area of policy as a means of determining how long-term political liberalization could be made compatible with short-term stability. A group of experts was convened by then Commission president Romano Prodi to identify ways of deepening dialogue across civilizations, leading to new proposals for educational exchanges, higher quality media coverage, and civic meeting places across the Mediterranean.[22] A Dialogue on Cultures and Civilizations was established, along with bilateral sociocultural programs with individual Mediterranean partner states. Significant new funding was directed toward cultural and social exchanges.[23] Many existing EMP networks were strengthened. The Euromed Parliamentary Forum was converted into a more strongly institutionalized Euromed Parliamentary Assembly, while a new extended format of the Euromed Civil Forum was initiated in January 2004; a more structured Euro-Mediterranean

Non-Governmental Platform was formed to coordinate the forum, beginning from April 2005. The EU's program of university exchanges was extended to Mediterranean partners. The Euromed trades union forum and the Euromed economic and social committee engaged in more regularized dialogue on political as well as socioeconomic rights. A new Euromed youth platform was created in 2003, along with an enhanced cross-Mediterranean program of cooperation between municipalities. Euromed Heritage, a program funding the preservation of historical sites and monuments, saw its budget significantly increased to €45 million, one of the largest of all MEDA funds. The Euromed Audiovisual program was a particular focus for new funding and activity, with a series of initiatives under the label of "Knowing the Other." At the bilateral level, France and Germany in particular framed their human rights work within the scope of cultural cooperation budgets. The Catalan government proposed a Euro-Mediterranean Committee of the Regions, while in 2005 a series of twinning arrangements commenced between regulatory and standards agencies in Europe and the southern Mediterranean.[24]

The new Ana Lindh Euromed Foundation, established in 2004 and opened for business in 2005, provided the most high-profile new avenue for cultural cooperation. The first workplan for the foundation included a number of initiatives aimed at developing "democratic citizenship." It was this realm of social, educational, and cultural exchange that attracted most new proposals in preparation for Barcelona's tenth anniversary summit. France and Spain proposed an increased focus on regions within southern Mediterranean states, through programs that would indirectly enhance civil society access to local governments.[25] Some in the southern Mediterranean states observed that it was in relation to politically couched cultural projects that Arab governments most notably changed their views, apparently recognizing that greater willingness to engaging at this relatively soft level might help neutralize a harder-edged US focus on democracy promotion.

These relatively soft, apolitical initiatives were, observers highlighted, subject to their own limitations. The share of overall European aid going through civil society bodies remained lower in the Mediterranean than in other developing regions.[26] Bodies such as the Civil Forum remained bereft of an official role in EMP policymaking. Tensions over the Arab-Israeli conflict ensured that many cultural and social projects were frustrated, with states such as Syria and

Lebanon often refusing to participate alongside Israeli representatives.[27] The plethora of new education projects made no apparent link to new clampdowns on student protests in the region. Within the Euro-Mediterranean parliamentary assembly, Arab politicians blocked toughly worded statements on a number of acts of political repression, such as the detention of Egyptian opposition leader Ayman Nour. Staff at the Anna Lindh Foundation acknowledged a range of concerns affecting their planning, including the unlikelihood of the foundation being able to support southern organizations not officially sanctioned by their governments; the cool reaction of radical groups themselves toward a venture seen as controlled by governments; the difficulty of getting European visas for many potential Arab participants; the tendency for much youth work simply to add funds to governments' own national youth programs; a very limited initial budget of €11 million; and a reluctance on the part of most European and Arab governments to develop indicators to assess the broader political impact of cultural and social initiatives. One symbolic omission cast doubt on the EMP's permeation to the grassroots level in Arab societies: only in 2005, ten years after its signing, was an official Arabic version of the Barcelona Declaration made available.

Proposals to include moderate Islamists within such networks were invariably blocked by southern Mediterranean governments, and were in any case not pressed by southern EU states. The much-vaunted interest in engaging with moderate Islamists took the form of the latter's inclusion in broad-ranging dialogue forums, without a significantly more proactive defense or promotion of these groups' still heavily comprised political rights. A single, clear European line on which Islamist groups, if any, could and should be included within cooperation projects remained conspicuously absent—this after a number of member states had proposed the elaboration of such guidelines. Most member states argued that engagement should be with already officially sanctioned Islamist parties, through the Euromed Parliamentary Assembly. Commission officials admitted to being less willing than in other areas to assume a lead role in engaging with Islamists, due to the political sensitivities of this issue. It was noted that most Islamist groups themselves remained reluctant to accept backing from European governments. In Spain, Italy, and France, 9/11 engendered a notable effort from governments to engage with Islamist—especially Muslim Brotherhood–linked—groups living *within* European societies; but this was not matched by rapprochement with similar organizations based in the Maghreb and Mashreq. In private, diplomats from some member states still questioned the wisdom of the very notion of engaging with Islamist groups as supposed vehicles of democratic change. The largest share of cultural-religious events focused on the situation of Islam in Europe, rather than the lack of Islamists' democratic rights in the Arab world.

The claimed link between such sociocultural approaches and democratic capacity was rarely demonstrable. Such initiatives placed far more emphasis on recognizing differences and specificities than on the common validity of democratic norms. One diplomat acknowledged that the purposeful use of such forums for political reform objectives was "a game we haven't played yet." Critics berated the EU for a one-sided, overly instrumental, and unrealistic perception that such regional projects could be used to socialize away cultural differences between Europe and Arab states.[28] Northern states complained that southern EU states judged cultural initiatives as an alternative to, more than an instrument of, democracy promotion. Prodi's group of experts itself expressed concern over its cultural recommendations being pursued as a substitute for other areas of policy.[29] If cultural diplomacy became an EMP forte, its pertinence to the fostering of democratic dynamics appeared far more questionable than was claimed by many policymakers.

A parallel argument was that the new security context warranted a strengthening of economic cooperation with Maghreb and Mashreq states, with this still judged by policymakers to be the area of greatest European influence, the EMP's real bread and butter. In 2002 the Euromed Internal Market Programme was created, with the aim of integrating southern Mediterranean partners into the web of regulations governing the EU's single market. This strand was given significant further impulse by the European Neighbourhood Policy, from mid-2004. Considerable support was offered to help implement the Agadir agreement, a new commitment to subregional economic liberalization between Morocco, Tunisia, Jordan, and Egypt. Progress was made on streamlining rules of origin and the implementation of trade facilitation measures. Additional funding was made available for the Euro-Mediterranean Energy Networks infrastructure project. The Facility for Euro-Med Investment and Partnership was established in October 2002, providing €1.5 billion of credit for southern Mediterranean states. Notoriously subject to delays in disbursement of infrastructure funding in its first years of operation, MEDA had by

2003 achieved a payments/commitments ratio of 90 percent. Many European ministers revealed that they had taken as a lesson from 9/11 the need for greater circumspection in pushing forward with socially disruptive economic adjustment. The "backloading" of economic liberalization obligations was said to be a new guiding objective. Several ministers suggested that the EU would not push to meet the slated 2010 deadline for Euro-Mediterranean free trade.[30] Indeed, by the middle of 2005 only Tunisia and Morocco were set to remove tariffs on manufactured goods by the planned date, and only in June 2005 did the Commission introduce proposals to begin liberalization in services and investment with southern Mediterranean states.[31] Perhaps most significantly, at the EMP tenth anniversary summit the EU committed to opening its agricultural markets, albeit through wording that included a number of possible caveats and qualifications.

The evolution of these economic approaches was seen to provide a means, in the words of one national diplomat, of bringing in politics "though the back door." The importance was emphasized of EMP forums involving the Economic and Social Committee, EU Chambers of Commerce, and trades unions, all facilitating the dissemination of "best practice" in independent regulatory structures and the monitoring of economic and labor rights. Several member states opined that the EU could and should gradually develop pressure for political reform primarily through this more economically focused framework, rather than as a separate democracy strategy. Diplomats from these states argued that it was through economic initiatives that Islamists could most readily be incorporated. Indicative of its concern to mesh the political and economic spheres, the UK supported capacity building for businesswomen in Egypt. However, if weakness in the linking of economic and political reform strategies was an Achilles heel of the EMP prior to 9/11, this imprecision persisted as new initiatives were elaborated between 2002 and 2005. Despite much rhetoric asserting that economic change would lead to political reform, one official acknowledged that in practice "we are just crossing our fingers" that these would eventually lock together. It was difficult to discern any concrete new measures aimed at actively harnessing economic instruments to the aim of engendering democratic dynamics. Some, mainly north European, diplomats worried that the shift in EU policies toward supporting social stop-gap measures would actually discourage the kind of restructuring needed to dilute the overbearing control and nepotism of state structures in the southern Mediterranean.

In addition, the tensions that erupted in relation to Morocco's refusal (until 2005) to negotiate a new fisheries agreement demonstrated that well-defined sectoral interests could still cut across engagement aimed at the longer-term goal of promoting democratic change. As the Bush administration introduced plans to create a US–Middle East free trade area by 2013, explicitly linking economic and political conditionality, the EU ran some risk of losing the comparative advantage it had potentially held in its influence over the underlying economic preconditions to democratization.

The European Neighbourhood Policy

From the middle of 2004 the focus was increasingly on the decision to complement the Barcelona Process with the new European Neighbourhood Policy, which purported to foster a "ring of friends" on the EU's new postenlargement periphery. This initiative bred some confusion over how the linking together of southern Mediterranean states with countries such as Ukraine, Moldova, and Georgia would relate to the EMP. The Neighbourhood Policy reflected suggestions that disaggregating Maghreb and Mashreq policy had become essential to freeing up political reform cooperation with those states more willing to progress in such areas.[32] The ENP offered the "new neighbors" participation in many areas of EU economic cooperation, and in particular the single market, and was said to be based on an "everything except the institutions" logic. It also contained a notable political reform dimension. The stated hope was that the framework could help overcome, in the words of one southern EU member state's diplomat, "a Euro-Med fatigue" increasingly evident in EMP forums.

Reflecting the declared aim of differentiating more between individual states, the ENP provided for bilateral action plans covering each neighboring country. Morocco, Jordan and Tunisia—along with the Palestinian Authority and Israel—were the first to negotiate such action plans. These accorded commitments related to democratic reform a more prominent priority than did existing association agreements, and included human rights programs agreed with the respective governments. By the middle of 2005, Egypt and Lebanon were also negotiating their action plans. A list of reform priorities more specific to each state was compiled, with the involvement of civil society organizations and parliaments. Political dialogue was driven toward "single theme" discussions to avoid, in the words of one diplomat, "hot air" generalities. While the 2003 communication on democracy and human rights had stressed dialogue "below the political level," the action plans were more explicitly based on the notion of comprehensive political-level engagement.[33] Progress on a series of reform benchmarks would be reviewed in 2007, which would, it was hoped, generate a competitive dynamic between countries eager to attract more European resources. In preparation for this, a €45 million MEDA Neighbourhood Programme was established for 2005–2006; it was proposed that the range of budgets covering the new neighbors— MEDA, Tacis (grant-financed technical assistance to thirteen countries of Eastern Europe and Central Asia), and EIDHR—would be folded into a single European Neighbourhood and Partnership Instrument to streamline funding, beginning in 2007.

The approach embodied in the Neighbourhood Policy constituted mainly quantitative not qualitative evolution. European policies toward democratic reform remained cooperative rather than coercive. The Spanish government stressed that the Neighbourhood Policy must not undermine the "sense of family" built up under the Barcelona Process; in light of the fact that the ENP had been devised by the EU and then offered on a take-it-or-leave-it basis to Arab states, key diplomats in Madrid suggested that the partnership dimension should now be firmly emphasized. They were adamant in their argument that, however frustrating progress at the multilateral level in the Barcelona Process, relations with Arab states should not be "bilateralized." EU diplomats at the most senior level revealed that the Neighourhood Policy had been made possible in particular due to a shift in French thinking, but that this shift was as yet "nothing dramatic." French diplomats acknowledged that some degree of reform dimension was seen as desirable to offset the emerging role of the US-inspired Broader Middle East Initiative through the ENP. If the Forum on the Future helped galvanize EU deliberations, it also encouraged many European governments to stress even more strongly the EU's partnership-based approach to reform, to distinguish policy from what was perceived as the United States' more heavy-handed strategy. Italy remained conspicuously unengaged in these debates, which were eclipsed by Berlusconi's orientation toward strategic alliance with the United States; a limited Italian aid budget for the Middle East was (outside the Palestinian Territories) divided mainly between Egypt and Tunisia and bereft of any notable political reform profile.[34] Much European discussion focused on the precise relationship between the Barcelona Process and the Neighbourhood Policy, leaving internal EU debates divorced from wider discussions over Arab reform.

The EU remained deliberately vague on the question of which kinds of reform would be rewarded with which sums of additional aid. Where initial action plan drafts talked of firm, objective benchmarks, more discretionary language gradually crept back in.[35] Both the Commission and southern EU member states insisted on a dilution of "positive conditionality" commitments, unconvinced of the merits of firm linkage between EU benefits and Arab states' relative willingness to reform. The Commission's guidelines eventually suggested only that future proposals would be made "in light of" a review of progress under action plans, and that some Mediterranean partners "could" be offered upgraded relations.[36] Senior officials acknowledged that they sought to keep conditionality linked to the very general "overall level of shared values" demonstrated by partner states, rather than at the level of detailed reform stipulations.[37] Like the Barcelona Process, the ENP talked primarily in terms of shared goals and co-ownership, through workplans drawn up in collaboration with governments in the south. The Neighbourhood Policy included no new operational language on democratic conditionality, while under bilateral action plans southern Mediterranean governments would sit on the committees charged with monitoring their own performance against political benchmarks.[38] Only one member state, Britain, offered its own proposed action plan language aimed at enhancing commitments to benchmark political reform; the UK argued that both the ENP and the Barcelona Process needed to be more "outcome-focused rather than process-driven."[39] Clear incentives were not provided in terms of what the eventual Neighbourhood Agreements—which were envisioned to supplant association agreements in three to five years—might actually include. Civil society organizations lamented that human rights commitments under the ENP represented a step back from the 2003 guidelines.[40]

The claimed specificity of action plans to the challenges of individual states also looked overstated. The new detail on political reform in practice resided in "democracy" being broken down into sectoral categories more than previously. But these categories were largely generic; each action plan included some reference to recent or forthcoming developments in each respective country, but the guiding aims were virtually identical across different states—international human rights instruments, women's rights, freedom of expression and association, decentralization, judicial modernization, public administration capacity building, political party reform, and social rights.[41] Little could be gleaned from the action plans as to where the main blockages to reform really existed in each southern Mediterranean state and what the EU intended to do to address these. The areas identified as priority sectors for support continued to be NGOs, women's rights, and standard human rights legislation. Little more was committed to reform political-level institutions such as political parties or parliaments. The action plans included over 200 stated objectives, but with no ordering of priorities. Such was the degree of general replication from the Europe agreements of the 1990s that the first action plan drafts had reputedly circulated without every mention of the Eastern European state in question having been substituted for the Arab counterpart!

The logic of "everything bar the institutions" was bereft precisely of what was arguably the most potent leverage over democratic reform in southern and eastern Europe, namely the prospect of governments gaining voting rights and thus formal influence over EU policies as a quid pro quo for political liberalization.[42] The prospect of more formal integration into single market regulations did not address the Mediterranean partners' long-standing complaints against EU protectionism in agriculture and textiles. Concessions on these issues were resisted by southern EU member states during Neighbourhood Policy negotiations—despite the new wording agreed upon at the tenth anniversary summit. Spain and France still insisted that Arab governments only raised the agriculture issue as a negotiating ploy and, in the words of one diplomat, "not because it is really important to them." Moreover, at the behest of (some) member states the approach to the possibility of Mediterranean states being granted internal market provisions on the free movement of workers became increasingly noncommittal. Indeed, the inclusion of permanent safeguards on free movement in negotiations with Turkey set a precedent that rendered EU concessions on this issue less likely. It was increasingly recognized that the Commission had been guilty of over selling the Neighbourhood Policy and that the Council had reined back the rhetoric as it became clear that what was on offer was very much less than "everything but the institutions." It was also argued that the ENP still failed to offer a genuine partnership on addressing open conflicts in the region, for many Arab organizations a vital situational factor relevant to democratic potential.[43]

The Commission's proposal to create a single Neighbourhood Policy financing instrument from 2007 involved the incorporation of EIDHR funds in a way that threatened to leave strategy toward the region without a pool of resources earmarked specifically for democracy assistance. The emphasis shifted toward using mainstream MEDA funds, from which each Mediterranean state was allocated between €2 and €5 million for democracy and human rights projects for 2005–2006; unlike under the EIDHR, the use of these funds had to be negotiated with Arab governments. The Commission reacted to concerns expressed by civil society organizations by proposing a Euro-Mediterranean democracy and human rights conference in 2006 to debate future strategy—an idea the Egyptian government lambasted as unacceptable "interference."[44] Within debates over the EU's 2007–2013 financial perspectives, however, the UK, Denmark, and the Netherlands resisted the prospect of significant increases to middle-income Maghreb and Mashreq states and pressed instead for a larger share of resources to be directed at the poorest developing states.

Backing Controlled Reform

European strategies were aimed at supporting change afoot in a number of Mediterranean partner states that was implemented by governments in a cautious and controlled fashion. In these cases, many aspects of European policy were sufficiently tepid to legitimize reforms that were at best cosmetic, with efforts to pursue a cooperative approach to more meaningful change successfully diverted by Arab regimes.

Morocco

Under Mohammed VI Morocco became the main hope for a cooperative approach to Arab reform. European states commenced a range of new initiatives with the Moroccan government. Many of the EU's new regional networks and initiatives were built around prominent participation from Moroccan civil society groups, seen as among the most autonomous and dynamic in the southern Mediterranean. A €34 million project on judicial reform broadened the scope of previous work to focus on the more sensitive issue of strengthening judges' political independence. While over 80 percent of total EU aid to Morocco still came from the Commission and the French government,[45] a number of other donors launched reform projects. Morocco was a priority recipient of funds from the UK's new Engaging with the Islamic World fund, particularly through projects on financial sector modernization, judicial reform, and the social consequences of economic change. The German development ministry ran projects on decentralization, election organization, and the gender effects of Morocco's economic policies. The first meeting of a reform-oriented EU-Morocco Reinforced Political Dialogue was held in June 2004, and Morocco was the first state to negotiate a bilateral Neighbourhood Action Plan, with human rights elements.

However, limits to the king's willingness to undertake comprehensive reform and to the EU's ability to gain purchase over such a process soon became apparent. Morocco was excluded from the EIDHR's target states in the context of the government intimating it was ready to accept unhindered human rights funding through mainstream, government-to-government EU budgets. In practice, Moroccan ministers subsequently scuttled a number of political reform initiatives forwarded on this basis. Elements of European policy were notable less for their gentle encouragement of further change than for their appeasement of the king's reining in of the reform dynamic. The French government was not only silent on the jailing of prominent journalists in Morocco—even when this affected French journalists—but was critical of the demonstrations held by Moroccans in Paris that such clampdowns on press freedoms provoked. After the May 2003 terrorist bombings in Casablanca, the Moroccan government introduced tough antiterrorist provisions with negative human rights repercussions. Several European states responded by backing the Moroccan government through new security cooperation. Paris and Rabat established an intelligence-sharing "French-Moroccan axis."[46] During his October 2003 visit to Morocco, President Chirac made no mention of reform issues; offered firm support for Morocco's position on Western Sahara; and declared his main aim to be winning Moroccan support against the invasion of Iraq.

There was ad hoc and exploratory European engagement with the Party of Justice and Development (PJD), but not with its rival Justice and Charity movement (still barred from political activity). When the king stepped in to determine the structure of the broad-based coalition government, after the September 2002 elections, and exclude the PJD, there was no EU reaction. The United States was equally circumspect; the State Department initially clashed with the

National Democratic Institute in relation to the latter's new parliamentary training program with PJD representatives. The EU was equally silent on the continuing ban from political activity of the Justice and Charity organization. If the European approach had been predicated on the notion of persuading the king to implement a top-down process of political liberalization, it was not clear by 2005 that the EU was exerting any critical pressure to encourage Mohammed to take more significant steps in this direction. With the United States negotiating a bilateral free trade agreement with Morocco and making the latter the sole Arab state qualifying for funding from the Millennium Challenge Account, European governments faced new competition for influence over Rabat. This competition was of particular concern to the French government and represented a ratcheting-up of the long-standing Moroccan foreign policy strategy of playing off Paris and Washington against each other.[47]

Most notable in the wake of 9/11 were the tensions that erupted between Morocco and the center-right Spanish government of José María Aznar. Morocco refused to sign a new agreement to extend fishing rights previously granted to Spanish trawlers, while Spanish farmers and fishermen took to the streets to protest the (in fact modest) tariff reductions granted to Morocco under the association agreement. In October 2001 Morocco withdrew its ambassador from Madrid accusing Spain of (pro-Polisario) interference in the Western Sahara and angered by Spanish accusations that Rabat was being uncooperative in the control of migration. Morocco's "invasion" of the uninhabited rock of El Perejil then took relations to a new low point. If these contretemps did come with a slightly greater degree of criticism of Morocco's democratic shortcomings than had been customary from Spain, observers characterized Aznar's approach to such issues as one of neglect. Indeed, Spain explicitly kept democracy off the formal agenda so as not to complicate bilateral disputes even further. The management of Spain's relations with Morocco in this period was taken over by the prime minister's Moncloa office, undercutting the incipient work of the development ministry's human rights department. Moreover, many Spanish civil society aid projects were suspended because of the El Perejil incident. In the closing period of the Aznar administration the focus was firmly on restoring more positive diplomatic relations with Rabat.[48]

Significantly, as these tensions mounted, Paris demonstrated greater solidarity with Rabat than with the Aznar government. Slighting the Spanish emphasis on Saharawi self-determination, President Chirac insisted on referring to Western Sahara as Morocco's "southern province." France vetoed a proposed ESDP statement backing the Spanish position on El Perejil—leaving Europe's supposedly common defense policy unable to react to the invasion of one of its own states' territory, and requiring Colin Powell to step in to avert a conflict. The aim of Spain's new Socialist government to normalize relations with Morocco, after the March 2004 elections, was built primarily around a security orientation.[49] Joint Spanish-Moroccan patrols commenced in the Mediterranean in July 2004, and the two countries sent a joint police mission to Haiti. In October 2004 a new forum of "triangular cooperation" between Madrid, Paris, and Rabat was established on antiterrorist cooperation and illegal migration. Spain's €50 million bilateral aid program for Morocco in 2005 did include a reinforced targeting of judicial reform and decentralization, with a particular focus on strengthening local government in the north of Morocco.[50] However, with the Spanish Socialist Workers' Party (PSOE) reactivating its history of close cooperation with the Moroccan socialist party, there was a conspicuous absence of any push for political reform at the diplomatic level. At the beginning of 2006, for example, Spain blocked a Swedish proposal that the EU issue a critique of the Moroccan press code.[51] Human rights activists in Morocco and Spain criticized the PSOE government's change of policy on the Western Sahara, which apparently brought Spanish policy into line with the positions of Rabat and Paris, favoring Saharawi autonomy within Morocco.[52] The significance of this shift for the Palace's authority could not be underestimated, given the core importance of the Western Sahara issue to domestic Moroccan politics.[53]

Algeria

European policy toward Algeria was similarly seen after 9/11 primarily in terms of shoring up the position of President Bouteflika. Reform potential was judged as best served by strengthening presidential powers.[54] If some European governments had begun to despair of Bouteflika's hesitancy to reform Algeria and expected the military imminently to ease him from office, in the changed environment after 2001 the president won less ambivalent international backing. As a peace deal held together and Bouteflika remained unchallenged by the military, European governments were drawn to Algeria's model of the formal elements of democratic process being developed within a context of continued military influence and a government-controlled incorporation of moderate Islamists.

Some elements of cooperation in the field of democracy and good governance became more practicable and acceptable to the Algerian government than in previous years. Algeria was included as a target state for the EIDHR in 2002. The EU's priorities in Algeria were defined as stability and security, fundamental liberties, and good governance. New initiatives were launched on judicial reform, with a focus on the transparency of and access to the legal system and training for women judges; the insertion of human rights issues into the education syllabus; human rights training for magistrates; police reform; the media; the rehabilitation of areas affected by terrorism; the strengthening of local administration; and information programs on democracy. The basic aim was defined by EU diplomats as being to cooperate with the government on modest parcels of human rights education and awareness building. In 2004, €15 million of MEDA funding was allocated to judicial reform in Algeria. One of the main priorities of the Commission's governance focus was to press the Algerian government to budgetize—and thus increase scrutiny over—revenues from the national oil company, Sonatrach.

At the end of 2004, ten EIDHR microprojects were awarded to Algerian civil society organizations, focusing on the prevention of violent behavior among young people, children's rights, and human rights monitoring.[55] The biggest Commission allocations were a €60 million allocation for professional training and an NGO-run program offering assistance to the victims of terrorism. The security-oriented design of political reform priorities in Algeria was seen in the large amounts of funding that went to initiatives ostensibly aimed at reform of the security services. In 2005, a €10 million second phase of the MEDA Algerian policing project began, with a particular focus on strengthening border patrols. The EU insisted that this entailed an upgraded human rights dimension, but it was also widely agreed among policymakers that Algeria represented one of the most egregious cases of European governments being unwilling fully to share information on their bilateral military cooperation.

In Algeria, Morocco, and Tunisia, French policy was acknowledged by the Quai d'Orsay to be heavily conditioned by presidents' personal links to Jacques Chirac. Chirac's visit to Algiers in March 2003—the first by a French president since 1962—led to new cooperation agreements between France and Algeria, which included a commitment to assist in ongoing democratic reform.[56] It was still the case that only the Commission and France ran significant aid programs in Algeria, both with annual allocations approaching €100 million; no other European donor gave more than €15 million. French aid focused strongly on education and assistance to the victims of terrorism, with the French development agency given additional autonomy in Algeria to invest dynamism into these priority areas. Significantly, in 2004 the French development agency also recommenced a governance program in Algeria. Priorities within France's bilateral aid program included administrative modernization and the strengthening of cultural links between Algerian and French civil society organizations. The Spanish government also funded new work on judicial reform and prison conditions. German aid concentrated on small-scale social work, for example through the Friedrich Ebert Stiftung, which became the first European foundation to open offices in Algeria.

Undoubted progress on basic democratic norms was made, but the EU also indulged a number of maneuvers of doubtful democratic legitimacy. Bouteflika's May 2003 ousting of his prime minister, Ali Benflis, in favor of an army-backed figure, elicited no response. The EU's judicial reform program proceeded as Bouteflika began removing a number of judges who had incurred his displeasure. In response to its diplomatic tensions with Morocco, the Aznar government openly sought to develop an alliance with Bouteflika, given substance through a new gas pipeline deal and generous debt relief, and militating further against human rights criticism from Madrid. The presidential elections of 2004 were given a clean bill of health by European Parliament observers, the Organization for Security and Cooperation in Europe, and the United States, and won their most unqualified praise from the French government; the US and French reactions went beyond the standard welcoming of election results to a more or less overt endorsement of Bouteflika.[57] Analysts highlighted that crucial manipulation had occurred prior to the election—in terms of media bias and the disqualification of notable Islamist candidates—sufficient to secure a rather unconvincing 83 percent vote for Bouteflika. Questioned about this manipulation, French foreign minister Dominique de Villepin reassured that France would not "interfere in Algeria's internal affairs . . . out of respect and friendship for the Algerian people" and the two countries' "common conscience . . . [and] . . . common destiny."[58] In part concerned at deepening US counterterrorist rapprochement with Bouteflika, Chirac rushed to Algiers three days after the elections to congratulate the president, with no mention of imperfections in the procedures preceding the vote. Negotiations followed for a Franco-Algerian Friendship Treaty and one of France's biggest ever loan deals. Several north European states were slightly more circumspect, while still accepting the basic validity of the elections. Chancellor Schröder used an October 2004 visit to Algiers to congratulate Bouteflika on his "impressive" democratic reforms.[59]

The EU saw the incorporation of a number of moderate Islamist parties into the Algerian parliament as having helped undermine any remaining relevance of the Front Islamique du Salut (FIS). Avowedly reluctant to rock the boat while a peace of sorts uneasily held, European governments agreed that the way forward lay in Bouteflika's idea of extending dialogue and the amnesty deal with Islamist combatants. Support for reform was seen as best going through Bouteflika's national commission for reconciliation, with gentle encouragement from some European states for the government to allow this commission more autonomy and transparency. Aid projects were invariably run through government-sanctioned partners; the EU's media program, for example, was implemented through the journalists' union linked most closely to the regime. EU diplomats judged that Algeria differed from Syria to the extent that, in the former, outside actors could "work with the grain" of domestic developments. The French position was that, in the words of one Quai d'Orsay official, "things are going in the right direction in Algeria."

The waters of European-Algerian relations were not entirely smoothed, however. Progress on trade liberalization remained halting, with hydrocarbon-rich Algeria showing distinctly less enthusiasm than other Mediterranean partners for free trade with Europe, and Algeria lagged behind other EMP partners in relation to its prospective Neighbourhood Action Plan. This was acknowledged to have compromised the EU's political purchase. Talks on counterterrorist cooperation were also described as "prickly"; Algeria complained that it had in vain sought such assistance during the 1990s, long before 9/11 magnified Europe's own concerns. Some diplomats lamented that support for partial political reform was not without its problems. Algeria continued to resist some European aid projects, for example holding up for some time one Commission initiative on journalist training and another on displaced people; obliging the Friedrich Ebert Stiftung to dilute a number of activities; and preventing a part of the Spanish development budget from being channeled through NGOs. Problems encountered with such initiatives had by 2005 led the Commission to debate the feasibility of funding being channeled through more independent "Algerian" NGOs registered in France—to circumvent the EU's own rule that only groups officially licensed by authorities in the recipient country were eligible for assistance.

Some policymakers questioned the longer-term sustainability of controlled reform. It was recognized that the government-backed Islamist parties—Al Nahda and the Social Movement for Peace—were losing ground due to their perceived co-option. Of the newer parties, Islah—seen by some as a FIS proxy—was now the second largest party in parliament, while the Wafa party remained banned. On these trends and restrictions the EU was silent. While the EU supported a number of NGOs and governance reforms, policymakers recognized the absence of concrete engagement on what observers identified as Algeria's most pertinent reform challenge, namely to fashion a process for the negotiated withdrawal of the military from politics. Diplomats recognized that by 2004 their political focus was on the issue of the "disappeared" victims of the 1990s conflict, not on broader institutional reform. Relations assumed their most critical edge over the Algerian parliament's resistance both to the proposed liberalization of family law and to elements of free trade negotiations, in particular to the prospect of Algeria being obliged by WTO rules to lift restrictions on trade in alcohol.

Egypt

Much of the post-9/11 debate on Middle East reform centered on Egypt, and in particular on US strategy toward the Mubarak government. Egypt's pivotal role in Arab politics and long-standing alliance with the United States ensured that this was the country where the prospect of democratic change was seen to hold both unparalleled catalytic significance and short-term strategic risk. In contrast to US policy, EU policies toward Egypt were subject to little far-reaching reassessment after 2001. European strategy reacted in little tangible fashion to 9/11, but rather continued along its path toward incrementally establishing a hold over gradualist reform.

In its new 2002 strategy for Egypt, the EU suggested that the latter had made "more progress than is apparent on the surface" and welcomed the 2000 elections as the fairest for a generation.[60] Of all

Mediterranean partners, it was in Egypt that the social development and economic flavor of the EU approach to reform was perhaps most notable. This persisted after 9/11, with few signs of a more directly strategic approach toward the question of Egyptian democracy. Egypt received two-thirds of its standard development aid from the EU, a large proportion of the bigger US aid allocation going to military cooperation. The Commission defined its main concern in Egypt to be with fostering more autonomous civil society capacity.[61] A new structured dialogue between the state and NGOs on social development was coordinated and EU statements became more critical of restrictions on NGOs, with more representations being made against prohibitions under the new NGO law. One notable case of European pressure in this regard was in relation to the Egyptian Human Rights Organization, which after eighteen years of precarious existence received a license in the summer of 2003. Egypt's (belated) inclusion in EIDHR funding for small-scale microprojects was used to prepare projects on the empowerment of women in public life and training to help local groups undertake election monitoring.

Significantly, under the auspices of prominent Egyptian civil society figures, a dialogue commenced between the Muslim Brotherhood and diplomats from some European states. When word of this was made public, however, both sides, in the words of one diplomat, "got cold feet," and the talks were aborted. The major European governments insisted they had no official contact with the Muslim Brotherhood. When the latter issued its pro-democracy manifesto in March 2004, sixty of its members were arrested by President Mubarak, with little critical European response. Civil society liberals, including many long critical of trends in political Islam, were well ahead of the EU in their engagement with Muslim Brotherhood potential reformers. After debate on this issue took place subsequent to the EU's April 2005 statement suggesting a need to engage with faith-based organizations, the Muslim Brotherhood reaction was ambivalent; in part seeking to protect its own position, the Brotherhood insisted that any such engagement should go through the Egyptian government.

Alongside this civil society focus, coordination with reformists within the political elite was increasingly sought. At the rhetorical level, no European government was as outspoken in its criticism of Egypt's democratic shortcomings as was President Bush on the occasion of his April 2004 meeting with President Mubarak. Heir apparent Gamal Mubarak was feted as a reformer in a number of European forums, including the UK Labour Party conference. While the constraints of Egypt's NGO law restricted more political civil society initiatives, human rights training was pursued more through legal reform programs funded through, and controlled by, the state.[62] European legal reform was slightly, though not radically, broader in scope than the largely technical focus of US programs, the latter being confined mainly to case processing capacity. A principal emphasis was penal reform, with a €1 million project on Egyptian prison conditions initiated by the Commission in 2002. Support was provided for the new National Council for Human Rights, a government-controlled body interpreted by many as a largely cosmetic response to international, particularly US, pressure. In 2004 the UK began new projects offering human rights training to lawyers and support for a women's rights ombudsman. Sweden's €2 million allocation through the respected Alexandria Institute included a priority focus on women's participation in subnational public administration. Most donors funded significant education reform programs in Egypt, in cooperation with reformist ministers.

Other aspects of policy continued to militate against a focus on reform in Egypt. Most significant in this sense was Mubarak's role in negotiating a Hamas ceasefire in the Occupied Territories in 2003. Participants in the first EU-Egypt association council held in June 2004 acknowledged that discussions had focused nearly exclusively on the Arab-Israeli conflict, with little concrete discussion of political reform in Egypt itself. Caution was compounded by the Iraq conflict. Additional Commission support for Egypt was released in early 2003 as a means of mitigating the effects of the imminent conflict in Iraq. In trade policy Egypt found itself caught in transatlantic crossfire, when the United States suspended free trade talks with Cairo after Egypt refused to back the United States against the EU in a series of ongoing WTO disputes. A few days after the September 2004 National Democratic Party national conference—which committed the party to economic reform while ruling out political liberalization—the UK launched a major new initiative on trade, investment, and financial reform with the Egyptian government. Progress on EU-Egypt trade measures was not interrupted by a disappearance from the NDP agenda of the much-intimated lifting of emergency law provisions.

European reaction was absent to a series of repressive new security operations launched by Egyptian forces in the autumn of 2004, which by the spring of 2005 had rounded up several hundred Muslim Brotherhood supporters. The granting of a license to the al-Ghad party was generally attributed to US, not European pressure, this not having been an issue targeted in any concrete way though EU diplomacy.[63] The EU reaction to Ayman Nour's imprisonment was relatively restrained alongside the United States response, which included the cancellation of a Condoleezza Rice visit. The Egyptian government in fact refused to receive an EU troika delegation that was dispatched to express concern, on the rather implausible grounds that Egypt did not recognize "collective bodies" (this of course being the same "collective body" whose aid and trade cooperation Egypt appeared to have no trouble in recognizing). When Nour was handed a prison sentence at the end of 2005, curiously just after failing to win a seat in the parliamentary elections, the EU issued a more strongly worded statement—notable alongside the lack of criticism of actions against Muslim Brotherhood members—but still declined to take concrete action. It was at Egypt's behest that a statement adopted at the EMP ministerial in May 2005 included a new reference to "non-interference" within its paragraph on human rights. Egypt also objected to the formation of a democracy and human rights subcommittee within its draft Neighbourhood Action Plan, justifying this position by referring to the lack of such a forum in Israel's Action Plan.

As debate over political reform became more vibrant during 2005, US policy appeared to become more critical than that of the EU. The Bush administration criticized the NDP crackdown on protests against the referendum on Mubarak's proposed constitutional change—which activists saw as insubstantial—while the European reaction was more cautious. The Brownback amendment to the State Department's 2005 appropriations bill allowed USAID to direct democracy funds to Egyptian organizations in consultation with an independent board of prominent Egyptian activists.[64] No similar step was taken by the EU to broaden its range of civil society partners. After some internal debate, it was agreed that the EU would not push hard for an invitation from the Egyptian government to observe the 2005 parliamentary elections; such an invitation was ruled out when the Egyptian government barred external monitoring. More cautiously, the EU sent a fact-finding mission to Cairo at the end of September to discuss the prospects of monitoring the November parliamentary elections, which it presented as sending a signal to the Egyptian authorities that these elections would be watched with a more critical eye. A

European Parliament delegation was, however, unceremoniously rebuffed by Egyptian authorities. Unlike the United States, the EU offered no concrete support for the range of groups that pushed—unsuccessfully—for provisions to allow for unrestricted domestic monitoring of the elections; also in contrast to the EU, the United States expressed reluctance in practice to move forward with its free trade negotiations with Egypt because of the conditions surrounding these elections.

Jordan

With notable similarities to their policy toward Morocco, European governments placed great faith in the reformist intentions of Jordan's new king. This policy appeared unduly optimistic while Abdullah tightened political freedoms and declined to reverse his suspension of parliament during 2002. Awkwardly for European states, one of the reasons cited by the king for suspending parliament in 2001 was the latter's blocking of EU-related economic reforms.[65] Elections were eventually held in 2003, and as Jordan seemed to return to a reformist path, it became the Arab state most open to political cooperation with the EU. Unlike most other Mediterranean states, Jordan did agree that the Commission would be the sole authorizing body for human rights projects under MEDA. In Jordan a large number of European donors were willing and able to run a relatively broad range of reform projects, in particular on women's rights, judicial reform, and media freedoms—although French assistance to anglophone Jordan continued to be negligible. Several European states offered assistance in response to the king's intimated willingness to liberalize the law governing political parties. Several also developed low-level engagement with the officially sanctioned Islamic Action Front and even included some of its representatives in grassroots development projects.

If the most prevalent view among European diplomats was that the king represented the best hope for Jordanian reform, some tensions nonetheless remained. Abdullah refused to allow EU observers into the June 2003 elections and imposed new restrictions on external support for political parties. Evident imperfections in the 2003 elections met with no open European criticism. While analysts lamented the electoral gerrymandering undertaken with the express aim of limiting Palestinian representation, European diplomats judged this relatively uncritically as a move necessary to preserving Jordanian support for the Middle East peace process. A prominent concern was that many civil society organizations pushing for more far-reaching political reform were also those most strongly opposed to the normalization treaty with Israel. In practice, the EU aid program agreed with the Jordanian Ministry of Planning, excluded support for opposition-minded groups, and channeled the largest share of funding to so-called NGOs run by members of the royal family.

The elite orientation in European governments' aim to back rather than undermine Abdullah also manifested itself in the nature of EU support for judicial reform, which was limited to the issues of capacity and caseload management; and, unlike US funding, EU support focused on the judicial system's treatment of human rights issues rather than its broader institutional reform.[66] This orientation was also seen in the significant amounts of security cooperation undertaken with the Jordanian armed forces. UK diplomats insisted that the long-standing British relationship with Jordanian forces gradually took on more of a reform direction, with traditional defense diplomacy work reduced and with priority, it was claimed, given to training the security forces to intervene in domestic disturbances in a less heavy-handed fashion. While these elements were undoubtedly developed and support enthusiastically given to the king's effort to improve human rights standards in army and police operations, much defense cooperation remained of a traditional kind, shoring up some of the least reform-minded parts of the Jordanian polity. Some Jordanians frowned at the European support offered to civil society reformists previously involved with the Jordanian intelligence services.

Much significance was attached to the convening of the EU-Jordanian subcommittee on human rights at the beginning of 2005, presented as the first of the new bilateral forums focusing specifically on democratic reform in southern Mediterranean partners. Within the scope of the EU-Jordan Neighbourhood Action Plan, commitments were made to increase support to civil society, to anti-corruption campaigns, and in particular for the Jordanian National Centre for Human Rights.[67] However, the proposals introduced at the same time by the Jordanian government for new restrictions on political parties and professional associations raised further questions about the impact of the EU's strongly elite- and partnership-based approach. After the November 2005 bombings in Amman, policies in Jordan took on more of a security than a reform orientation.

Tunisia

In the case of Tunisia, European criticism sharpened after 9/11, only then to subside. In response to President Bin Ali's restriction of political space, Tunisia was in 2002 identified as a target state for the European Initiative on Democracy and Human Rights. Despite objections from the Tunisian government, the EU offered new funding for the Ligue Tunisienne des Droits de l'Homme. When this group's activities were then constantly broken up by the authorities and licenses delayed, the Commission protested and held back a number of aid packages. It was significant that both France and Italy did for the first time acquiesce to more forceful pressure against Tunisia. The Dutch ambassador invited the head of the Ligue to EU heads of mission meetings, eventually and crucially winning the support of the French ambassador for this move. Tunisian attempts to restrict the political aspects of other areas of aid, for example in the area of judicial reform, led to further cutbacks in EU funding. The Commission resisted Tunisian efforts to divert a €22 million judicial reform project from training in EU rights standards to the purchase of computers and other hardware, putting this project on hold as a consequence. Tunisia was the only Mediterranean state excluded from funding for new human rights microprojects. However, as the broader political situation in Tunisia deteriorated there was no decision to take more significant punitive action. The fact that most of the aid held back was that earmarked for democracy and human rights projects was acknowledged to have actually played into the hands of the Tunisian government. The Commission accused several member states of having "pulled back" after registering a symbolic protest against Bin Ali. Tunisia remained the second (to the Palestinian Authority) highest per capita recipient of overall EU aid in the Middle East.[68]

Northern EU member states complained of southern European governments remaining soft on Bin Ali. If the French position had evolved slightly, its declared approach was to use long-standing contacts to work for change from within Bin Ali's ruling Constitutional Democratic Rally party, while President Chirac declared the Tunisian president to be a leader in human rights advances.[69] Paying an early visit to Tunisia, new Spanish prime minister José Luis Rodriguez Zapatero similarly congratulated Bin Ali on his "democratic advances"; Spanish aid to Tunisia increased steadily after 2003.[70] In response to the October 2004 elections, which returned Bin Ali with 96 percent of the vote, the EU congratulated the president on his victory and the holding of "multiparty elections with a choice of candidates"—contrasting dramatically with the unequivocal European condemnation of the (at least partially competitive) Ukrainian elections held the same week.[71] Spain and other southern member states insisted that EU pressure be confined to the issue of Tunisia's hindrance of EU aid projects, rather than broader issues of political repression. This caused a diplomatic spat with the more critical US and chagrin on the part of Tunisian liberal activists—whose much-vaunted "internal voices," they complained, had once again been ignored. Less than two months after these elections, the Spanish defense minister signed an agreement to provide the Tunisian security forces with new equipment to help bear down on illegal immigration.[72] Even in this more conflictive case, a gradualist elite-oriented preference was still evident. After the intimations of a more muscular approach, the attacks of 9/11 and a short time later those against German tourists in Tunisia itself seemed in fact to imbue greater caution in European policy toward the Bin Ali regime.

Engaging the "Rogues": Syria and Libya

If in most of the above cases European policies purported to be aimed at latching onto the first stirrings of political opening, how did the EU react toward the region's more immovable autocratic regimes?

Syria

Syria appeared to represent one of the clearest cases of division between a European proclivity for positive engagement and a US policy of threat and coercion. In the wake of 9/11 neither the United States nor the European Union revealed significant interest in Syrian democracy. Syria's willingness to cooperate through counterterrorist coordination and intelligence sharing on Al-Qaida suspects won Syria exclusion from President Bush's infamous "axis of evil."[73] Even as the tentative political opening of President Bashar's first months in power was gradually reversed, the EU concluded that 9/11 had increased the urgency of concluding an association agreement with Syria. The EU's main aim was to prevent Syria falling behind other Mediterranean partners, with the Baathist regime the only EMP government not to have concluded an association agreement by the autumn of 2003.[74]

Transatlantic divergence emerged as the United States tired of Syrian obfuscation: Bashar's reluctance to sever links with Hamas, Islamic Jihad, and Hizbollah, his accelerated efforts to develop chemical weapons capacity, and then his apparent attempts to challenge the US presence in Iraq by facilitating the movement of jihadists across the Syrian-Iraqi border. Citing these factors, the Bush administration tightened its policy against Damascus. After initially holding back his support, in December 2003 President Bush signed the Syria Accountability and Lebanese Sovereignty Restoration Act. Sanctions against Syria followed in May 2004; Syria was not offered a place in the US-Middle East free trade area, and officials began to brief that military action against Syria was an option now on the table. Significantly, this evolution in US policy strongly conditioned European strategy. EU officials admitted that the tougher US line made them more determined to deepen engagement with Syria, in particular through expediting the conclusion of association agreement negotiations. US pressure on the EU not to sign the association agreement predictably increased most European governments' determination to do just that. The Syrian regime appeared to react in kind: recognizing its need for European forbearance to offset US coercion, Damascus adopted more compliant positions in its negotiations with the European Union, including in relation to the standardized democracy clause. Negotiations were concluded in December 2003.

Signing of the agreement was then delayed, however, by a standoff over the EU's new nonproliferation clause. The new agreement with Syria was the first since the EU agreed in November 2003 to include in all third country agreements a standard clause aimed at toughening up nonproliferation commitments. Damascus objected to having to sign up to language enjoining it to adhere to the Chemical Weapons Convention. The UK consequently blocked the signing of the association agreement. London gained some support from Germany, Denmark, and the Netherlands, albeit with these states influenced by slightly different motives—Berlin's traditional tilt toward Israel contrasting with the Danish and Dutch stated concern with human rights issues.[75] Other states urged flexibility on the WMD clause, again citing the priority of first establishing a formal agreement with Syria. Several accused the UK—and Tony Blair personally—of drifting toward a fundamentally more coercive approach and seeking to do the United States' bidding in Damascus. Some variation was indeed evident within the UK government between diplomats responsible for security policy and the relevant geographical departments, the latter appearing more inclined to stress the priority of implementing the association agreement. The agreement was finally unblocked in September 2004, when Syria agreed to sign the nonproliferation clause. One European diplomat acknowledged that during this period "WMD took so much effort that . . . there was no scope for a two-pronged attack" on internal political issues as well.

Again, the balance was decided in favor of attracting Syria into far-reaching economic and political engagement with Europe. One central theme was the EU intent to use the association agreement as a base from which to push and help prepare for Syria's entry into the WTO—still opposed by the United States. European governments listed the same strategic concerns as the US administration in relation to Syria—chemical weapon development and Syrian support for Hizbollah—but linked these to regime change in a less direct and instrumental fashion. While European diplomats insisted that the association agreement's importance lay in its providing a "tool for reformers," the logic was, in the words of one diplomat, "getting these other things sorted out first." The French, German, and Spanish governments were certainly unwilling to punish Syria in any way for Damascus's apparent meddling in Iraq: indeed, for these states, unity with Syria on the Iraq invasion tipped the scales more toward an alliance-building rather than a reform-promotion dynamic during 2004. Most Europeans argued that if Bashar retightened political control during 2004, it was in response to US threats and the deepening instability in Iraq; the ousting of another Baathist Sunni minority–controlled regime was causing some nervousness in Damascus.

Behind the high-politics differences, there was further contrast between, on the one hand, the absence of US development aid to Syria (the latter disqualified by virtue of it being defined as a "state sponsor of terrorism") and, on the other hand, European efforts to increase reform-oriented funding. A number of EIDHR projects in Syria were initiated in 2001, convening networks to support peoples' involvement in local-level decisionmaking, and funding training, educational work, and publications on human rights. A Citizenship Guide was compiled in conjunction with the Friedrich Naumann Stiftung and launched by the Commission in March 2005.[76] A new €2 million tranche of MEDA funding was allocated to assist decentralization in Syria. The European approach laid primary emphasis on strengthening the position of reformists within government and the capacity of modernizing ministries, such as Labour and Social Affairs. To this end the French government provided administrative reform experts to cooperate on strengthening the presidential office, and the Commission began to divert funds in a similar direction.[77] France also initiated a program on judicial reform; the UK supported reform dialogue with what were judged to be Syria's most promising modernizers, and also offered assistance on reforming the governance of Syria's nascent financial markets; Denmark funded women entrepreneurs, public sector modernization, and administrative reform linked directly to the implementation of the association agreement; and the German government supported initiatives on public administration reform, in particular with the Syrian State Planning Commission. The Friedrich Ebert Stiftung launched a range of initiatives, before being barred from Syria. The restricted scope for implementing meaningful reform projects in Syria, relative to the political space available in more reformist countries, ensured that the country remained a limited recipient; but this was partially offset by an attempt to include Syrian organizations within regional projects.

In June 2004 the Commission released a €40 million grant for Syria small businesses and coordinated a seminar in Damascus on improving conditions for European investment. The Commission launched an €80 million economic and social support program for 2005–2006, which listed a number of reform-related and institution-building commitments: support for a national-level small enterprises lobby; a focus on creating a "more supportive regulatory framework" for civil society; and an aim to strengthen civil society, measured by increased dialogue between the government and NGOs and an increase in the number of NGO registrations. Only €2 million out of the €80 million was set aside directly for civil society, and the Commission acknowledged that ministries would remain key parties in initiatives involving civil society partners. Apart from the Commission, only the UK funded Syrian NGOs, and to a very modest extent (€0.4 million for 2003).[78] A new €0.5 million call for democracy and human rights microprojects in Syria was launched at the end of June 2005—this being delayed from the 2004 budget, and the subject of pressure from the European Parliament—with priorities identified as "women, children, and people with special needs." The Commission delegation in Damascus gained a waiver of the rule that only officially registered NGOs could apply for funds; this had for some time ruled out Syrian groups based from necessity in Lebanon, which the Commission was keen to support.

Bashar's plans for economic reform were cited by diplomats as providing a valuable access point for such types of cooperation, judged to be most useful in terms of broader social and political reform over the longer term. These approaches were preferred to backing exiled opposition groups. Indeed, in mid-2003 the French government opined—somewhat at odds with most accounts of developments within Syria—that opposition groups had in fact "gained progressively in autonomy."[79] The group of 700 democracy activists that presented another reform petition in March 2004 did not benefit from concrete European backing. Damascus's spring 2004 clampdown against Syria's Kurds also failed to provoke explicit public condemnation from the EU—even though the pardoning of 312 Kurdish activists one year later was widely linked to general Western concern over this issue. A key European judgment was that Bashar and his closest advisers were reform minded and merited support against the old guard within the political elite—regime evolution rather than regime change defined as the goal. One report quoted a French diplomat as justifying such logic by the need to recognize that Bashar was essentially "in synch with his people."[80] After signing the association agreement, key Syrian ministers claimed that economic reform would indeed help lead to political liberalization.[81]

The European tack contrasted with Washington's increasingly critical approach, evidenced in US engagement with exiled opposition groups such as the Syrian Democratic Alliance and the Reform Party of Syria. However, the transatlantic difference was slightly narrowed by the US administration's clarification that it sought "change in regime behavior, not regime change," as well as by reports that the Reform Party of Syria was also in dialogue with some Brussels-based European diplomats.[82] The Syrian perspective on the EU policy of engagement was complex and often difficult to read. For one expert, such "ambiguity without" reflected "Syria's ambiguous transition within." On the one hand, Bashar welcomed a European focus on democracy and human rights as a means of strengthening his hand against the regime hardliners inherited from his father; on the other, EU partnership was pursued as a classic strategy of balancing, designed to offset stronger US pressure for political change. The delicacy of this internal balancing act contributed to the fluctuations witnessed in Syrian positions toward the EU, across the political, economic, and security domains.[83]

Just as decisions were being made to unblock the association agreement, attention turned to Syria's de facto rule in Lebanon. By their own admission, European governments had not responded to the gradual tightening of Syrian control over Lebanese politics during 2003–2004 for fear of overloading the demands imposed on Damascus. Syria showed itself increasingly intent on frustrating EU engagement in Lebanon, blocking absorption by the latter of many areas of European funding and preventing Lebanese representatives from attending many even relatively innocuous EMP forums. European caution was reflected in the limited amounts of aid channeled to Lebanon; practical reform work was seen as unavoidably compromised by Syrian interference. The exceptions were €30 million yearly allocations from France and the Commission, Lebanon's two largest donors of mainstream aid. French funding priorities were listed as civil society, administrative reform, and the promotion of francophonie, as well as police and military cooperation.[84] In the latter area, the French undertook a significant amount of security cooperation for capacity building of Lebanese forces, ostensibly to deploy less heavy-handed tactics than their Syrian counterparts. Cooperation programs that were implemented again focused at the local level on fostering interfaith education and exchanges. A judicial reform program was hindered by a dispute with Lebanese authorities over the balance between rights-based training and the purchase of equipment. European states opposed the US push for a blanket proscription of Hizbollah, recognizing the latter to be the fastest growing political organization in Lebanon, as witnessed in the municipal elections of spring 2004. A number of European embassies commenced low-level dialogue with Hizbollah, with the aim of backing the group's political arm against the militia wing, although concrete cooperation toward this objective remained impracticable. A principal European argument was that unlocking the Syria-Lebanon impasse required more pressure primarily in relation to the peace process, especially the Golan Heights track, to remove the reasons for Syria's presence in Lebanon.

Then in September 2004 Syrian interference to prolong pro-Damascus president Emile Lahoud's term in office and additional troop deployments in Lebanon provoked a joint French-US UN Security Council resolution (1559), calling for Syria to pull back and allow free elections in Lebanon. Such joint action between Paris and Washington was significant against the backdrop of Iraq-related disagreements, of course, although motivations differed slightly: France seemed motivated by a desire to protect Francophile prime minister

Rafik Hariri (who did soon decide to resign), while for the United States this Security Council action represented another step in the gradual tightening of policy against Syria. French national diplomacy comprehensively overshadowed joint EU involvement. Paris insisted most strongly on the association agreement being made conditional on implementation of UN resolution 1559. After Syrian troops withdrew in May 2005, Paris insisted that new coordination between France, Britain, and the United States had taken shape to hone in on Syria's "residual presence" in Lebanon, in particular in the form of intelligence agents.[85] Hizbollah sought to protect its own position by claiming that Paris was not in agreement with Washington's attempt to use resolution 1559 to push for the disarming of resistance groups.[86] The Dutch and Italian governments pressed for Hizbollah at this stage to be placed on the EU list of terrorist organizations but did not win backing from other member states.

In 2004 France and Sweden alone had pressed debate over the need for assistance to ensure clean elections in Lebanon. Only after Rafik Hariri's assassination in February 2005 did other states engage significantly on the fate of Lebanese democracy. Lebanon's Neighbourhood Action Plan was, at this stage, made explicitly conditional on democratic elections and a widening of Lebanese political autonomy—to which the caretaker government in Beirut reacted in critical and uncooperative fashion. In February 2005, €0.5 million was made available for Lebanese NGOs from the EIDHR, a funding allocation again delayed from 2004. Paris leaned most strongly on the caretaker Lebanese government to issue an invitation to EU election observers; the decision to send a European team was coordinated with the US administration, who as a consequence agreed to stand aside. The EU observers expressed concern over the decision not to reform the electoral law, and over the number of seats not subject to competition but rather allocated in accordance with power-sharing trade-offs.[87] The British foreign secretary also expressed concern over bias in the pre-existing electoral law.[88] After the elections, France was the state most critical of the share of power accorded pro-Syrian forces. In the summer of 2005, two conferences on Lebanese reform were organized in Paris, incorporating a core group of governments, including those of the United Kingdom and the United States, and aimed at mobilizing new funding. The Commission and other European donors were not convinced of the need to direct significant new funding at Lebanon. Quai d'Orsay diplomats insisted there was a need and intent to make additional support "more firmly conditional" on political reform. A difference between Europe and the United States perceived by diplomats related to Washington's attempt to use the eruption of democracy demonstrations in Lebanon as a means of tightening pressure for political change in Damascus, a strategy that did not win enthusiastic EU support. Observers predicted that a retightening of US pressure against Damascus and for Hizbollah's disarmament would soon break the Franco-American alliance. As of early 2006, however, French judgment that Syria remained unwilling to cease completely its orchestration of Lebanese politics, combined with British impatience with Bashar's actions in relation to Iraqi border crossings, sufficed to ensure that Paris and London were themselves considering ways of tightening policy against Damascus. This evolution in policy became more pronounced as UN inquiries uncovered high-level Syrian involvement in Hariri's murder.

Libya

While Syria had long ceded its status as most problematic Mediterranean state to Libya, policy toward the latter underwent a dramatic shift, which commenced prior to 9/11 but accelerated notably in the wake of the terrorist attacks. The United Nations Security Council suspended (without definitively removing) sanctions against Libya following the 1999 deal on the handing over of suspects in the Lockerbie trial. For a long time Europe's backmarker on relations with Libya, the UK lifted additional bilateral sanctions and quickly developed links with Tripoli. Negotiations between London, Washington, and Tripoli led to agreement in December 2003 that Libya would abandon its WMD programs. To their considerable chagrin, European governments were not consulted by the UK on this deal. Britain's main role was in conveying the offer to Colonel Qaddafi of normalization with Washington—although the United States was reported to have been concerned that this was leading the Blair government into too cozy a relationship with the Libyan regime.[89] Significantly, the UK-US lead role persisted beyond these early stages of WMD talks; as late as October 2004 a new US-UK-Libyan arrangement was established as the principal forum for discussing proliferation issues and defense reform.[90] Meanwhile, European Commission president Romano Prodi embarked—not without causing some unease on the part of Chris Patten and Javier Solana—on something of a personal diplomatic campaign aimed at accelerating EU engagement with Libya. In December 2003 he claimed to have offered Qaddafi immediate EMP accession and new top-level contacts. He even intimated at the prospect of bringing Libya straight into the European Neighbourhood Policy as a way of bypassing the more problematic political aspects of the EMP.

The actual lifting of sanctions on Libya had to await the negotiation of compensation deals with France in relation to the 1989 bombing of a UTA flight and with Germany for the 1986 bombing of a Berlin disco. A deal on the former was concluded in January 2004 and on the latter in September 2004. During 2004 a procession of ministerial visits ensued. In January 2004 the Libyan foreign minister visited Paris, where he was promised a new French aid package. A trip back to Libya by the French trade minister followed shortly after, with a party including seventy businessmen. At a further meeting between Prodi and Qaddafi in February 2004, the Commission president offered to send officials to Libya to help prepare the country for accession to the EMP. By the autumn of 2004, Silvio Berlusconi had made three visits. The Libyan foreign minister visited Britain, paving the way for Tony Blair's visit to Colonel Qaddafi's desert tent. Chancellor Schröder visited in October 2004, with a large contingent of German businessmen, and Jacques Chirac arrived in November. Member states began increasing their embassy personnel in Tripoli.

These moves appeared to point toward an engagement with Libya in no way conditional upon or concerned with domestic reform. The detention of a prominent Libyan human rights activist early in 2004 occasioned some criticism from the United States, much less from the EU; the campaigner was released (temporarily) in March after appeals from members of the US Congress, but without visible European governmental pressure. When agreement was finally reached in September 2004 to a formal lifting of sanctions, only Denmark and Ireland registered concern over the absence of human rights conditions. In no discussions, strategy documents, or dialogue meetings was there mention of the continuing persecution of the Libyan Islamic Group. European governments welcomed limited changes made— Qaddafi's decision to allow in an Amnesty International mission, talk of repealing emergency law provisions—but were silent in respect of subsequent human rights reversals. The United States initiated a dialogue specifically on human rights; the EU did not. A conference of Arab civil society activists, meeting to prepare for the EMP's tenth anniversary, strongly criticized the EU's move to unconditional engagement with Libya.[91]

The Commission's acknowledged priority focus was cooperation over migration. A number of states moved quickly to initiate talks on arms contracts, this area being recognized by diplomats as the sector quickest in responding to the new rapprochement with Libya. Some governments alluded to the intense competition between European states in these areas; the early jostling for positions in a newly opening market was acknowledged to be cutting across discussion of common EU foreign policy positions. All member states agreed that the main potential existed in the area of economic reform, where genuine movement was detected on the part of the Libyan government. State subsidies were cut and new licenses granted to foreign companies to export to Libya through local agents.[92] Much hope was explicitly placed in new business-oriented prime minister, Shukri Ghanam. Notably, like the EU, Washington moved to back Libya's candidature for WTO entry—a convergence of view made more significant by the fact that this issue most commonly represented a major point of transatlantic difference in relations with difficult states.

Engagement on economic reform was, in particular, the stated priority for a new UK strategy toward Libya. Britain supported projects on administrative reform associated with market liberalization and capacity building for Libya's patronage-ridden judicial system. Some low-level dialogue was undertaken with the Qaddafi Human Rights Foundation; the UK and other European governments were keen to support reform through this organization, run by Qaddafi's apparently more Western-oriented son. The UK also provided a sizeable package of assistance to help Libya move from WMD to conventional defense, as a quid pro quo for Qaddafi agreeing to a nonproliferation deal. It was claimed that removal of the arms embargo was important in part to remove constraints on engaging in security sector reform activities with Libyan forces, with the training of border guards an early priority.

Italian pressure for a quick lifting of the arms embargo was motivated by the desire to sell Libya equipment to stem the flow of illegal migrants to Italian shores. Indeed, the Italian government announced that it would in any case ignore the embargo to sell patrol boats, helicopters, jeeps, aircraft, and night vision equipment to Libya. In return Qaddafi suggested a plan to rename the main coast road Via Berlusconi![93] Italy also offered €6 billion in (colonial) war compensation;

was the largest European aid donor, channeling almost as much aid to Libya as all other Middle Eastern states put together; and facilitated a €5 billion investment in Libya by ENI, the Italian multinational oil and gas company. A high-level Italian-Libyan Security Committee was created in 2002 and Rome pushed new forms of security cooperation through the 5 + 5 Dialogue, expressly so as to offset Libya's exclusion from the EMP. The European Parliament criticized Italy's repatriation of a large number of Libyan citizens and its funding of migrant detention camps within Libya itself.[94] The French government announced it was contemplating the transfer of nuclear technology to Libya, while a €1 million grant for health-related projects was granted Libya from the EU's Rapid Reaction Mechanism.[95] Despite the lifting of US sanctions, at the beginning of 2005 the EU was still supplying 90 percent of Libya's imports.[96] Ahead of the EMP tenth anniversary meeting, a number of European governments launched a new diplomatic effort to bring Libya into the partnership; in fact, it remained Qaddafi who was not keen on acceding to the Barcelona Process. Some diplomats suggested a Neighbourhood Action Plan might provide the means of unblocking this impasse and offering a tailored strategy that circumvented Libya's problems with the more general conditions of the Barcelona Process—principally Qaddafi's refusal to participate in regional forums with Israel.[97]

Conclusion

If most areas of the Euro-Mediterranean Partnership developed slowly during the late 1990s, the breadth and depth of the partnership's *acquis* strengthened notably after 9/11. European influence consolidated itself sufficiently to constitute a significant factor in political developments across the Maghreb and Mashreq. While there were new elements that represented a very tangible reaction to 9/11, most aspects of EU policy exhibited incremental continuity from efforts initiated in the mid-1990s. The new international security environment provided a fillip to ongoing European strategies in this part of the Middle East, rather than the kind of watershed moment that 9/11 appeared to produce in US perceptions (or at least rhetoric) toward key states such as Egypt. In this region where all the elements of the EU's much-vaunted soft power were increasingly embedded, European influence proved very much less than profoundly transformative of the Arab polities on its southern periphery. EU policy was heavily reliant on the notion that democratic norms could spread by osmosis through southern Mediterranean governmental and civil society bodies adopting norms from European organizations.

Barcelona Process discussions often appeared to take place in a self-enclosed world, concerned with procedural issues disconnected from broader Arab reform debates. Nuanced differences between member states on issues such as the use of conditionality, the pace of economic reform, or the rightful type of engagement with Islamists survived any centrifugal impact of 9/11. Many aspects of EU policy expressly served to legitimize top-down liberalization that was so gradualist and bounded that its genuinely reformist credential was equivocal. The EU reliance on a meaningful prompt to political reform flowing from cooperation in economic, social, and cultural spheres remained based on hope more than genuinely crafted and substantiated opportunity. A logic of security through mutual understanding was stronger than one of security through democratization. In parts of the region, the prioritization of direct security imperatives—weapons of mass destruction, widening terrorist networks—indubitably compromised the more modest and low-profile initiatives aimed at long-term underlying transformation. But as the EU broadened its range of policy instruments and reform-relevant resources, and moved to tighten the operationalization of some of its strategic tools, at least the contours of a more proactive approach toward security could be detected in the Maghreb and Mashreq. New tough, outspoken US language on democracy had galvanized debate; arguably, European norms had begun to weave themselves more intricately into the southern Mediterranean's political consciousness. Imprecision both in political will and in the design of policy instruments certainly detracted from this potential; but by 2006 a range of political reform initiatives was more firmly elaborated than hitherto.

Notes

1. For instance, Chourou, "Security Partnership and Democratisation," pp. 163–188; Lia, "Security Challenges," pp. 27–56; Spencer, "Rethinking or Reorienting," pp. 135–154.
2. *Financial Times,* 15 November 2000, p. 18.
3. Biscop, "The European Security Strategy."
4. Tanner, "NATO's Role," pp. 101–113.
5. *Euromed Synopsis,* no. 262, 4 March 2004.

6. Leveau, "La France, L'Europe et la Méditerrannée," pp. 1019–1032; Gillespie, "Spain and the West Mediterranean."

7. Commission of the European Communities, *Communication from the Commission to the Council,* see especially pp. 11, 13.

8. Intervention by Javier Solana at the Opening of the Forum on the Future, Rabat, 11 December 2004, http://www.ue.eu.int/solana, p. 4.

9. Schmid, "France and the Euro-Mediterranean Partnership."

10. Department for International Development, *Regional Action Plan,* www.france.diplomatie.fr/cooperation/dgcid.

11. Commission of the European Communities, *EIDHR Programming Update 2004.*

12. Holden, "The European Community's MEDA Aid Regime," pp. 347–363.

13. Rheinhardt, "Civil Society Cooperation in the EMP."

14. Cofmann Wittes, "The Promise of Arab Liberalism," p. 69.

15. Commission of the European Communities, *MEDA Regional Indicative Programme 2002–2004,* p. 10.

16. Quoted in Balfour, "Rethinking," p. 18.

17. European Council Secretariat, Presidency Conclusions for the Euro-Mediterranean Meeting of Ministers of Foreign Affairs, pp. 29–30, November 2004, Council document 14869/04.

18. Commission of the European Communities, *Regional and Bilateral MEDA Cooperation.*

19. Euromesco, *Barcelona Plus,* p. 50.

20. Tanner, "Security Cooperation."

21. *Middle East International,* no. 736, 22 October 2004, p. 26.

22. Report by the High Level Advisory Group, established at the Initiative of the President of the European Commission, *Dialogue Between Peoples and Cultures in the Euro-Mediterranean Area.*

23. *Euromed Synopsis,* no. 196, 26 September 2002, p. 2.

24. *Euromed Synopsis,* no. 306, 3 March 2005, p. 3.

25. Franco-Spanish Non-Paper on the MEDA Programme, 16 February 2005.

26. Ebeid and El Kady, "The Politics of Arab Reform," p. 10.

27. See Euro-Mediterranean Human Rights Network, *Rule of Law,* p. 81; Lannon, "Parlements et société civile."

28. Attina, "The Euro-Mediterranean Partnership Assessed," pp. 181–199; Volpi, "Regional Community Building."

29. High Level Advisory Group, *Dialogue Between Peoples.*

30. See comments by Hubert Vedrine, *Agence Europe,* 26 April 2002, p. 2.

31. Cameron and Rhein, "Promoting Political and Economic Reform," p. 5; *Euromed Synopsis,* no. 321, 30 June 2005, p. 1.

32. Emerson and Tocci, "The Rubik Cube."

33. Menéndez, "Arab Reform," p. 26.

34. Balfour, "Italy's Policies."

35. Tocci, "The European Neighbourhood Policy," p. 10.

36. Commission of the European Communities, *Communication to the Council on Commission Proposals for Action Plans.*

37. Commission official quoted in Kelly, "New Wine in Old Wineskins."

38. Emerson and Noutcheva, "From Barcelona Process," p. 11.

39. Foreign and Commonwealth Office, "Achieving a Common Vision."

40. Euro-Mediterranean Human Rights Network, *Barcelona Plus 10.*

41. For action plan texts, see http://europa.eu.int/comm/world/enp/pdf/action_plans.

42. Tocci, "The European Neighbourhood Policy," p. 7.

43. Aliboni, "Promoting Democracy," p. 12.

44. Commission of the European Communities, *Tenth Anniversary of the Euro-Mediterranean Partnership;* BBC Monitoring Service, 2 June 2005.

45. Montes and Migliorisi, *2004 EU Donor Atlas,* p. 107.

46. BBC Monitoring Service, 15 September 2004.

47. Willis and Messari, "Analyzing Moroccan Foreign Policy," p. 61.

48. For an account of Spanish-Moroccan tensions, see Feliu, "A Two Level Game," p. 100; Gillespie, "Spain and Morocco"; and Tanner, "North Africa," p. 143.

49. *El País,* 16 March 2004.

50. Agencia Española de Cooperación Internacional, *Plan Anual de AECI 2005,* p. A.2-23.

51. *El País,* 3 January 2006.

52. Gillespie, "Spain and Morocco."

53. Willis and Messari, "Analyzing Moroccan Foreign Policy," p. 61.

54. Commission of the European Communities, *Algérie,* p. 30.

55. *Euromed Synopsis,* no. 297, 22 December 2004.

56. *Le Monde,* 5 March 2003.

57. *Le Monde,* 11 April 2004.

58. www.diplomatie.gouv.fr/actu/bulletin, interview with Al-Jazeera, 13 January 2004.

59. *Daily Star,* 18 October 2004.

60. Commission of the European Communities, *Egypt,* p. 9.

61. Quotes from Commission of the European Communities, *Egypt,* pp. 34–36.

62. Grunert, "Loss of Guiding Values."

63. *Middle East International,* no. 739, December 2004, pp. 17–18.

64. Council on Foreign Relations, *In Support of Arab Democracy.*

65. Lucas, "Deliberalization in Jordan," pp. 137–144.

66. Jones and Emerson, "European Neighbourhood Policy," p. 11.

67. For background, see www.europa.eu.int/comm/external_relations/Jordan.

68. Montes and Migliorisi, *2004 EU Donor Atlas,* p. 24.

69. *Le Monde,* 14 October 2004.

70. Agencia Española de Cooperación Internacional, *Plan Anual de AECI 2005,* p. A.2-43.

71. *European Commission Weekly News Digest,* 4 November 2004; "Declaration by the Presidency on Behalf of the EU on Presidential and Parliamentary Elections in Tunisia," 13932/04, 25 October 2004, http://europa.eu.int/comm/external_relations/newsdigest.

72. *El País,* 11 December 2004.

73. Abrahams, "When Rogues Defy Reason," pp. 45–55.

74. *External Relations Weekly Digest,* 15–21 September 2003, http://europa.eu.int/comm/external_relations/newsdigest.

75. Allaf, "Point of No Return," pp. 12–14.

76. *Euromed Synopsis,* no. 309, 31 March 2005.

77. International Crisis Group, *Syria Under Bashar (I),* pp. 20–21.

78. For all these figures, see Commission of the European Communities, *EMP Syria National Indicative Programme 2005–2006.*

79. www.diplomatie.gov.fr/actu.

80. International Crisis Group, *Syria Under Bashar (I),* p. 18.

81. *Daily Star,* 3 November 2004.

82. *Middle East International,* no. 748, 15 April 2005, and no. 752, 10 June 2005, p. 25.

83. Hinnebusch, "Globalization and Generational Change," pp. 94–97.

84. DG Cooperation Internationale et Développement (2002) Documents Stratégiques Pays: Liban, www.diplomatie.gov.fr.

85. Quai d'Orsay statement, 28 June 2005, www.diplomatie.gouv.fr/actu.

86. *Middle East International,* no. 749, 29 April 2005, p. 7.

87. *Euromed Synopsis,* no. 318, 9 June 2005, p. 2; *Euromed Synopsis,* no. 320, 23 June 2005, p. 3.

88. See Jack Straw's speech to the Fabian Society, www.fco.gov.uk, 10 March 2005.

89. *Financial Times,* 26 January 2004.

90. Dunne, "Libya: Security Is Not Enough," p. 4.

91. *Daily Star,* 4 November 2004.

92. *Arab Reform Bulletin* 3, no. 5, June 2005, p. 6.

93. BBC Monitoring Service, 22 September 2004.

94. Balfour, "Italy's Policies."

95. BBC Monitoring Service, 27 November 2004.

96. *Middle East International,* no. 739, 3 December 2004, p. 26.

97. Aliboni, "The Geopolitical Implications," pp. 1–16.

5

Palestine:
State Building in Hard Times

It was routinely suggested that developments in the Palestinian Occupied Territories lay at the root of Arab disaffection and international terrorism. By the time terrorists struck in the United States on 9/11, disillusion over the Oslo peace accords had already taken root among Palestinians. In September 2000 what was termed the Al-Aqsa Intifada (also called the Second Intifada) broke out; Israel subsequently regained military control of significant parts of the Occupied Territories; and a spiral of tit-for-tat violence was unleashed. To structure international efforts to mitigate the conflict, the Quartet was formed of the United States, the EU, Russia, and the United Nations. A Roadmap toward a final settlement was presented, but the momentum provided by this plan soon dissipated. While the hard-line policies of Ariel Sharon's government inflamed Palestinian sentiment, the paucity of the political reforms accepted by the Palestinian Authority (PA) also triggered unrest within the Occupied Territories. After Yasser Arafat's death in November 2004, the process of Palestinian institutional reform appeared to be unlocked, and was posited as integral to a renewal of the peace process. The challenge of Hamas's rising popularity soon became a priority concern, however, and lay behind the postponement of parliamentary elections from July 2005 to January 2006. There was further urgency in the development of Palestinian institutions after Israel unilaterally withdrew from the Gaza Strip in the summer of 2005. The Hamas victory in the January 2006 elections then sent shock waves through the region and raised further challenges for the international community.

This chapter outlines the evolution of European policy in response to these events. While the broad evolution is sketched of European positions toward the peace process in the direct sense of negotiations between Israel and Palestine over a final settlement to the conflict, this is not the chapter's primary focus; this question has received exhaustive attention, which has clearly highlighted the EU's secondary role at this level of diplomatic mediation.[1] Rather, the focus here is on an area where the EU did position itself to exert a significant impact, namely the development and reform of Palestinian institutions and political structures. The EU's policy response to the growing violence after 2000 was notable. A generous increase in resources supported emergency relief and the provision of basic services in the Occupied Territories, and played arguably the major role in keeping the Palestinian Authority afloat, albeit in circumscribed form. Moreover, the chapter shows that the EU did use this support to leverage the beginnings of a process of institutional reform, aimed at improving the quality of Palestinian democracy, while also seeking to avoid a perception that it was attaching primary blame to the PA for the collapse of the peace process. However, the account suggests that the EU's influence was on second-order reform issues, which failed to change underlying power structures of the PA. Even after Arafat's death the shift in European strategy was truncated by the desire to support the new president, Mahmoud Abbas, in the face of Hamas's surge in popularity; the EU was still struggling to know how best to approach the latter in the run-up to the January 2006 elections. The chapter argues that the case of Palestine was one that evidenced areas of tangible European influence, but one that also suggested a failure to maximize the EU's potential impact on political developments.

The Al-Aqsa Intifada and Palestinian Reform

On the back of a long history of relief and development work in the Occupied Territories, going back to the early 1980s, the EU provided over half the funding that supported the setting up of the Palestinian Authority quasi-state institutions in the wake of the 1994 Oslo accords. The overwhelming share of European funding was channeled to the PA executive, and in particular the Negotiations Support Unit, with few conditions or benchmarks aimed at enhancing transparency and accountability. From the mid-1990s, the EU imposed firm conditions on the PA in relation only to macroeconomic policy and fiscal reform, not issues of democratic quality or good governance. The EU provided €18 million in support of the 1996 Palestinian elections, but few European objections were then raised in response to Arafat's postponement of subsequent polls. Little protection was offered against the PA's arbitrary arrests, narrowing of associational space, or restriction of Islamist welfare organizations.[2] Most European funding went to providing direct support for the PA's operating budget. From 1997 the EU was covering PA budget deficits; the payment of public sector salaries; and provisions for the centralization of fiscal revenues to the PA as part of the establishment of new structures for macroeconomic policymaking. All this support continued while PA appointments and payments had become a form of social benefits system. A major category of assistance was support for creating a strong police force, this forming the subject of one of the first Common Foreign and Security Policy Joint Actions. In 1997 an association agreement was signed, in formal terms with the Palestine Liberation Organization (PLO) but de facto providing a significant impulse toward the PA's standing as an international actor.

Funding for Palestinian NGOs more than halved after the mid-1990s. No pressure was exerted when the PA created its oxymoronic NGO Ministry, aimed at controlling civil society activity. Only at the very end of the 1990s was there a slight reversal of the drop in civil society funding. A new European Initiative on Democracy and Human Rights program offered €1.7 million for an NGO consortium on human rights and democracy in the West Bank and Gaza. While the Occupied Territories attracted funding from the MEDA democracy fund, and later from the EIDHR, these projects often funded initiatives more related to the peace process than to democracy strictly defined—funding covering projects on, for example, the protection of medical facilities, stopping property destruction, and legal assistance for the victims of attacks. The EU funded more work on Arab rights in Israel than Arab rights in the West Bank and Gaza. These funding priorities were justified as an effort to transform broad national movements into organizations running state-like institutions and the switch from NGOs fighting for independence into personnel running practical administrative functions. The EU was widely seen as instrumental in pressing Arafat to rein back on use of the death penalty. However, it was agreed that the EU used most of its capital with Arafat to persuade him not to declare statehood ahead of Israeli elections in 1999, probably against the majority will of Palestinians.[3] As quid pro quo, in its 1999 Berlin declaration the EU gave its firmest and most explicit support to date for the principle of Palestinian statehood.

While routinely criticized for not challenging US diplomatic primacy, the EU's bigger failure arguably lay in its inability to use the low-level cooperation of the Euro-Mediterranean Partnership to generate underlying dynamics more favorable to the peace process during the late 1990s. The EU presented as its most distinctive idea for reviving the peace process the promotion of civil society links between Arabs and Israelis. It explicitly declined, however, to link the Euro-Mediterranean Partnership's social and economic benefits to the parties' respective positions toward the various tracks of the peace process. No parallel of the Regional Conditionality applied by the EU as a conflict-resolution instrument in the Balkans was developed. Rather than the Arab-Israeli conflict being assuaged through a technicalization of relations under the EMP, ostensibly technical dossiers were adversely affected by security tensions. Israel refused to recognize the EU-PLO association agreement; blocked the preferential import of European goods to Palestinian territories; and provided Israeli origin certificates for goods made in the Occupied Territories, thus gaining trade preferences to which Israel was not entitled.[4] The struggle for tariff preferences was drawn into the conflict, rather than the EMP's low-level economic dimension providing sufficient incentive for moderation in the high politics sphere. The one area where the EU could have had a really significant impact was in halting the slide of the Palestinian economy, but nothing effective was done to ensure that Palestinian producers could actually export to the European market and circumvent obstacles imposed by Israel. No critical response was forthcoming to Israel's closure of parts of the Occupied Territories, undermining the EU's economic engagement with the Palestinians.

In response to the outbreak of the Al-Aqsa Intifada in September 2000, European governments shifted their support to more basic emergency relief. The ratio of development aid to emergency assistance shifted from 7:1 in 2000 to 1:5 by 2002.[5] Overall, donors doubled aid to the PA budget after the beginning of the Intifada. Total EU (Commission plus member states) aid rose to €500 million per year beginning in 2001. This accounted for 35 percent of total aid flows to the Palestinians; six of the PA's top ten funders in 2001 were EU donors. The logic was that if the PA collapsed completely, Israel would have no interlocutor in the peace process. After September 2000 the Commission channeled €10 million per month to support the PA budget to offset Israel's withholding of revenues. It was largely EU aid that kept the PA budget afloat, enabled PA salaries to be paid, and gave the PA some form of existence—all this while aid promised by Arab states failed to materialize in significant quantities. Donors observed that the Occupied Territories were one of the few areas where effective coordinating mechanisms were established on the ground, and where coordination among EU donors preceded discussions in other forums. The EU viewed its persuasion of the United States to resume direct assistance to the PA during this period as a significant success.[6] USAID launched a $33 million Palestinian civil society program in 2000,[7] although with the United States having an aid office only in Tel Aviv, the provision of basic relief through a strong presence on the ground was seen as a comparatively robust aspect of European endeavors.

While the immediate trigger of the Second Intifada was Ariel Sharon's inflammatory visit to the Al-Aqsa shrine, one (contested) view was that more indirectly it also reflected an underlying and growing disillusionment with Arafat's leadership among Palestinians. Hamas rose to prominence through providing the kind of local-level social benefits that the Palestinian Authority had failed to provide. The arbitrary and repressive provision of security had bred discontent. Some argued that the PA lacked the credibility and popular legitimacy to sustain any clampdown against suicide bombers after each periodic rounding up of suspects. Links were suspected between PA security forces and violent militia. Heavy-handed attempts to crush Islamist organizations had simply radicalized these groups. The common view was that Arafat had backed the uprising in part to shore up his own position vis-à-vis Hamas, and by the time he did try to temper the violence he found his authority undermined.

European diplomats began to acknowledge more candidly that the EU had miscalculated, to the extent that support for Palestinian security forces had contributed more problems than solutions. The EU was one of the most forthright sponsors of the International Task Force on Palestinian Reform—made up of the Quartet, Canada, Norway, Japan, the IMF, and the World Bank—with the Commission chairing this forum. After pressure from the Quartet, the PA elaborated its 100 days reform plan in mid-2002. To assist this, the International Task Force began to elaborate initiatives in relation to financial accountability, judicial reform, elections, local government, regulatory reforms, civil society, and security sector reform.

Work inaugurated by the Commission in 1999 that had advocated benchmarks on a range of reform questions—including limits to presidential powers, strengthening of local government, strengthening of the Palestinian Legislative Council (PLC), better budgetary scrutiny by the PLC, judicial independence, clearer separation of the PA and PLO, an end to emergency rule provisions, and press freedom—began to inform policymaking in Brussels. The Palestinian reform agenda began to be explored by the EU at this stage, some time ahead of its pursuit by the United States. The EU gradually built transparency benchmarks into its budgetary support, for example insisting on a freeze on new hiring and the transfer of monies to a single IMF-monitored account. During 2002 the EU began to raise the need for a dispersal of the leadership's power.

This focus on political reform was cautious, however. Emergency service provisions continued to dominate the EU response to the Intifada and Israeli incursions. Many suggested that EU financing of the PA budget was effectively bearing the cost of Israel's reoccupation of the Occupied Territories, removing from Israel the obligation to provide such funding. Aid focused mainly on the socioeconomic ramifications of the conflict, including, for example, support for rebuilding Palestinian housing. Such support also effectively substituted the fast-collapsing Palestinian "state" for social NGOs as primary service providers, arguably undermining local democratic accountability. Some more political initiatives commenced, including through support for the Palestinian Center for Human Rights, the Palestinian Human Rights Monitoring Group, and the Palestinian Center for Peace and Democracy.

Generous European support for infrastructure projects—the building of the Palestinian Legislative Council headquarters, the construction of Gaza International Airport—was not accompanied by more forceful diplomacy. The physical products of many EU projects were swiftly destroyed in Israeli attacks, with little in the way of concrete European reprisals (beyond a claim for compensation that was not carried through). EU special envoy Miguel Angel Moratinos was with Arafat when his compound was shelled in March 2002, and even this failed to engender a concrete policy response against Israel. The EU declined to heed the call of the European Parliament (EP) for suspension of arms transfers to the Israelis and Palestinians—although some states, such as Germany, did hold back some sales on an ad hoc basis. When the EP called for the EU's just-forming Rapid

Reaction Force to be deployed in the Occupied Territories, ministers acknowledged this was not even remotely likely. A clear majority of member states came to declare their support for a suspension of the EU-Israel association agreement, but a minority—Germany, the Netherlands, and the UK—opposed and blocked consideration of this option.

The EU still also failed to use the potential of its economic leverage. One of the most serious results of reoccupation was the decline in the number of Palestinians employed in Israel, from 100,000 in 1999 to fewer than 10,000 in 2003. Yet there was some concern among Palestinians that the EU actually worked with this trend, pushing more on direct EU-Palestinian links than on more integration between Israel and the Occupied Territories economies. Israel continued to frustrate Palestinian trade with the EU. Frequent commitments were forthcoming to ensure a more effective linkage between the peace process and the EMP—especially from external relations commissioner Chris Patten—but little concrete follow-through could be observed. In this period, it was suggested that the EU's primary concern was to avoid controversy with Israel in order to help itself secure a diplomatic role, through its inclusion in the Quartet.[8]

The Roadmap and the Limits to Reform

In June 2002 President Bush explicitly committed the United States to supporting the creation of an independent Palestinian state, making this conditional on PA reform and the removal of Arafat. The three-stage Roadmap toward a final settlement was presented under the auspices of the Quartet in October 2002. European governments played a significant role in the elaboration of the Roadmap. Indeed, the latter was based on a Danish presidency proposal, itself worked up from a German paper.[9] After its pivotal 1999 Berlin declaration, the EU's approach to the peace process became more sharply political. The EU stipulated with increasing force and clarity that the Palestinian state must extend to 1967 borders; that Israel must halt and reverse settlement construction and cease its attempt to irreversibly change the facts on the ground; that Israel's new security barrier was illegal; and that fundamental human rights standards were being breached through Israeli incursions into the Occupied Territories. In practice, no punitive EU measures were taken against Israel on these issues. The EU was influential mainly through crisis management activities, the EU special representative intervening to defuse a number of "microsecurity" crises—negotiating temporary ceasefires and mediating hostage standoffs, for example. Increased support for peace projects involving cooperation between Israeli and Palestinian civil society organizations was still seen as the most concrete expression of the EU's attempt to underpin the formal diplomacy of the peace process. Rather than pursuing new initiatives of its own, the EU prioritized its involvement in the Quartet and in efforts to ensure a reengagement of the Bush administration. The EU's elaboration of the Roadmap was presented in this light, as a concrete and balanced plan that would facilitate the United States' reengagement.[10]

Crucially, there was an increasingly inextricable link between these EU positions on the peace process per se and the nature of its focus on Palestinian institutional reform. The Roadmap envisaged an initial focus on strengthening Palestinian security services, to be followed by new Palestinian elections, which would open the way for a major donors' conference. Linked to the Roadmap, both the post of prime minister and the cabinet were to be strengthened in relation to Arafat. In practice, Arafat continued to limit the powers of Mahmoud Abbas, nominated as prime minister in April 2003. Abbas's attempt to bring in a tough new head of security services, the US-backed Mohammed Dahlan, triggered a dispute with Arafat that led to the prime minister's resignation. Arafat loyalists remained prominent.

On such issues, the Roadmap superficially embodied unity between the EU and United States. However, what the Roadmap also did was to provoke new differences over the sequencing of reform. The EU rejected President Bush's insistence that institutional reform occur prior to final settlement negotiations, as well as the notion of democratic reform being promoted primarily as a means of "getting Arafat out" (or even more disingenuously, of the United States setting reform hurdles so high that they would not in practice be obliged to exert any pressure on Israel).[11] It was universally felt that the United States' demonizing of Arafat would boost his standing and give him more incentive not to cooperate. There was EU unity in favor of the widespread view that the creation of a Palestinian state must occur together with reform of the PA into a full nation-state democracy, and that Palestinians must see that democracy meant something in terms of securing progress on a final settlement.[12] The European Union criticized the United States for failing to accept that Israeli withdrawal would itself feed into the kind and extent of PA reform that was feasible.

For the EU, reform conditions under the Roadmap were too front-loaded. However, diplomats admitted that this concern was subjugated to the desire to make sure that US reengagement was sustained. Abbas himself said he would not tolerate any bypassing of Arafat. The basic logic of the EU position was that Arafat's style of governance needed changing, but that he individually still had legitimacy as a symbol of the independence struggle. Paris was most skeptical over the institutional reform agenda; French diplomats unenthusiastically endorsed the Roadmap as the only means of attaining a new US involvement[13]—although it was, ironically, President Chirac who then called for new elections as a way, in French eyes, of boosting Arafat's position to negotiate with Israel. The Germans remained more skeptical on the utility of elections at this stage. Notwithstanding these differences, there was significant European unity on the general stance toward the issue of how reforms should be sequenced.

Despite the misgivings, the EU did attempt to harness the Roadmap for a further ratcheting up of the focus on broader democratic and governance reform. With an increased €250 million aid package at its disposal, the Commission urged a move away from short-term humanitarian aid, with the Roadmap having formalized at the political level a commitment to institution-building initiatives. The Commission sought further to tighten transparency and accountability benchmarks. This involved the Commission insisting on the creation of a single treasury account, tougher auditing provisions, and pension reform; holding back a large tranche of new EU aid until Abbas's appointment in April 2003 provided for stronger parliamentary government; holding back €10 million for election support until a new election law was passed, providing for an independent Palestinian Electoral Commission; and linking €7 million of judicial reform assistance to the adoption of a new Law on the Independence of the Judiciary. In part as a way of reducing the risk of fraudulent PA use of European aid, in the middle of 2003 the EU scrapped its €10 million a month direct budgetary transfer, in favor of more targeted parcels of aid to pay off particular PA bills, with a new €80 million package targeted in particular at covering debts accrued by the private sector. Particular focus was placed on supporting the reformist finance minister, Salem Fayyed. In relation to a number of these forms of conditionality, the Commission came into conflict with other members of the International Task Force concerned that holding funds back would actually make reform more difficult. At the same time, the PA's association agreement at this stage opened up further areas of work on procurement and other governance issues, including some with a peace process read-over. In the words of one policy-maker, the European pressure on corruption and financial misman-agement moved from "soft" to "hard" conditionality.

More pressure was exerted on Arafat to widen the political space available to NGOs receiving European funds. New funding for civil society organizations was made available from a number of different sources, including the EIDHR—the Occupied Territories became a disproportionately heavy priority under the latter budget. New EIDHR projects included support for media and grassroots democracy in Palestine; changes to the nature of media coverage in Israel; the rights of Palestinian women in Israel; and the funding of a new jour-nal to monitor the PA aimed at reporting on executive abuses not published in mainstream media. New human rights training courses were funded for security services under the umbrella of the EU secu-rity adviser's office in Ramallah. A continuing security focus was seen in a new Joint Action aimed at helping the Palestinian Authority in its fight against terrorism, but it was claimed that this built in a more prominent human rights training component than previously.[14]

Additional funding was forthcoming from some European gov-ernments. Democracy and governance allocations to Palestine for 2004 included €10 million from Germany, €15 million from Den-mark, and €24 million from Sweden. Spanish aid to the Occupied Ter-ritories doubled between 2000 and 2004, while Palestine accounted for nearly half of Italian aid to the entire Middle East after 2002.[15] A £30 million UK aid package targeted administrative reform and streamlining ministerial structures. DfID initiatives were oriented more toward civil society, reflecting concern with the donor focus on governmental structures designed to make the PA more accountable to the international community than to Palestinian civil society. A new initiative on service delivery NGOs reflected an effort to give aid funding a profile more akin to that in other recipient states. Euro-pean influence within the International Task Force on institutional reform was, according to diplomats, focused on addressing this issue of local ownership.

European governments were, however, still reluctant to shift the focus too far toward institutional reform and away from direct efforts aimed at peace process negotiations. European donors talked of their belief in the need for democratic reforms but also of their reluctance to use up political capital on this issue. A high-profile meeting in London in December 2002, called ostensibly to discuss institutional reform, in practice focused overwhelmingly on the Roadmap, and actually excluded experts involved in democracy and human rights programs on the ground in the Occupied Territories. Proposals forwarded by Joschka Fischer and others for a UN protectorate, to be charged with implementing reforms to the PA, in fact raised question marks precisely over the local "ownership" of democratic reforms. Projects funded by European donors and foundations were in practice still aimed more at the peace process than at democracy per se, with aid priorities including the reinsertion of political prisoners, dispute resolution techniques, projects fostering dialogue between PLC and Knesset moderates, and technical advice on lobbying the EU to use its association agreement to press Israel. The peace process link was seen in the disproportionate orientation of funds toward NGOs based in Ramallah.

European governments still reined back from a strongly critical stance toward Arafat. When Silvio Berlusconi visited the Middle East in June 2003, he both refused to meet with Arafat and unilaterally promised a strengthening of EU-Israeli links. He thus incurred the wrath of other member states and was shunned by Abbas in return.[16] Conditionality and pressure focused mainly on relatively technical auditing devices, rather than on the underlying power structures of the PA. In terms of concrete policy initiatives and funding priorities, the concern was less with comprehensive democratization and more simply with greater transparency to prevent PA funds being siphoned off to violent groups. When the United States announced that it was withdrawing its judicial reform program, the EU committed to taking over this area of work, and it was less insistent on the complete overhauling of the legal system. One diplomat suggested that the EU remained "cautious" over political reform, eschewing any "off-the-shelf template." The largest slice of European institution-building aid continued to be channeled through the government-controlled Negotiations Support Unit, even as negotiations ceased and it was realized that such support had little spillover capacity-building impact through other parts of the government. The PLC, often referred to as the great hope of the democratic opposition, did not now receive significant European support.

Broader diplomatic factors also limited the extent and effectiveness of the institutional reform focus. The key point during this period was when Israel, after years of pushing for stronger prime ministerial autonomy from Arafat, undermined Abbas by refusing to lift checkpoint restrictions or halt settlement activity. The EU did little—either itself or through pressure on Israel—to give Abbas a chance to consolidate an independent reform-oriented power base. Increasing French opposition to US designs in the Middle East further undermined France's legitimacy with Israel: Sharon refused to see Dominique de Villepin during the latter's visit to Israel in late May. The United States was keen to restrict direct EU involvement in policing the Roadmap; the EU was instead allocated responsibility for building the PA state and institutional reform. The latter was seen as an area where the EU could offer a distinctive imprint. Israelis increasingly charged the EU with not having fulfilled its task of building a strong democratic PA during the 1990s, one capable of providing not only security but also the kind of basic social and economic services the lack of which had unleashed radicalism among Palestinians.

Thus, by late 2003 the reform process had stagnated, violence resumed with even greater ferocity, and the Roadmap appeared to be leading nowhere. Arafat regained the initiative, appointing a new personally loyal security adviser, which caused Abbas to resign in September 2003. Ahmed Qurei, seen as closer to Arafat, replaced Abbas. The EU again did little to shore up Abbas. Israel threatened to "remove" Arafat and refused to deal with Qurei. The United States blocked a Syrian-sponsored UNSC resolution condemning Israel for this threat against Arafat; a majority of EU states supported the resolution. More direct Palestinian appeals for European help were increasingly heard. Significant response was seen by EU diplomats as particularly difficult during Italy's six-month tenure of the EU presidency. In late October the United States dropped its opposition to Israel's security fence; the EU's angry reaction took the Quartet to the point of collapse. Over the autumn of 2003, as violence intensified, the United States shifted back to requiring less of Israel, more of the Palestinians.

Security Imperatives

European thinking on security challenges also evolved against this backdrop of Roadmap stagnation, Israeli incursions, persistent suicide attacks, and growing social instability in the Occupied Territories. An apparently significant change was registered in September 2003 when the EU added Hamas to its list of groups defined as terrorist organizations. European governments had increasingly espoused some degree of rapprochement with Hamas, showing some sympathy with Abbas's decision to offer Hamas political partnership in return for a ceasefire. In contrast to the US pressure on Abbas to move immediately and forcefully to disarm Hamas, EU diplomats spoke of the need to recognize the organization's social presence and to bring it into the political process. EU security officer Alistair Crooke initiated a process of dialogue that included inviting Hamas representatives to town hall meetings between different local groups, which he mediated. The United States criticized European governments for funding some apparently innocuous social organizations whose members included personnel from Hamas's political wing.[17] Incurring US anger, the EU moved to isolate Islamic welfare organizations only where links were demonstrated to Hamas's military wing—Germany, for example, did ban the Al-Aqsa Foundation when it uncovered direct use of funds for military purposes; European donors argued that otherwise cooperating on social issues with such groups kept access open to Hamas politically.[18] Recriminations were intensified by claims that Commission funds had ended up supporting educational materials that incited violence. (A subsequent in-house inquiry cleared the Commission on this point.)

The change of position registered in September 2003 was in part due to US pressure and in part consistent with general post-9/11 shifts in counterterrorist strategies. It also, however, reflected an impatience that the more engagement-oriented line toward Hamas had produced little moderation from the latter. France held out longest against the shift in policy, insisting on the inclusion of a clause that would make it easier to take Hamas off the terrorist list again. That Paris did acquiesce to the change demonstrated the depth of European concern. Javier Solana's 2002 efforts to mediate a ceasefire between the PA, Palestinian security forces, and Hamas appeared to have been unsuccessful, as Hamas resumed violent attacks in the autumn of 2003. When Crooke was withdrawn from the Occupied Territories at the end of September—a move reputedly pushed by PA officials unhappy at European contacts with Hamas—the EU's links with Hamas dried up.[19] Only two member states thereafter admitted to low-level contacts with the organization; Jack Straw insisted in early 2005 that low-level British contacts with Hamas officials be discontinued. Diplomats in the Occupied Territories complained of a lack of sustained political backing for on-the-ground engagement, with Javier Solana, in the words of one high-level official, being "pushed forward and then reined back" by successive presidencies.

Notwithstanding the decision to include the organization on its list of terrorist groups, the EU line toward Hamas retained some of its distinctiveness vis-à-vis US and Israeli approaches. European donors justified their increased allocations of aid to basic service provision in the Occupied Territories as a means of providing alternative sources of welfare to those provided by Hamas, and thus a more surreptitious means of undermining the latter's appeal. European diplomats commonly argued that Hamas could not be defeated by force and repression; rather, some form of credible and effective state had to be constructed—and *allowed* to be constructed—in order to undercut the mutual assistance and community policing networks that had given Hamas such a deeply embedded presence in society. Some claimed that if Hamas committed itself to elections and won a significant share of seats, the EU would "accept the consequences." The preference in many European chancelleries was for support to be directed at fashioning a broad national dialogue or pact, including Hamas, to take reforms forward in a negotiated and consensual fashion. The problem, according to one influential European diplomat, was that beyond the warmer words the EU had in fact failed to engage with Islamist welfare organizations in a way that provided concrete benefits and could be used for political leverage. In these difficulties around getting Hamas to engage, one critic saw the price paid by European governments for shunning moderates in the organization during the latter half of the 1990s.[20]

Similar issues emerged in relation to the EU's broader security role. As US security monitors arrived in the middle of 2003, French foreign minister Dominique de Villepin advocated an EU "inter-positional" force. The UK was reportedly considering the deployment of special forces.[21] However, Israel remained adamantly opposed to the Europeans adopting a security monitoring function. Indeed, security sector support that had been provided by the EU had occasioned one of its most humiliating foreign policy experiences. Much European-funded hardware—such as forensic laboratories—was unceremoniously destroyed by Israel, and Palestinian forces were prevented from using and carrying a lot of the equipment provided by European governments. Political sensitivities ensured that the notion of an EU police mission was not considered feasible.

A criticism from Palestinians was that European security support had been provided in an uncoordinated way, leaving forces with a mish-mash of British, Dutch, and Danish equipment that was not always fully interoperable. Early in 2004, an EU Coordination Unit for Palestinian Police Support (COPPS) was created, to consolidate and enhance the European security profile. New commitments were made to provide Palestinian forces with more modern equipment, but also to train officers to intervene in a less heavy-handed fashion and to avoid further aggravating tensions. The British development ministry funded a police adviser, for the first time linking the provision of equipment with support for civil society input into debates over policing doctrine in the West Bank and Gaza. A stated EU aim was, in a break with the past, to try to tie police support to a reform of the criminal law system. A big European diplomatic push was instrumental in the security forces being placed more tightly under the control of the prime minister's office. The Dutch government released a particularly significant package of new security cooperation to the PA in the middle of 2004, while also using its EU presidency to push for Hizbollah to be added to the list of terrorist groups.[22] COPPS was significantly strengthened with new funds at the end of 2005.

Limitations and tensions persisted, however. The European Commission lamented that COPPS in practice declined to focus on the crucial issue of strengthening the democratic control of security forces. Several member state governments expressed concern that too much additional police cooperation would be interpreted as the EU seeking to control the Palestinians at Sharon's behest. Some European police officials opined that the fixation with training was misplaced, with Palestinian forces already over-trained and hampered mainly by a lack of political motivation deriving from the broader political context in the Occupied Territories. A common fear was that new initiatives in the field of security were widely perceived on the ground as counterterrorism dressed up as support for political reform.

Security sector support was increasingly seen as a critical issue as Sharon progressed with his proposal for a unilateral withdrawal from the Gaza Strip. This plan received immediate US backing but initially appeared to occasion a split within the EU, with Britain, Germany, and the Netherlands reacting more favorably than other member states. The more skeptical states began to see some virtue in Gaza withdrawal as some key Palestinians, such as Marwan Barghouti, came out in support of the plan. In broad diplomatic terms, the main concern among Europeans was to ensure that Gaza withdrawal assisted a comprehensive final settlement rather than, as Sharon apparently intended, being accompanied by a tightening of Israeli control over the West Bank. The question debated within the EU, without firm resolution, was how to prepare for filling the dangerous institutional vacuum that Israel's departure from Gaza would produce, and yet not simply freeing up Israeli resources and manpower for deployment in the West Bank, or provoking divisions among Palestinians, to Israel's advantage. Again, such strategic thinking vis-à-vis Israel clashed to some degree with a focus on better governance in the Palestinian Territories. Most states in the EU also shied away from the notion—supported both by Israel and some opposition Palestinians in Gaza—of using withdrawal as an opportunity to create new governance structures that would circumvent Arafat and the PA.

Solana announced plans for a postwithdrawal security sector initiative. Acknowledging that a direct European security role in Gaza was unlikely to be accepted, a primary element of EU policy was to back the idea of Egyptian forces helping to provide security and train Palestinian forces after Israel's withdrawal—given the record of Egyptian security forces this arguably sat uneasily with EU human rights commitments. Some consideration was given to the use of Canadian and Norwegian troops—relatively uncontroversial nations, to both sides—to help in what would be the necessary provision of security at border crossings between Gaza and Israel. Both Israelis and Palestinians lamented that Europeans seemed willing to contemplate only modest training proposals, exhibiting limited thinking on how to establish effective and democratic governance within Gaza. On the economic side too, Europeans were reluctant to launch new cooperation if withdrawal were not part of new moves toward final settlement; concern was expressed that after withdrawal Israel would increasingly close off the Gaza economy. Notwithstanding such doubts, European policymakers also insisted that with key figures on both sides wanting Gaza withdrawal, "for the first time we have real leverage." In particular, the EU moved to stipulate detailed conditions that disengagement must increase the freedom of movement across the border, which would start to make the successful administering of EU projects easier. After Israel did pull out from Gaza in August 2005, despite the erstwhile reluctance the EU did proceed to dispatch border guards to the Refah crossing, albeit with a tightly drawn operational mandate.

After Arafat

By the early part of 2004 significant change appeared to be afoot within Palestinian politics. As Hamas and Islamic Jihad won more elections to student councils and professional bodies, and came to rival Fatah in terms of overall national support, Fatah sought a more systematic rapprochement with Hamas. The apparent shift in Hamas positions on participating in mainstream politics fed into debates over the holding of new elections. Elections, called for June 2004, were once more postponed. Popular frustration was then further triggered by Arafat's appointment of his cousin to head the security forces in Gaza. This unleashed protest in Gaza and caused Qurei briefly to resign. The PLC suspended its activities for a month in September in an attempt to push Arafat into agreeing to reforms and new elections. By October a firm schedule for different levels of elections had still not been put in place.

Some evidence emerged of growing European frustration with Arafat's continuing reluctance to implement reforms. European diplomats judged that some degree of reassessment was needed due to the increasing divisions among Palestinians, with Arafat no longer enjoying the same degree of consensual backing within the Occupied Territories. Despite this, the EU retained its policy of dealing directly with Arafat. EU special representative Marc Otte acknowledged that the EU was still doing little in terms of engaging the young guard in Fatah—and even less so potential new leaders outside Fatah. The EU's insistence on meeting Arafat ratcheted up tension with the Sharon government: Israel cancelled the visit of French foreign minister Michel Barnier in the summer of 2004—with Sharon adding a call for Jews to leave France due to an increase, he alleged, in French anti-Semitism. Most European states were notably less explicit than the United States in backing Mohammed Dahlan, Arafat's emergent rival in the Gaza Strip.

Some Europeans did begin to push more explicitly for elections. DfID's new strategy asserted that "a renewal of the democratic mandate of Palestinian institutions could add some impetus to the reform movement," and thus provide conditions for switching the focus away from basic humanitarian and emergency assistance to a more significant effort in the field of institution building. The UK committed an increased 15 percent of its aid, from late 2004 to 2006, to measures aimed at strengthening accountable government.[23] To the extent that concerns were present over the need for democratic reform, an indirect and local focus continued to be prominent. By early 2004 the UK was helping to set up local committees around housing reconstruction projects, the logic being that prevailing support for Islamist welfare organizations could be channeled into alternative representative bodies focusing on specific development issues.

European donors expressed a frustration that the relatively large amounts of institution-building aid forthcoming since 2001 had generated few reform dynamics. The EU line had been: "We help build the Palestinian state first, then we aim to perfect democracy." By the middle of 2004 more European diplomats were willing to question the wisdom of this approach. One diplomat acknowledged the fact that the priority focus on financial transparency in the PA had had little benefit to ordinary people. Large amounts of European aid allocated for institutional reform remained unspent. The PA leadership was seen to have judged that the EU was bluffing in its relatively timid threats to withdraw support. Palestinian civil society organizations had themselves tired of the institution-building focus of European programs, arguing to diplomats that these had been ineffective and divorced from citizens' desire for tangible and qualitative change. Pessimism grew over the effectiveness of long-term capacity building in the prevailing circumstances of renewed Israeli incursions and crisis in the PA. Rather, the priority was on keeping the peace process at least on "life support," with some in the EU arguing that funds should be deployed more to raise awareness and influence opinion inside Israel.

The UK, Germans, and Dutch were more eager to press for elections. Others in the EU questioned this as representing the US agenda; even some of the more Atlanticist states recognized that the case for pressing for elections had been complicated by the US position toward Arafat. The basic calculus on the holding of elections appeared to have changed: some estimated that a poll was now more likely to oust than reconfirm Arafat. A number of member states sought to block EU aid for local elections, for fear of Hamas winning seats. Despite such doubts, some Europeans did begin to play an active role on the ground in preparing for elections. A number of member states sent electoral monitoring teams to the Occupied Territories to assist with preparation of the electoral census—several, such as the Spanish team, had their movements restricted by Israel. As initial preparations did commence for municipal elections in December, the EU criticized the fact that the Electoral Commission still lacked full independence from Fatah, with the latter agreeing to hold a first round of elections only in the districts where it looked likely to win. When Israel closed a number of polling stations registering voters for elections in East Jerusalem, no EU reaction was forthcoming.

As these debates were intensifying, Yasser Arafat's death on 11 November 2004 changed the whole political context. Mahmoud Abbas's victory in the January 2005 elections was widely interpreted as Fatah having retained control. The US and Egyptian governments openly backed Abbas, leaning on the less-favored Marwan Barghouti not to run. The Fatah old guard prevailed in preventing the elections from offering genuine democratic competition. In reaction, Hamas did not join the Israeli-Palestinian ceasefire concluded in February 2005.

The EU sent 260 observers to monitor the January 2005 elections, its biggest ever election mission. The head of the EU delegation, Michel Rocard, criticized Israeli restrictions on the movement of election candidates.[24] It was reported that Israel did relent on some restrictions for fear of the EU withdrawing funds from the PA, which Israel would be obliged to cover.[25] The observer mission also identified concerns on the Palestinian side, including the "misuse of public resources in favor of one candidate"; the arbitrary extension of voting times specifically to bus more Fatah supporters in to the polling stations; the fact that the PA openly mobilized in support of Abbas; and Abbas's securing of 94 percent of election-related air time on television.[26] In relation to this last concern, Rocard complained that the Palestinian media were "acting as if there is only one candidate."[27] Despite such manipulation, European donors moved to increase support to the PA and Abbas. Critics argued that this revealed a continuing ambivalence over genuine democratization, in the name of security.[28] Ariel Sharon disdainfully suggested that after the elections Europeans should limit themselves to assistance for "desalination, roads, and buildings for refugees."[29]

Tensions with Israel were apparent as Tony Blair sought to shift the focus onto postelection institution building at a meeting in London in March, which Israeli officials did not attend. The London meeting produced a 17-page document laying out what was by now a standard menu of reform work required of the Palestinians: a new electoral law, completion of rolling municipal elections by the end of 2005, pension reform, a civil service law, abolition of state security courts, increased civil society input through the National Reform Committee, strengthened reporting of security structures to civilian bodies, and a streamlining down to three security forces. The document stated that reforms "should open the way" to new aid commitments.[30] Blair's initiative was criticized from both sides: some resented the impression that the PA was being singled out for pressure; others (including some EU donors) feared that the new document would be used by the Palestinians to claim that previous broader reform commitments had been supplanted.

External relations commissioner Benita Ferrero-Waldner used the London meeting to update the distribution of the Commission's €250 million package: €70 million would go to the World Bank Reform Trust Fund, and another large chunk through the UN Relief and Works Agency (UNRWA); €7 million was destined for the judiciary, through MEDA funds; €14 million was allocated to support the introduction of a new electoral law and a strengthening of the Central Election Commission; and €5 million would go to the anticorruption task force, for training auditors and financial controllers.[31] One EU diplomat suggested that the Commission's postelection priorities were to strengthen the separation of powers; firm up good governance benchmarks; and ensure that formal judicial reform translated into de facto judicial independence—the last an increasingly acknowledged gap in EU policies hitherto. The new European Neighbourhood Action Plan signed with the PA explicitly placed the construction of a democratic Palestinian state as its priority objective. A new program of EU assistance to Palestinian civil policing identified its aim as transformational change in security provision and complementarity between police restructuring and broader judicial reform. Even if in the short term the plan appeared to focus mainly on the provision of equipment, EU officials argued that they had developed a broader and more reformist approach to security sector cooperation than the United States—this as President Bush dispatched a new team of security advisers to the Occupied Territories.[32]

Abbas gradually asserted himself against Arafat loyalists and implemented a number of reforms, strengthening provisions for parliamentary scrutiny, increasing fiscal transparency and broadening judicial independence. Even if Abbas remained cautious on the pace of reform, observers detected the emergence of a decisionmaking culture based more on the rule of law, distinct from Arafat's preference for dealing with the perpetrators of violence outside the legal system on a personal basis. Both internal and external reform commitments soon faced a challenge, however, in the shape of Hamas's decision to participate in the parliamentary elections scheduled for July 2005, a move that followed the organization's success in municipal elections, where they won a swath of seats. Blatantly in order to head off a strong Hamas showing in the July elections, Abbas announced that these elections were to be postponed until January 2006. The Fatah old guard pushed for a delay to elections even beyond early 2006, while also postponing the long-awaited Fatah general conference in order to head off pressure from reformists.[33]

The EU was not strongly critical of the postponement of elections. EU support had already commenced to help draw up a new legal framework for the elections; to increase voter registration; and to strengthen the Central Election Commission with a view to preventing state resources from being used to back Fatah candidates as had happened in the presidential elections. After some internal debate, the EU had decided to press Abbas to hold the elections; the official European line was that Hamas needed to be given the opportunity to participate fully in democratic politics. By May 2005 a number of EU member states were pushing for Hamas to be taken off the terrorist list, complaining that without such a move European engagement with the organization in the run-up to the elections was hindered. The United States was widely seen as favoring a postponement; the fact that the delay was announced immediately after Abbas's meeting with President Bush in Washington led to speculation that the United States had actively leaned on the Palestinian leader to postpone the poll.[34] European ministers claimed that they had wanted the elections to go ahead, and urged the PA to "set as soon as possible a date for the organization of free and fair legislative elections."[35] However, despite all this reasoning, no concrete critical response followed the postponement. In the autumn of 2005 quiet diplomacy prevailed, aimed at ensuring that the new polling date in January 2006 would be respected.

When Ariel Sharon's hospitalization in January 2006 led some Palestinian politicians to raise the possibility of a further delay to elections, the United States was more overtly insistent than the EU that the January poll proceed as planned. Nevertheless, the EU also supported the principle that elections be held, as it became clearer that a Hamas victory was highly possible, and offered €1.4 million of support for their organization. It was in the immediate run-up to the elections that EU commissioners and officials began to suggest that in the event of a Hamas victory the EU would withdraw its aid if the group were not to renounce violence—a position frequently highlighted by Fatah during the electoral campaign. In practice, as the implications of Hamas's win were assessed in the immediate aftermath of the elections, many European diplomats cautioned against precipitate action and feared that withdrawing aid would actually be tantamount to punishing President Mahmoud Abbas for the Hamas victory. An EU that had for some time advocated Hamas's political inclusion was revealed as having had no preplanned coherent response to a Hamas victory that many had been warning was eminently possible. The condition was imposed that Hamas should renounce violence, but little detail was pronounced on the precise steps that would lead up to the suspension of aid, or conversely what concrete moves from Hamas would suffice to avoid the withdrawing of funds.

European policymakers expressed concern that a strong political case existed not for withdrawing funding but that there were legal complications flowing from Hamas being on the EU list of terrorist organizations. With members of the Palestinian security forces expressing reluctance to accept the electoral results, the continuity of the EU's Refah border and police reform missions was seen by diplomats as particularly problematic. One contemplated route forward was to divert more funding to civil society organizations and UNRWA. European strictures were at one level similar to those of the United States, insisting on Hamas in some form (even if not through an immediate change in its charter) publicly declaring its acceptance of Israel's right to exist. It also emerged, however, that the Bush administration was drawing up plans far more quickly to starve a Hamas government of financial assistance—although some diplomats claimed that in private US policymakers recognized the virtue of other international funds continuing in order to avoid complete collapse in the Occupied Territories. The European hope was that Hamas would form a technocratically flavored coalition government, within which non-Hamas ministers would provide interlocutors for the international community. It was also suggested that the EU would see virtue in powers being transferred back to the presidency—after years of the Palestinians being enjoined by the EU to shift responsibilities in exactly the opposite direction.

Conclusion

In quantitative terms the EU's role in the Occupied Territories represented one of its most significant external relations engagements. In qualitative terms its approach was increasingly shown to have been unduly myopic. From 2001, the EU did adapt its strategy to place greater emphasis on long-term institutional reform; but this move was late and had relatively limited impact. European governments were united in criticizing President Bush's very direct attack on the person of Arafat; and yet, however narrow this US approach, it did spark debate on Palestinian democratization in a way that the EU's focus on low-profile transparency benchmarks failed to do. The attacks of 9/11 encouraged the EU to intensify a focus on reform that it had already begun to develop, but the origins of this shift lay in domestic Palestinian and Israeli developments.[36] With the PA so heavily dependent on European support, it might be asked whether the EU fell well short of exerting its full potential influence.

If Europeans rejected the US line of trying to push reforms in a front-loaded fashion, they could not break the circular logic of "No reform without peace; no peace without reform" that increasingly predominated.[37] The EU attempted to ensure that democratic reform and final settlement talks proceeded in parallel; as such simultaneity failed to emerge, some experts argued that the peace process could only be unblocked by moving straight to a final settlement, delinked from trends in internal Palestinian politics. In this sense, the EU was arguably guilty of underestimating the extent to which the PLO's legitimacy was integrally tied to the struggle for independence, thus rendering the granting of a fully sovereign Palestine a prerequisite to social debate and activism shifting to a focus on democratic values. This failure reflected in part one of the sharpest disconnects in European foreign policies between high-level diplomacy and the elaboration of in situ aid projects.

The EU's conception of the rightful ingredients of Palestinian reform exhibited a significantly instrumentalist logic, having its main focus on how reform could contribute to immediate improvements in security capacities. Support for a more prime ministerial political system contrasted with the EU's more common backing for strongly presidential polities in conflict scenarios. Some glaring omissions were evident in European funding: little work was supported to promote democratic capacity building among the Palestinian diaspora, for instance, whose size and weight was such a distinctive feature in the prospects for Palestinian democratization. The focus was clearly on governance and transparency, much less on trying to reform the underlying dynamics of Palestinian politics. Despite the rhetoric on the desirability of integrating Hamas into democratic politics, the concrete substance of European strategy invited the conclusion that the EU saw reform in terms of strengthening Fatah against Hamas. Supporting the principle of Hamas's participation in elections, the EU then did nothing to defend that principle when elections were postponed. It was as a result of this ambivalence that, after many had foreseen a significant change in policy after Arafat's death, in practice by the end of 2005 the EU was slipping back into the familiar strategy of placing its faith in a pro-peace and nominally pro-reform leader whose ability to deliver on either of these commitments was increasingly open to question.

When elections were eventually held, representing a significant democratizing step, the EU did not quickly have a strategy in place to harness the new juncture as an opportunity for influencing Hamas policies. If the Hamas victory in January 2006 was the result of a vote in large part against Fatah corruption, it must be asked whether EU indulgence of the latter had not in a small way actually contributed to the radical organization assuming power. Certainly, as the dust settled after these elections and the next steps in European policy remained unclear, the dramatic change in Palestinian politics raised a crucial challenge: could the EU now successfully use leverage gained from having pumped millions of euros into the Occupied Territories over the course of a decade to influence a now-governing Hamas?

Notes

1. Aoun, "European Foreign Policy," pp. 289–312; Emerson and Tocci, "The Rubik Cube"; Tocci, "The Widening Gap."
2. Asseburg and Perthes, "The European Union and the Palestinian Authority," pp. 28–31 and 39.
3. Ginsberg, *The European Union,* p. 123.
4. Tocci, "Does the European Union Promote Democracy in Palestine?"
5. Department for International Development, *Country Assistance Plan,* p. 12.
6. Chris Patten, "A Roadmap Paid for in Euros," *Financial Times,* 16 July 2003.
7. www.usaid.gov/wbg.

8. Soetendorp, "The EU's Involvement," pp. 283–295.

9. Asseburg, "The EU and the Middle East Conflict."

10. For an overview of the evolution of EU peace process policies, see Tocci, "The Widening Gap," and Asseburg, "From Declaration to Implementation?"

11. See Carnegie Endowment Forum, *Toward Democracy.*

12. International Crisis Group, *Middle East Endgame I.*

13. International Crisis Group, *A Middle East Roadmap to Where?* p. 24.

14. *Agence Europe,* 17/18 April 2000, p. 5.

15. Agencia Española de Cooperación Internacional, *Plan Anual de AECI 2005,* p. A.2-33; Balfour, "Italy's Policies in the Mediterranean."

16. *Financial Times,* 16 June 2003.

17. *Financial Times,* 27 August 2003.

18. International Crisis Group, *Islamic Social Welfare,* pp. 19–20.

19. International Crisis Group, *Dealing with Hamas,* p. 20.

20. Kepel, *Jihad,* p. 325.

21. Indyk, "A Trusteeship for Palestine?" pp. 51–70.

22. BBC Monitoring Service, 22 September 2004.

23. Department for International Development, *Country Assistance Plan,* p. 29.

24. BBC Monitoring Service, 12 December 2004.

25. *Middle East International,* no. 736, pp. 16–17.

26. Preliminary Statement of the European Union Election Observation Mission to the West Bank and Gaza: 2–4.

27. BBC Monitoring Service, 4 January 2005.

28. Alistair Crooke, "Forget Palestinian Security Reform," *Daily Star,* 12 December 2005.

29. BBC Monitoring Service, 30 December 2004.

30. Conclusions of the London Meeting on Supporting the Palestinian Authority, London, 1 March 2005, www.fco.gov.uk.

31. Speech to the London Meeting on Supporting the Palestinian Authority, 1 March 2005, http://europa.eu.int/comm/external_relations/news/ferrero/2005/sp05_126.htm.

32. EU Council Secretariat, "EU Assistance to Palestinian Civilian Police."

33. Y. Sayigh, "In-fighting Threatens Palestinian Democracy," *Financial Times,* 8 August 2005.

34. *Middle East International,* no. 752, 10 June 2005, pp. 4–5.

35. Council Conclusions, 16–17 June 2005, p. 37, www.consilium.eu.int.

36. International Crisis Group, *Middle East Endgame I,* p. 11.

37. Magan, "Building Democratic Peace in the Eastern Mediterranean," p. 115.

6

The Gulf and the
Arabian Peninsula:
Not-So-Benign Neglect

While significant attention and debate centered on other
parts of the Middle East during the 1990s, in the countries of the
Gulf Cooperation Council (Saudi Arabia, Kuwait, Bahrain, Qatar,
Oman, and the United Arab Emirates), along with Yemen, European
foreign policy was strikingly low profile. Precisely in the area where
concerns relating to the security of energy supplies were so acute,
politically the Gulf represented one of the EU's least developed areas
of foreign policy. If some focus on political reform had crept into
European policies elsewhere in the Middle East by the end of the
1990s, this was to an overwhelming extent absent in the Gulf. The
latter was the region where the autocratic containment of Islamist
radicals was indulged by the EU to its most undiluted degree. Even if
economic and energy supply issues compounded this orientation, in
practice engagement in these areas prospered only to a limited extent.
This chapter details the EU's efforts to enhance its profile in GCC
states and Yemen after 9/11, when the region was catapulted to the
frontline of international counterterrorist concerns; and analyzes the
EU's difficulties in correcting its previous neglect of the region.
Some increase in European attention to the Gulf was witnessed after
9/11; this included a cautious attempt to support political reform
dynamics—a shift in strategy reflecting in part new security thinking,
in part a response to the beginnings of political change in some countries in the region. However, the GCC remained the area where European purchase was weakest in the Middle East and where policy initiatives were the least comprehensive. The nature of economic, social,
political, and strategic engagement in the Gulf was of a qualitatively

171

different order than elsewhere. Oil was one factor explaining this, but another was the more rudimentary nature of economic and civil society structures, which militated against the effective deployment of standard EU forms of cooperation. While Yemen presented a qualitatively different order of challenge, and was a case where European development policies and resources were of significance, here too it proved difficult for the EU to gain traction in influencing the country's halting process of reform.

The 1990s: Oil and Defense Diplomacy

During the 1990s, European policy in the Gulf revolved around the twin pillars of energy supplies and defense cooperation, within the context of a limited overall political and economic engagement with the region. Relations were based on the 1988 Cooperation Agreement between the EU and the Gulf Cooperation Council. Of determinant importance was the EU's decision to seek trade facilitation and liberalization on this interregional basis. While the United States sought to deepen cooperation with individual GCC states, EU efforts were diluted to the level of the state most cautious in strengthening links, namely Saudi Arabia. Saudi Arabia stalled on EU trade liberalization proposals; Bahrain and the United Arab Emirates were the states most intent on such cooperation.[1] The regional approach most notably meant that the EU was reluctant to push for significant economic cooperation and liberalization until the GCC itself established a full customs union. Economic measures implemented under the Cooperation Agreement were insubstantial. Successive EU-GCC joint cooperation committees registered limited progress. On the one hand, oil-rich Gulf regimes perceived little need to open domestic markets. On the other hand, European petrochemical producers (at this stage) convinced EU governments to retain a defensive stance in this sector. European producers accused Gulf regimes of subsidizing petrochemical production; the GCC accused the EU of unjustified protectionism, and itself resisted European pressure to ease restrictions on foreign investment. The EU remained particularly protectionist on many superior refined oil products from the GCC.[2] In this regard, EU proposals for a carbon tax were another point of contention.[3] With most GCC exports already entering the EU free of duty under Most Favored Nation status, there appeared little enthusiasm for Europeans' advocacy of more reciprocal trade liberalization.

Unlike other Middle Eastern countries, Gulf states neither received nor sought European development aid, removing one source of potential leverage. Reflecting the GCC's possession of nearly half the world's oil reserves and its supply of a fifth of global production, energy cooperation was the priority for many European governments. The region was the source of over a quarter of EU oil imports. Despite the magnitude of oil imports, however, the EU's trade deficits with the GCC turned—in the case of most countries—into increasingly large surpluses during the 1990s. European deficits in visible trade (oil) became overall surpluses by virtue of Saudi Arabia, in particular, importing an increasing value of services from Europe. Overall, the share of GCC imports emanating from the EU declined during the 1990s; the share of the region's exports going to the EU remained negligible, at under 5 percent. Saudi Arabia's trade shares were highest, with one-third of its imports coming from the EU. Concerned by the paucity of their economic relations and influenced by the creation of the Euro-Mediterranean Partnership, in 1998 the EU and GCC committed themselves to negotiating a free trade area (FTA); in practice, little progress toward this goal was registered.[4]

While Saudi investment in the EU steadily increased, European investment in the GCC declined dramatically in the late 1990s, halving between 1999 and 2001.[5] Saudi foreign direct investment into Europe was higher than European investment in the kingdom. The limited degree of engagement from European commercial and public sector contractors was seen as striking. British business interests in the Gulf declined during the 1990s, reorienting to what were judged to be more attractive markets. German commercial interest was conspicuously limited relative to the country's efforts at engagement with Iran: Germany imported only a small share of its energy resources from the Gulf, and German investors cited concerns over instability and the absence of the rule of law as reasons for their disinterest in the Gulf.[6] In general, the paucity of economic interpenetration militated against European leverage. Into the new century, Germany and other European states were accused of sacrificing relations and political engagement with the Gulf on the altar of maintaining protectionism for petroleum products.[7]

In contrast, defense links with the Gulf intensified. The 1990s witnessed significantly increased arms sales to the region from the UK, France, Italy, and Germany. With Saudi Arabia devoting nearly a third of its GDP to military spending, a huge market was maintained for Western suppliers. This trend was facilitated by the success of the pro-Israeli lobby in the United States in urging restriction of US arms sales in particular to Saudi Arabia. The Saudi Arabian air force became highly dependent on British, rather than US, cooperation and technology. In 1993, the UK signed its largest ever oil-for-arms deal with Saudi Arabia, which led to the creation of a number of joint Anglo-Saudi companies. With trade outside the oil and defense sectors remaining limited, sales of defense equipment accounted for over half of UK and French exports to Saudi Arabia. A key strategic objective of GCC states was to dilute US prevalence in the region through these defense agreements with European powers, especially the UK and France.[8] By end of the 1990s, however, the United States began to re-close the gap with European suppliers. French suppliers, in particular, began to be eased out of the market for military equipment, their problems being compounded by the decision of the French government to withdraw from the policing of the southern Iraqi no-fly zone, in relation to which British and French personnel had been granted bases inside Saudi Arabia.[9]

Against this background, the formalized incorporation of human rights issues evidenced in other parts of the Middle East was largely absent in EU policies toward the Gulf. When the EU did discreetly broach human rights issues in the context of EU-GCC forums, Gulf ministers and officials pointedly brought discussions to a close.[10] The latter invariably argued that the problem was of an institutional nature, and that the GCC as a regional body was not authorized to deal with political issues. It was indeed the case that the GCC's limited degree of formal cooperation in political spheres proved to be a complicating factor for conducting relations on a region-to-region basis with the more deeply integrated European Union. Europeans also judged (correctly or not) this institutional argument to be a convenient smokescreen for a lack of political will to engage in dialogue on human rights. A commitment to a more broad-ranging political dialogue was agreed upon in 1996, but it was acknowledged by diplomats that in practice this failed to enable dialogue on questions of human rights and democratic reform. In such discussions, the focus was invariably on Gulf states' admonishment of European states for hosting political dissidents from the region. Even softer forms of civil society cooperation failed to develop to any significant degree. Funds were allocated for a university exchange scheme with the GCC, but this proposal did not prosper.[11] Gulf states offered little opening for cooperation on bottom-up governance reform; to the extent that very modest political liberalization occurred, it was in a tightly controlled top-down fashion.[12]

In sum, a largely unadulterated alliance-based logic persisted in the Gulf throughout the 1990s. If the radicalism of Saudi and other Islamist opposition was self-servingly overstated by regimes, it was a sleight of hand that the West seemed to accept. The standard view remained that the Gulf represented an island of pro-Western stability in a troubled region. At the same time, this was the area of the world where policies were arguably least Europeanized. The Gulf was the only part of the world where the Commission had no delegation; it was the region where UK bilateral influence remained most marked relative to common EU initiatives. In the key area of energy policy, neither the EU nor the GCC enjoyed strong competence over their respective constituent national members. While Europe's energy dependence was greater with the GCC than with EMP states, the GCC lagged behind Maghreb and Mashreq states in its relations with the EU. Instead of concerns over energy supplies engendering deeper relations across a broad range of issues, it appeared to have had the opposite effect.

Post–September 11 Reassessments?

In the wake of the terrorist attacks of 9/11, debates revived over possible political reform in the Gulf. Reforms were most far-reaching in Kuwait, least significant in the United Arab Emirates. In Bahrain, elections were held in 2002, reinstating parliament after a 27-year suspension, but the government then rowed back on reforms, narrowing parliamentary freedoms through constitutional change imposed by decree. Similar government-instigated reforms were introduced in Qatar, based around growing civic debate. GCC political liberalization was generally based on partially elected advisory legislatures combined with a cautious opening of public space to political debate.[13]

Within official European circles, diplomats reacted to the changed security environment by acknowledging that the EU had seriously neglected the Gulf and must rectify this area of weakness in its external relations. A new negotiating mandate for EU-GCC trade negotiations achieved agreement in late 2001. This commitment was enabled by the GCC bringing forward to 2003 the date for completing its own customs union. It was optimistically felt by many diplomats that this had cleared the way for an EU-GCC free trade area to be finalized even before its Euro-Mediterranean equivalent. The first session of a new EU-GCC Economic Dialogue forum took place in 2003. It was suggested that the key was to prepare subsequently to integrate the GCC and the Euro-Mediterranean area into a single free trade zone. Gerhard Schröder visited Kuwait in March 2005, pointing to a 30 percent increase in German-Kuwaiti trade during 2004 and announcing a new effort to boost investment.[14] Shell invested $2.4 billion in the development of a gas plant in Qatar. New proposals were also forthcoming in the security domain. A new mandate was agreed to negotiate a counterterrorism agreement with the GCC; an EU-GCC workshop was convened on terrorism; and the notion of supporting a Gulf regional security forum gained currency.[15] In sum, there were signs of an acceleration of relations and increased efforts to deepen the economic and security foundations of European links with the region.

Moreover, there appeared to be some commitment to incorporate issues of democracy and human rights into these intensified efforts. The outcome of the 13th EU-GCC joint council and ministerial meeting held in March 2003 still declined to make mention of cooperation on political reform and noted that a human rights table had still not been set up.[16] European diplomats suggested that the EU had pushed to launch a formal Human Rights Dialogue at this meeting, but that GCC states had not agreed to this, with differences persisting even at the very basic level of wording in joint declarations on international human rights instruments. The EU's stated aim was to link this new dialogue to the (then new) UN Arab Development Report, but GCC governments refused to acknowledge that this report provided such an opening. On his visit to the region in January 2004, French foreign minister Dominique de Villepin acknowledged these limitations and suggested France's aim was to "strengthen our political presence" and explore how "we can accompany the processes of political reform underway."[17] A March 2004 Commission report lamented that with the GCC the EU had so far only engaged in "limited political dialogue [which] has not reflected the strategic significance of the countries involved."[18] Some experts judged that space had opened up for a less timid strategy as the diversification of European oil supplies reduced dependence on Gulf supplies.[19]

There then appeared to be some movement, potentially breaking the logjam in European relations with the Gulf. The 14th EU-GCC joint council and ministerial meeting was held in Brussels in May

2004. Building on an April meeting on trade, energy, and economic cooperation, this committed the EU and GCC countries to a new high-level economic dialogue and the creation of a civil society forum. It stipulated that human rights and migration were to be included within the ongoing free trade negotiations. European and Gulf ministers insisted that in the wake of the Sana'a and Alexandria meetings on democratic reform there was a new "shared willingness to enter into dialogue on human rights," and consequently charged officials with exploring options for initiatives in this field. The meeting reported that free trade area negotiations were "heading to their conclusion." Intensified antiterrorist cooperation was also launched.[20] By 2004 the GCC was the EU's fourth largest export market, ahead even of China—with the head of the EU's new Riyadh delegation welcoming signs of a "growing partnership."[21]

Following this meeting, the EU's new Strategic Partnership with the Mediterranean and Middle East was concluded in June 2004. This was based on an initial Franco-German proposal, forwarded as a response to the initial US proposal for a Greater Middle East Initiative.[22] The strategy suggested that the EU would begin to develop "bilateral political engagement" with individual Gulf states wishing to cooperate on reform issues—an apparent shift of emphasis from the regional foundations upon which EU efforts had long been predicated. In this new document the EU also committed itself to investing more resources to support reform efforts in the Gulf. This Strategic Partnership gradually became the focus of efforts from a number of EU member states to intensify relations with the Gulf and gradually to gain a role in assisting incipient reform processes. This was pressed as a more strategic framework, circumventing what was judged by some governments to have been the ineffectual and overly low-profile, technical approach led by the Commission in talks with the GCC throughout the 1990s. An assessment of progress under this framework was to be carried out under the Luxembourg presidency in the first half of 2005, with a view to concluding new measures.[23]

A number of European governments made available defense advisory capacities to various Gulf states. There was a significant focus on the security of economic exclusion zones across the region, although European governments' efforts to convene regional programs on this topic were impeded by Gulf states' reluctance to cooperate with each other. NATO's Istanbul Cooperation Initiative (ICI), agreed upon in June 2004, signaled the organization's first effort to reach out to the Gulf. Excluded from NATO's Mediterranean Dialogue during the 1990s, the GCC was now to be the subject of a separate security initiative. Of apparent significance, the ICI included a commitment to improve "security governance" in the Gulf. This was to embrace cooperation on defense reform and civilian oversight of security forces, albeit without the formal acceptance by all partners of the principle of democratic control of armed forces as applied in the Partnership for Peace framework in Eastern Europe.[24] The defense minister of one European country strongly backing the extension of security reform work into the Gulf suggested that the ICI's purpose was to "demonstrate alternative solutions" to the problems of internal law and order to Gulf security forces. The initiative was pushed in particular by the UK, but its scope was reined back by southern EU states that insisted on NATO retaining a preferential and more institutionalized Mediterranean Dialogue. French and Spanish post-Iraq ambivalence toward NATO also cut across the effort to deepen security cooperation in the Gulf. Indeed, the logistical support offered by states like Qatar to the US invasion of Iraq introduced a new element of broader political tension between the EU and the GCC.[25]

Some European support for political reform commenced. Significantly, much of this focused on parliamentary training, representing a different focus from elsewhere in the Middle East. The British government provided support for a project on participatory democracy in Bahrain, which included training for prospective female parliamentary candidates; improved campaigning techniques for women activists in Kuwait; public sector training and capacity building for the attorney general's office in Oman; transparency in accounting standards in the Omani civil service; a program for Arab women parliamentarians, run in Kuwait, Oman, and Bahrain; work in the Gulf states under the OECD-UNDP good governance initiative; strengthening the role of women in local councils across the region; and the drafting of a more liberal law governing the creation of civil society organizations in Bahrain.

The German development ministry embarked on a wide-ranging program in the region, including technical support for elections; women's roles in development; combating female genital mutilation; providing social care housing for women; support for social development funds; the training of television journalists; and technical advice and support to anticorruption and auditing committees. Sweden invested €300,000 in a program of parliamentary training for women, bringing Gulf women into programs coordinated from Cairo, in order to circumvent restrictions on directly funding relatively rich GCC states from development aid. Yemen, Bahrain, and Saudi Arabia were included as states eligible for European Initiative for Democracy and Human Rights funding for 2005–2006, the Gulf not having previously been included in this initiative. Kuwaiti ministers were reputed to have proactively petitioned Javier Solana for EU technical support on reform issues during the course of 2004. Seeking to fill a recognized gap in knowledge, the French government funded the setting up of a Euro-Gulf network of experts and exchanges. European governments cited as evidence of a concern with media freedom their criticism of the United States for regularly pressing the Qatari government to close down Al-Jazeera.

Despite these aspects of enhanced European strategy, problems continued to beset policy toward the Gulf. The UK complained that, notwithstanding the new EU strategic partnership, most European states were still not strongly engaged or interested in the Gulf. Brussels diplomats lamented that "the UK still has a monopoly" in the region. States such as Italy remained largely passive consumers of developments in EU-GCC relations.[26] The European Commission still had no delegations present in the GCC, other than its modest (one man) new mission in Riyadh—the Gulf being one of the few areas of the world where such representation was so limited. The number of personnel covering the Gulf both in the Commission and in some national ministries increased after 2004, but despite proposals from a number of member states no concrete moves were undertaken to ensure EU representation throughout the region, with increased resources going elsewhere. The Commission openly stressed a reluctance to assume the same prominent agency as in other parts of the Middle East, such as the southern Mediterranean or the Palestinian Occupied Territories. Commission officials lamented that the Strategic Partnership was member states' initiative and conceived by them as a way of correcting what was seen to be the failure of Commission-led trade talks, and that consequently the Commission could not be expected to take the diplomatic flak for beginning to press on more controversial political issues.

A major divide entrenched itself in European foreign policy coordination—arguably one of the sharpest within CFSP—between those pressing for the EU to retain a Mediterranean preference and those advocating a broader Middle East policy that included a significant focus on the Gulf. The former reined back EU ambitions and efforts in the Gulf, which in turn pushed the UK and France to continue to prioritize bilateral policies. Spain represented the main obstacle in this sense, insisting as a minimum that any new effort in the Gulf be accompanied by trade-off measures in the Mediterranean; complaining that the whole notion of a broader Middle East focus was overly reflective of US concerns and even harked back to British imperialism; and arguing that the only route into a more significant presence in the Gulf should be through encouraging the EU's southern Mediterranean partners to persuade Gulf states of the benefits of reform and partnership with the EU. Almost unnoticed amid the high-profile tensions occasioned by Iraq, this issue became one of the most conflictive issues of difference in EU foreign policy. Spain blocked a paper drawn up by the Dutch presidency at the end of 2004 that proposed means of reinvigorating relations in the Gulf. With the EMP's tenth anniversary approaching in the autumn of 2005, other member states complained of Spain "blocking everything in the Gulf" so as to defend a Mediterranean focus it judged to be increasingly under threat. Although by late 2005 Madrid was, according to EU officials, showing a slightly greater degree of willingness to support initiatives in the GCC, the review of progress made under the Strategic Partnership failed to agree upon concrete advances. While some member states pushed the idea of bringing the GCC, Iraq, Iran, and Yemen together into a single strategic framework, others again perceived this to be too indulgent of US visions. French diplomats saw themselves as playing a bridging role: with interests in both the Mediterranean and the Gulf, France pressed for a stronger EU role in the GCC, but sought to avoid this developing too quickly or too ambitiously, and thus taking focus away from the EMP. It was argued that the United States' insistence on developing the Greater, then Broader, Middle East initiative reinforced this reluctance on the part of some EU member states and "killed all chances of a healthy debate on what the EU should do in the Gulf."[27]

New political reform projects also suffered limitations. A number of European donors recognized that while there appeared to be greater political will among European politicians to work on human rights issues in the Gulf, it was difficult to justify aid resources going to relatively rich GCC countries for the strategic goal of political reform. No standard Commission development funds were available for GCC states, although a small amount was set aside under the proposed development and economic cooperation instrument proposed for the 2007–2013 EU budget. The EU's most senior aid official opined that the whole idea of putting Commission aid into the Gulf was "nonsense." Attempts to begin EIDHR microprojects were unsuccessful due to a lack of local civil society capacity and the fact that European NGOs themselves found it virtually impossible to work in this region. Member states' bilateral aid amounted to a handful of ad hoc projects, dwarfed in the case of several governments by defense cooperation agreements. Bahrain was a new focus of European political aid, but the Bahraini government often obstructed projects, restricting European participation in a number of conferences on reform. Human rights training through defense cooperation was limited and modest in nature, no more than a rather symbolic addendum. Many civil society programs, such as education exchanges, had to be prematurely stopped—with support for government-led educational reform an increasing alternative priority. The range of US political aid work was broader than that of European donors in the Gulf, encompassing projects on political participation, rule of law, press freedom, judicial reform, civil society, labor rights, and political parties.[28] Moreover, there was little EU reaction to reversals in political liberalization, such as the clampdown in Bahrain on emergent civil society groups; most member states acknowledged that, with limited capacity covering this area, they were no more than vaguely aware of such developments.

Meanwhile, EU-GCC trade negotiations remained blocked. Differences emerged over EU objections to Gulf regimes pricing gas and services at higher levels for foreign than domestic purchasers. On the GCC side, Saudi Arabia remained the main obstacle. After another failed attempt to conclude the FTA in April 2005, Gulf states angrily blamed the EU for being unwilling to remove protectionist measures in the petrochemicals sector. European diplomats emerged from the same meeting acknowledging that the talks "went badly" and that GCC states were still disinclined to accept, in the same way as EMP partners, the necessary political dimensions to a partnership with the EU.[29] The EU also complained that the GCC customs union was still unacceptably partial, from the EU's perspective, including many religiously based exemptions. The 60 percent rise in oil prices from 2004 to 2005 left Gulf regimes flush with funds and more strongly positioned to resist EU calls for the kind of economic liberalization that might engender a more autonomous private sector.[30]

Deeper differences emerged between EU member states over how far the regional focus should be maintained, with the UK, Dutch, Swedish, and Danish governments pushing hardest for enhanced cooperation with individual states as the central means of giving Europe a more effective presence in the region. Other member states were more openly critical of the way in which the United States' prioritization of relations with individual states was undermining the EU's efforts to build the GCC as a regional body. After the signing of a United States–Bahrain free trade agreement in September 2004, Saudi Arabia threatened to impose new tariffs against Bahrain in response, undermining GCC unity and thus the whole essence of the EU's strategic approach. Most GCC states increasingly stressed a desire for preferential bilateral links to the EU; but many in the EU were wary that, if taken too far, a new bilateral focus would fan rivalries between Gulf states. While EU missions were sent to a number of individual GCC states to explore deeper cooperation, trade commissioner Peter Mandelson clarified that the EU would not be willing to negotiate bilateral commercial agreements. As one diplomat explained: for the EU, the unity and stability of the GCC was seen as more important in security terms than the prospect of increasing leverage over reforms in individual states, such as Bahrain.

Diplomats acknowledged a lack of internal EU discussion on what were the "real aims" in the Gulf, or on what incentives might be offered to GCC states. After July 2004 there was in practice no detailed discussion of human rights. The report on progress under the Strategic Partnership at the end of the Luxembourg presidency in June 2005 acknowledged that relations in Gulf states still had to be moved beyond commercial issues.[31] Javier Solana suggested that the Iraq conflict required a change in European policy toward the GCC states, especially through support for a Gulf security forum, in a context in which the Gulf was increasingly "over-armed and under-institutionalized."[32] But officials acknowledged that by the end of 2005 the Strategic Partnership was bereft of substance. While GCC states in theory advocated European sponsorship of a regional security framework for the wider Gulf region, in practice they remained sensitive to concrete EU involvement in political issues; this was also an aspect of policy that divided the smaller Gulf states from the more resolutely skeptical Saudi Arabia. A number of member states were angered at the failure of presidency representative Jack Straw to allude to EU policy at all during visits to the region in the second half of 2005. One Brussels diplomat opined that despite the post-9/11 efforts, there was "still no EU policy" in the Gulf.

Grappling with Saudi Arabia

Against the background of these new European efforts and initiatives, Saudi Arabia presented a special set of challenges. This was where state-society relations appeared most brittle, and where gaining purchase over political change was most complicated. Concerns over Saudi Arabia were at the forefront of post-9/11 policy reassessments, 15 of the 19 hijackers being Saudi citizens. Tensions with Western governments grew over the amounts of funds being channeled through Saudi Islamist charities to radicals, despite the Saudi regime insisting that it was attempting to clamp down on such transfers. In New York talk emerged of the Saudi government being taken to court over the 9/11 attacks, for allegedly giving succor to Al-Qaida. The kingdom was shaken by terrorist attacks in May and November 2003, and in April and May 2004. The most dramatic attack in the oil town of Khobar, which left twenty-two dead, was claimed by the Al-Qaida Organization in the Arabian Peninsula. While the Saudi security forces responded forcefully to these attacks, reports rumored that the terrorist organization was enjoying some support from within the ranks of the security services. Following the terrorist attacks and hostage-taking in Khobar, some observers foresaw the beginning in Saudi Arabia of Algerian-style endemic violence and civil conflict, although others dismissed such alarmism as an overreaction. In September 2003, reports emerged of Saudi Arabia embarking on a strategic review that included the option of acquiring a nuclear capability.[33]

Crucially, the apparent beginnings of a reform process were witnessed. A first reform petition was presented to the government in January 2003; a second followed in September 2003. Crown Prince Abdullah opened a National Dialogue, three rounds of which were held in June 2003, December 2003, and June 2004, respectively. Unprecedented street demonstrations erupted on the occasion of the government-backed human rights conference held in October 2003. The *majlis* expanded in size and was given increased powers to debate legislation and propose amendments. Elections to municipal councils were held in early 2005. In 2003 the king allowed the creation of the Saudi Journalists' Association, a formally independent civil society body. Women were granted increased rights to establish companies; workers were given the right to establish labor committees within the workplace. Abdullah was seen to be confronting the more conservative members of the ruling family. After Abdullah succeeded King Fahd in 2005, he moved to release a number of human rights activists. It was widely argued that the basic underlying alliance between the Al-Sauds and Wahhabi Islam had fractured, accompanied by a desire for change deriving from a two-thirds drop in incomes between the late 1980s and 2003.

Of course, the extent of reform was highly curtailed. The increase in petitioning through the *majlis* was significant, but the latter remained a body appointed by the king. A vague commitment to have half the members of the *majlis* elected showed no signs of being implemented. In response to demonstrations and criticism, a number of petitioners were arrested. This happened most notably in March 2004, when liberals pressed to be allowed to set up an independent human rights organization; the regime set up its own shadow human rights forum and arrested thirteen reformists—all but three of whom were released after agreeing to restrict their activities. A law introduced in 2004 made it illegal for government employees to sign petitions and to criticize the government to the press. Municipal elections were held, but local administrations still lacked meaningful power and responsibility. Political parties were not allowed to run in these elections, only individuals; and candidates were screened by the government. Most notably, women were barred from either running or voting, although the regime suggested they would be allowed to participate in the following elections in 2008–2009. Moreover, it was reported that the elections were subject to pervasive vote buying. In practice a degree of government control was exerted over the new journalists' association. Chambers of commerce were the bodies with the greatest degree of genuine autonomy, although it remained unclear whether the business community would ultimately be drawn away from the regime toward support for the liberal reformers—it did not throw its weight in any unequivocal or public sense behind those calling for political opening. According to Transparency International levels of corruption increased notably in Saudi Arabia after 2003. Analysts doubted whether there was sufficient common ground between liberal and Islamist reformers to put the regime under serious pressure.[34]

The shock of seeing Al-Qaida activity within Saudi itself seemed to give a new impulse to pressure for reform, but also to tougher security measures. As oil prices surged to historic highs, the West once again needed to rely on Saudi Arabia's promise to relieve pressure by releasing reserve supplies. This added to reliance on Saudi's market-regulating role, which had already grown due to instability in Venezuela and Nigeria. Despite some diversion of supplies, the West still depended on Saudi for a quarter of its oil supplies. It was widely judged that provision of this market-balancing function was facilitated by Saudi oil remaining under the regime's control. Increased deployments of soldiers were also necessary to guard pipelines and refineries.[35]

US positions toward Saudi Arabia fluctuated in the wake of 9/11. On the one hand, the Bush administration in some of its rhetoric did become less cautious in criticizing human rights abuses and democratic shortfalls. A July 2003 US government report was thought to have accused middle-ranking Saudi officials of offering support to the 9/11 hijackers, and criticized the Saudi government for its reluctance to share intelligence related to the attacks. The United States moved to withdraw its military bases in Saudi Arabia. In November 2003, two congressmen introduced the Saudi Accountability Act, which sought to make continued US cooperation contingent on Saudi counterterrorist cooperation. The State Department for the first time named Saudi Arabia as a "country of particular concern" in its 2004 Religious Freedom Report.[36] Some in the administration began to surmise aloud that the existence of a more amenable, US-backed government in Iraq would provide more scope for increased US pressure on Saudi Arabia. However, the spate of terrorist attacks within Saudi Arabia placed a higher premium once again on counterterrorist cooperation with the Saudi authorities and seemed to dilute the emphasis placed on democratic reform by the United States in the immediate aftermath of 9/11. In early 2005 the State Department launched a review to rebuild the fast-weakening economic links between the United States and Saudi Arabia.[37] In May 2005, the three petitioners remaining in detention were given long prison sentences, this occurring one week after a meeting of Abdullah and President Bush at which human rights issues were expressly subordinated to discussions on cooperation needed to control the effect of the record high oil prices.

Against this background of changes in Saudi Arabia and in US policies, the EU struggled to gain a significant purchase, while adopting a more measured discourse on political change in the kingdom.

The economic prism was still seen as key to European influence. Diplomats claimed that the main change in policy triggered by 9/11 was a strengthened determination to conclude the EU-GCC free trade area. At the end of August 2003 the EU and Saudi Arabia reached agreement on a bilateral package of access conditions relating to Saudi Arabia's prospective accession to the WTO. This appeared both to clear a major obstacle to Saudi Arabia's entry into the WTO (the kingdom was the only GCC state at this stage still not a member of the trade body), and also to galvanize EU-GCC negotiations. The Saudis agreed to reduce restrictions on European investment and business operations in the kingdom and to stop the practice of selling gas more cheaply to domestic firms than internationally.[38] The opening of a delegation of the European Commission in Riyadh in April 2004 added to the sense of optimism and signaled an increased commitment to make progress and invest in local representation to facilitate this.

By the end of 2004, however, differences on trade once more dominated talks, with delays in the EU-GCC FTA resulting primarily from Saudi Arabia's continued reluctance to open up to EU exports. Significantly, EU negotiators claimed that such reluctance to liberalize trade was linked by the ruling family to their desire to limit the reach and pace of political change. European cooperation on those reforms requisite to WTO entry was undercut until late 2005 when the United States finally agreed on its bilateral terms with Saudi Arabia. Moreover, European efforts were overshadowed by the record increases in oil prices, the latter ensuring that the value of Saudi oil exports between 2002 and mid-2005 was greater than for the whole of the 1990s.[39] Despite this the EU aim remained to secure Saudi Arabia's accession to the WTO, which duly took place in December 2005.

Much new security cooperation was forthcoming after 9/11. In the wake of the terrorist attacks, the British government provided increased assistance for the Saudi National Guard—which included helping the latter formulate a new internal security doctrine—as well as to the country's army and ministry of defense. The UK increased arms sales to the kingdom, from £20 million in 2001 to £29 million in 2002.[40] In April 2004 France concluded a €7 million deal to provide Saudi Arabia with a surveillance system for the kingdom's borders; this even became entangled in domestic French politics as President Chirac and his rival, Interior Minister Nicolas Sarkozy, fought to claim credit for the arrangement.[41] (By late 2005 this deal was still awaiting final signature, held up in part due to US lobbying.)[42] Several

European governments acknowledged an intensification of intelligence cooperation with Saudi security services.

European ambivalence was evident over the prospects of usefully assisting political liberalization in Saudi Arabia. One European ambassador was quoted as justifying European passivity toward Saudi reform with the judgment that: "If there were an election today, bin Laden would win by a landslide."[43] It was immediately after UK foreign secretary Jack Straw's March 2004 visit to Saudi Arabia that the thirteen liberal activists were arrested, eliciting some critical reaction from the United States, less from European governments. Spain was notable in bringing up the rear in this regard. Reflecting its general unease with any drift away from the EU's Mediterranean policy toward a broader Middle East strategy, Spanish diplomats argued that the EU could play no useful part in pressuring Saudi Arabia—that this was a role only the United States could sensibly attempt to play; Saudi Arabia was not much in need of EU trade or aid and as a result "they impose conditionality on us, not us on them." One European diplomat opined that it was "unreal" to think that the EU could make any impact in pushing political reform in Saudi Arabia. Many EU diplomats felt that increased US criticism immediately after 9/11 had strengthened the Saudis' desire to cooperate with the EU, but that as US pressure seemed to subside, Saudi willingness to compromise in talks with the EU also lessened. Diplomats admitted that there was little ministerial debate on Saudi Arabia, with the country's plight overshadowed by policy challenges in Iran, Iraq, and the Palestinian conflict. Amid rumors of a $6 billion Franco-Saudi fighter plane contract, President Chirac welcomed Prince Abdullah to Paris praising the regime's "ambitious program of change."[44]

At the same time, the UK government's criticism of human rights abuses became more vocal. With the UK's Al Yamama defense contract coming to an end and Saudi Arabia not looking to place similarly large follow-up contracts, commercial defense interests were less dominant than in the past.[45] Many Saudi reform petitioners had begun to engage in dialogue with a number of European embassies. In February 2005, the UK held a seminar with reformists in the Saudi government on the challenges facing political reform, at which Jack Straw claimed a commitment to support "managed change" (a follow-up event was organized for late 2005). The Saudi initiative also launched in February 2005 for a new center on counterterrorism elicited a cool response from European diplomats precisely because it was feared to be a diversion from the underlying political root causes of problems in Saudi Arabia; a UK official was quoted as saying that there needed to be more effort aimed at "understanding the process by which younger people get radicalized."[46] The UK appeared to be more tolerant of Saudi opposition group activity in London than the United States was comfortable with. There were growing tensions between the Saudi government and the UK over London-based opposition groups, in particular the Movement for Islamic Reform (MIRA), which lay behind the organization of protests in Saudi Arabia in December 2004; however, when the United States froze MIRA assets in December 2004, the UK did follow suit. The group was later linked to the website on which responsibility for the 7 July 2005 London bombings was announced.

Some timid and small-scale efforts emerged to encourage and press forward Saudi's limited political opening. UK funding was made available to support vocational training; the chambers of commerce; the new journalists' association; businesswomen and the role of women in economic life; and training for judges. Funding was also provided to assist Saudi cooperation with the UNDP-OECD good governance initiative. The largest slices of UK reform support went to projects on education, economic reform, the development of financial services markets, technical assistance for the removal of FDI barriers, and an assessment of the impact of WTO entry. It was Saudi Arabia's apparent keenness to cooperate on preparations for WTO entry that was seen as providing the most significant leverage and access point for European governance and reform-oriented assistance. Saudi accession to the WTO was seen by the UK (in the event, correctly) to be a closer prospect than an EU-GCC free trade deal. Underpinning the centrality of this economically flavored focus on reform was the fact that Saudi Arabia remained the UK's largest export market in the Middle East. Initiatives on security sector reform were broadened from a traditional security focus with the national guard to a concern with police accountability; this was approached in particular by attempting to engage Saudi forces through region-wide initiatives held in the smaller Gulf states.

The Danish government was approached by members of the Saudi *majlis* for a twinning program but decided against supporting such an initiative with an unelected body. The Danish foreign affairs committee visited Saudi Arabia in October 2004 to reconsider the prospects for cooperation with representatives of the *majlis* but concluded that there was "not much to go on." The Danish government did, however, begin exploratory work, with the stated aim of "looking for the agents of reform," recognizing an uncertainty about where these were to be found. Denmark made funding available to support the new Saudi journalists' organization, seeing this as potentially the most promising entry point in Saudi Arabia. Denmark also pushed, including through the EU level, the idea of offering technical cooperation to make it possible to have segregated voting for women in the municipal elections in 2005—thus undercutting the ostensible reason given by the Saudi government for excluding women from the vote. Most EU member states were against pressing such an offer.

Chancellor Gerhard Schröder visited Saudi Arabia in the autumn of 2003 calling for Europe to pay more attention to developments in Saudi Arabia. But Germany also refrained from the same degree of bilateral security dialogue that it developed with other GCC states, due to its concerns over human rights in Saudi Arabia—concerns which surfaced in particular in tensions over alleged extremist teachings in a school run by the Saudi embassy in Berlin.[47] The EU did formally protest the Saudi regime on the decision to bar women from the elections, and got a somewhat belligerent response from the Saudis. The Commission offered no funding or projects in relation to the elections, an initial hesitancy compounded by the fact that assistance would anyway have had to be suspended after the decision not to allow women to participate.

In terms of rhetoric and engagement, by far the main focus of European states was on widening women's rights. Aims expressed by the Commission emphasized the issue of "women's role in economic life" also as a main entry point to reform-oriented work in the kingdom. As with European governments, the Commission's other focus was on the chambers of commerce and the journalists' association, seen as the two areas offering the best access to genuinely critical and somewhat independent civil society activity. In general, however, Europeans tended toward an indulgence of government-operated human rights "NGOs." Diplomats admitted to not thinking in terms of full-blown democracy in Saudi Arabia: more than anywhere in the Middle East here the old fear of democracy benefiting anti-Western radicals was still evident after 9/11. Aims were couched rather in terms of very gradually pushing to widen political space, particularly at the municipal level in the wake of the elections, the latter being seen, for all their imperfections, as giving international actors some degree of purchase and reference point. A problem referred to by the more reform-leaning EU states was that Saudi Arabia simply lacked valuable civil society partners and interlocutors. Saudi authorities did not accept the offer of cooperation in governmental capacity building, and unlike other GCC states did not respond positively to the offer of security sector reform cooperation under the NATO Istanbul Cooperation Initiative. A further complaint was that the broader lack of significant EU presence and engagement made any form of pressure more difficult. At the EU-GCC ministerial in April 2005 Saudi officials blocked efforts to initiate discussions on political reforms and human rights, angrily asserting that this amounted to "unacceptable interference." European diplomats argued that WTO entry would be the crucial factor in generating a more cooperative attitude toward political dialogue, as well as to opening the way to concluding a free trade agreement; by early 2006 it remained to be seen whether this would indeed prove to be the case.

Yemen: A Failing State?

Outside the GCC, and characterized by chronic poverty rather than oil wealth, Yemen presented Western powers with a different set of policy challenges. Unlike GCC states, Yemen received significant amounts of European development aid. A new, more extensive EU-Yemen cooperation agreement was signed in 1997. The EU established itself as Yemen's principal donor, accounting for 15 percent of the country's aid at the end of the 1990s—with a mixture of postconflict aid, poverty reduction, and civil society support undertaken.[48] Significantly, this development aid profile gained little purchase on political reform dynamics in Yemen. Newly unified Yemen held its first elections in 1993, but after northern forces emerged victorious from the subsequent civil war in 1994, political repression increased. Pluralism was restricted and the moderate Islamist party Islah was ejected from a power-sharing deal; the main southern party, the Yemeni Socialist Party, boycotted elections in 1997; and further manipulation allowed President Ali Abdallah Saleh to emerge a comfortable victor from elections in 1999, consolidating his hold on the country's leadership that he had held since 1978.

Yemen became an increasing security concern to Western powers, as between 2002 and 2004 terrorist attacks were perpetrated against the USS *Cole,* the British Council, and a French oil tanker. The country increasingly resembled a collapsed state, with weak governmental capacity, deepening poverty, and little control over its own borders; it was widely seen as a frontline state in counterterrorist challenges. Yemeni civil society became increasingly vibrant, but following 2003 elections President Saleh further tightened his grip on government.

New talks were pursued with Yemen, with the declared aim of incorporating the latter into the overall framework of Europe–Middle East trade integration. A new EU-Yemen political dialogue also commenced in July 2004. This contained probably the strongest human rights focus in the region, with European diplomats arguing that Yemen's keenness to present itself as a leading reformer could and should be harnessed to hold the country's political elite to greater account. However, diplomats acknowledged that the EU expressly steered clear of setting concrete political benchmarks for its cooperation with Yemen, after some internal debate on this. As with GCC states, a key entry point with Yemen was judged to be in pushing governance reforms related to prospective WTO entry. The Commission allocated €70 million to Yemen for 2002–2004, although only €27 million for 2005–2006. The largest bilateral donors in 2004 were Germany (€40 million) and the Netherlands (€25 million). The UK's aid program in Yemen increased from £2 million in 2002–2003 to £6 million in 2005, with a further increase to £10 million slated for 2006, the priority aim of this funding defined as addressing the root causes of conflict and terrorism.[49] French aid rose from less than €4 million prior to 2002 to €8 million in 2005, with a further doubling planned for 2006. By 2004 the EU's overall share of Yemen's aid receipts had increased to over 20 percent.[50]

Yemen was a case where significant difference existed between the EU's developmental focus and the United States' more direct security focus. The most striking change in US policy after 9/11 was an increase in military aid from $200,000 in 2001 to $2.7 million in 2003 and the undertaking of new covert operations in the country.[51] US development assistance, through economic support funds, was a limited $15 million for 2005, well below total EU allocations. Despite this European general developmental and governance-oriented purchase, however, at the bilateral level European policies were also often centered overwhelmingly on enhancing counterterrorist cooperation, as evidenced during a Saleh visit to Paris in April 2004. Indeed, a raft of new European cooperation was forthcoming in Yemen, much of which had a strong security orientation. The UK and Italy offered increased support for the Yemeni coast guard, while the French government provided police advisers to Yemen's interior ministry. In February 2005 France and Yemen signed a new military and security cooperation agreement, focused in particular on Paris providing equipment and manpower—mainly from its largest foreign military base in Djibouti—for joint Franco-Yemeni patrols in the Red Sea.[52]

While such security cooperation intensified, so did European political reform assistance. A new NGO support program totaling €5.3 million was funded by the European Commission between 2002 and 2005. UK-funded reform work in Yemen included training for district court judges, parliamentary capacity building, and professional training for women. A DfID "drivers of change" assessment of the country carried out in early 2005 concluded that the country was at increased risk of instability and indicated that more aid would be shifted out of standard infrastructure projects into civil service and security sector reform and the strengthening of local government capacity and accountability. The UK and Dutch governments agreed to support the Yemeni government to organize a conference on women's rights, this after GCC regimes scuttled Yemen's proposal to hold this as an EU-Gulf regional initiative. The Westminster Foundation for Democracy also began to plan parliamentary training projects in Yemen and Bahrain. Denmark developed a parliamentary twinning program with Yemeni politicians, while a French-funded program of parliamentary training also started. A number of European donors increased or commenced support for decentralization in Yemen. Most European initiatives, including the relatively large German and Dutch aid programs, worked overwhelmingly with Yemeni authorities, for example supporting the government-controlled supreme commissions on elections and corruption.

The results of such initiatives, however, were disappointing. If European policy had been strongly predicated upon an apparent belief that Yemen was one of the Middle East's most reformist states, by the beginning of 2006 the EU assessment of relations with the Saleh government was increasingly pessimistic. Diplomats perceived a declining willingness on the part of the Yemeni government to cooperate on reforms. At a political dialogue meeting in September 2005 officials claimed that for the first time the EU had sought to pressure Yemen strongly, including through suggesting a possible reconsideration of future increases in development assistance. European donors were influenced by a World Bank decision in late 2005 to cut assistance to Yemen by a third as a result of the country's worsening governance indicators. At the end of 2005 Yemen was also disqualified by the US administration from eligibility for Millennium Challenge Account funds on the grounds of deteriorating democratic and governance criteria. The year 2006 began with European governments and the Commission claiming to be seriously questioning the merit of further support for the Saleh government. Plans were stepped up to fund monitoring of the 2006 presidential elections, as doubt remained over whether Saleh would desist from running for election once again.

Conclusion

The attacks of 9/11 and other terrorist incidents produced a revitalized European effort to strengthen policies toward the states of the GCC and Yemen. This remained, however, the part of the Middle East where European presence was weakest, both in terms of the breadth of policies and diplomatic effort and representation. It was the area where EU economic incentives were least effective; where the European philosophy of using economic engagement for political influence prospered least; and where the EU's declared preference for bottom-up approaches was least congruent with the top-down dynamics of Gulf liberalization processes. Despite a change in rhetoric and a handful of new reform projects, in the wake of 9/11 the EU struggled to gain meaningful traction on economic and political change in the Gulf. The standard EU developmental focus established a foothold only in Yemen, and even here a significant investment of resources made limited impact on the country's precarious political balance. The Gulf was also the area where there was the sharpest duality in the EU perspective on the relationship between security and democratization: the notion of backing political reform here gained some resonance in European policy while the prospect of change, especially in Saudi Arabia, simultaneously awoke new fears and uncertainties.

Significant internal EU differences emerged over the notion of a broader Middle Eastern policy, more equally balancing initiatives in the Mediterranean with those in the states "east of Jordan"; in this debate the whole structure of the EU's strategy toward the Middle East was opened to debate. This reflected another key feature of EU relations in the Gulf, namely the divisions that pitted those governments exhibiting a strong interest in the region against those with minimal engagement. The UK, and to a lesser extent France, retained significant bilateral relations with Gulf states that were not eclipsed by EU-level strategy. Indeed, policy in this region also contrasted with that toward the Mediterranean in terms of the Commission's reluctance in the Gulf to be pushed into assuming a more political role. US policy toward political change in the GCC states and Yemen was also erratic and beset by tensions between democracy promotion and counterterrorist strategies; but in several areas US rhetoric and reform-oriented funding initiatives became more notable than European efforts. Gulf states continued to play the European Union and the United States off against one another. While to some extent this accorded European governments a degree of influence, it also narrowed the policy options seen as feasible. The European preference for extremely cautious political change in the Gulf was perhaps neither surprising nor without merit; but in some places in the region, reform was so gradual and limited that the expectations that it awoke among populations bred frustration that threatened to become increasingly destabilizing.

Notes

1. Overview from Wilson, "EU-GCC Relations," pp. 94–100.
2. Dosenrode-Lynge and Stubkjaer, *The European Union and the Middle East,* pp. 125–126.
3. Hollis, "Europe and the Middle East: Power by Stealth?" pp. 15–29.
4. For an account of economic relations during this period, see Nonneman, "Saudi-European Relations," pp. 631–661.
5. Commission of the European Communities, *The EU and the Gulf Cooperation Council.*
6. See respective chapters on the UK and Germany in the Emirates Center for Strategic Studies and Research, *International Interests in the Gulf Region,* namely: Hollis, "Britain's Strategic Approach to the Gulf," p. 146; Perthes, "Germany and the Gulf," pp. 76–79.
7. Moosbauer, "Relations with the Persian Gulf States," p. 121.
8. Baabood, "Dynamics and Determinants of the GCC States' Foreign Policy," p. 162.
9. Nonneman, "Saudi-European Relations," pp. 649–653; Boniface, "French Policy in the Gulf," p. 60.

10. Dosenrode-Lynge and Stubkjaer, *The European Union and the Middle East,* p. 141.

11. Nonneman, "Saudi-European Relations," p. 659.

12. Ehteshami, ""Reform from Above," pp. 53–75.

13. Crystal, "Political Reform."

14. BBC Monitoring Service, 2 March 2005.

15. Bertelsmann Foundation—Centre for Applied Research, *The EU and the GCC.*

16. Commission of the European Communities, Joint communiqué, 13th EU-GCC Joint Council and Ministerial Meeting, March 2003.

17. Statement at www.diplomatie.fr.gouv/actu/article:asp?ART=39735.

18. Interim Report on the EU Strategic Partnership with the Mediterranean and Middle East, European Council document 7697/04, March 2004.

19. Luciani, *An EU-GCC Dialogue,* p. 5.

20. Commission of the European Communities, Joint communiqué, 14th EU-GCC Joint Council and Ministerial Meeting, Brussels, 17 May 2004.

21. Savage, "The EU and the GCC," p. 6.

22. Koch, "GCC-EU Relations," p. 226.

23. Commission of the European Communities, *A Strategic Partnership with the Mediterranean.*

24. Tanner, "NATO's Role in Mideast Defence Cooperation," p. 109.

25. Baabood, "Dynamics and Determinants of the GCC States' Foreign Policy," p. 162.

26. Aliboni, "An Italian Perspective," p. 10.

27. Aliboni, "The Geopolitical Implications," p. 10.

28. US Department of State, *Supporting Human Rights and Democracy.*

29. BBC Monitoring Service, 6 April 2005.

30. Luciani and Neugart, *The EU and the GCC.*

31. Commission of the European Communities, *Euromed Report* 91, 20 June 2005, p. 2.

32. Speech by Javier Solana, "Helping Iraq," May 2005, www.consilium .eu.int.

33. *The Guardian,* 18 September 2003.

34. For background on Saudi reforms, see International Crisis Group, *Saudi Arabia Backgrounder;* Lacroix, "Between Islamists and Liberals," pp. 344–364; Gause, "How to Reform Saudi Arabia."

35. *The Economist,* 29 May 2004, pp. 72–73.

36. *Arab Reform Bulletin,* October 2004, p. 7.

37. *Financial Times,* 10 February 2005.

38. *Financial Times,* 31 August 2003.

39. *The Economist,* 6 August 2005, p. 34.

40. *Financial Times,* 14 October 2003.

41. *Le Monde,* 14 April 2004.

42. *Middle East International,* no. 749, 29 April 2005, p. 24.

43. Quoted in *The Economist,* 6 March 2004, p. 61.

44. *Middle East International,* no. 749, 29 April 2005, p. 24.

45. Emirates Center for Strategic Studies and Research, *International Interests,* p. 159.

46. *Daily Star,* 7 February 2005.

47. Emirates Center for Strategic Studies and Research, *International Interests,* p. 100.

48. International Crisis Group, *Yemen,* p. 8.

49. Department for International Development, *Middle East and North Africa,* p. 31.

50. For figures on European aid, see www.europa.eu.int/comm/external _relations/yemen.

51. International Crisis Group, *Yemen,* p. 8.

52. *Daily Star,* 28 February 2003.

7

Turkey: Success and Its Malcontents

The prospect of accession to the European Union gave Turkey's relationship to Europe a set of dynamics qualitatively different from those in other parts of the Middle East. For more than two decades the EU alternated between courting and rebuffing Turkey. In the post-1990s phase of these relations, Turkey's moves toward fully developed democracy, especially under Recep Tayyip Erdogan's Justice and Development Party (AKP) government, marched hand in hand with the EU's tortured steps toward granting Ankara an opening date for accession negotiations. From the mid-1990s relations between the EU and Turkey resembled a drawn-out and complex game of diplomatic chess, replete with psychological brinkmanship. Was the EU using its democratic entry conditions disingenuously to ward off Turkey's accession? Was Turkey merely shedding crocodile tears at each rejection, in truth unwilling to contemplate the reforms needed to enter the EU? Was each hoping the other would pull the rug out from under the façade of mutual commitment to accession, so as not to be revealed as the spoiler? Would such a moment inevitably arrive?

This chapter assesses these questions, in the context of the EU's December 1999 decision to accept Turkey's candidature and leading up to the October 2005 opening of accession negotiations with Ankara. The chapter examines why the EU equivocated for so long in offering Turkey a clear roadmap into the EU; the factors that accounted for its decision to make that offer at last; and the obstacles that thereafter remained on the path to Turkish accession. The analysis demonstrates how each party was increasingly entwined in the internal politics of the other, sparking both positive reinforcing change and negative counterreaction; and how, notwithstanding the opening of accession negotiations on 3 October 2005, many fundamental questions remained unresolved by 2006. The EU-Turkey relationship has become one of the most exhaustively analyzed of all European external relations; but this chapter focuses on a factor underplayed in most analyses, namely the derived significance attached to democracy in European security thinking toward Turkey. While there was growing focus on Turkish political reform as a concern in itself, diplomats commonly reached judgments on Turkey's internal politics that served their respective positions on the more traditional "containment versus engagement" continuum of security logic. Different parts of the overall EU foreign policy system reached contrasting judgments on this: for some Turkey was a buffer between Europe and the wider Islamic world; for others it was a bridge to that world. But *both* groups viewed Turkey's reform process through the lens of their respective other security logic. In this sense, the chapter suggests that support for democracy and support for accession were not as coterminous as often assumed—with profound implications for the unfolding of European policy toward Turkey.

The Pains of Rejection

Cooperation between the EU and Turkey initially developed under a 1963 association agreement, the first signed by the EU. European states suspended aid after the military coup in 1980, but diplomatic reaction was softened by the need to maintain Cold War alliances with Turkey. Turkey lodged a formal application to join the EU in 1987 but was turned down. European governments and the Commission did seek to find ways to include Turkey in an ad hoc fashion within specific EU schemes and initiatives. These were mostly blocked by the European Parliament, however, on the issue of Turkey's suppression of Kurdish rights. At this stage, it was the EP that became the principal target of Turkish anger. Unlike the situation under the Europe Agreements concluded with Eastern Europe's still fragile and partial democracies, during the early 1990s the EU provided little proactive assistance to help and encourage Turkey along the road to political reform. In contrast to the European caution, US aid increased significantly over the 1980s and into the early 1990s, with

Turkey becoming the third largest recipient of US aid (behind Israel and Egypt). Washington gave far stronger support to the Turkish state to combat the Kurdistan Workers Party (PKK), which Washington saw as an illegitimate destabilizing terrorist force—in contrast to the EU's more sympathetic focus on Kurdish rights. In 1992, the German defense minister was forced to resign after it emerged that tanks sold to Turkey had been used against the Kurds. Influenced by the country's growing Kurdish community, the German parliament became an increasingly outspoken critic of the Turkish government.[1]

An EU-Turkey customs union was negotiated and entered into force at the end of 1995, but the EP effectively held it in abeyance. The EU negotiated the customs union despite a period of deterioration in human rights conditions. More journalists were imprisoned in Turkey than in any other country. In 1994, thirteen Kurdish MPs were stripped of their seats and several imprisoned under the draconian antiterrorist code. A number of Members of the European Parliament (MEPs) did react strongly to this; most EU governments less so. In addition to governments' desire to conclude the customs union, Turkey's importance as a NATO ally ensured it increasing flows of arms sales. After the EP's refusal to sign the customs union agreement, the Turkish government did change a number of pieces of legislation, providing greater human rights protection under the Anti-Terrorist Law and enhanced trades union rights. The EP was pressured by member states and the Commission into signing the customs union after these relatively modest improvements had been secured. Greece also finally agreed to the customs union, along with a new EU aid package, in return for accession discussions starting with Cyprus. A mixed dynamic had already taken hold. On the one hand, the EU rejected Turkey's bid for accession; on the other hand, European governments were indulgent of the military's reinvigorated control over Turkish politics.[2] Insofar as there was a European human rights focus this was overwhelming on the Kurdish issue, not always seen as the principal reform challenge by the rest of Turkey's population.[3] The development of Caspian Sea oil supplies, requiring a pipeline across Turkey into European markets, became frequently cited as reason for stronger engagement with Ankara.

If the signing of the customs union seemed to offer a new start to relations, optimism was soon dashed. The EP struck back by withholding the release of funding made available under the customs union. European governments were furious; this was the case that did most to push governments into reducing the EP's scope for using its budgetary powers to frustrate CFSP objectives, in what would eventually become the Amsterdam treaty. Moreover, the customs union hadn't given Turkey one of the provisions it most sought: the free movement of workers. Ankara resisted discussion of human rights within political dialogue with the EU. The one part of the aid allocation that the EP had allowed through were funds for democracy and human rights NGOs. But most civil society projects were blocked by the Turkish government, which claimed that such proposals constituted an underhand means of the EU channeling support for Kurdish separatists. Support for the Turkish Human Rights Association was scuttled and only a limited range of basic human rights education went ahead. Aid for military training was the area of funding that increased fastest after 1995. In 1996, the Commission proposed Turkey's participation in two EC programs, Socrates and Youth for Europe, financing youth exchanges as a means of inculcating European values to young Turks; the EP refused to allow these schemes through, again citing the issue of Kurdish minority rights.

A pivotal moment came at the Luxembourg European Council in 1997 when the EU accepted the candidature of ten Eastern European applicants, but not that of Turkey. Not only was Turkey excluded from the first wave of EU applicants, it failed even to make it onto the list of second-wave countries, with the likes of Slovakia, Romania, and Bulgaria, which were given reinforced preaccession partnerships. Ankara complained that additional and more stringent entry conditions had been set for Turkey, the latter being obliged to refer unresolved territorial disputes—that is, with Greece in the Aegean—to the International Court of Justice, as well as to press Turkish Cypriots to accept a mediated solution in Cyprus prior to the island's entry in the EU.

In justifying its decision, the EU cited the military's ousting in June 1997 of the Islamist government of Necmettin Erbakan. This was the army's infamous postmodern coup, executed by prying away members of Erbakan's coalition, in response to perceived attempts by the government to Islamize the public sphere, particularly in the field of education. The EU had already reacted coolly to Erbakan's apparent hostility toward the EU, his declared preference for building alliances with Muslim states, and his proposal for an Islamic Common Market to rival the EU. Twin interpretations were again possible: for some, European governments had sought to defend Islamists' democratic rights despite their ambivalence toward Erbakan; for others, the EU had ratcheted up democratic conditionality as a defense against the rise of the Islamist Refah (Welfare) party.

The immediate fallout from the Luxembourg decision was severe and took relations between the EU and Turkey to a new low. Turkey threatened to boycott EU goods and the government committed itself to discriminating against EU bidders in the awarding of public contracts.[4] Turkey then suspended formal dialogue with the EU and declined to participate in the EU's proposed European Conference framework, a forum of more broadly ranging cooperation offered to non–first-wave applicants in the hope of placating Ankara. Turkey intimated that it would be prepared to impede NATO's enlargement until it was granted EU candidature. Attitudes in Turkey also hardened on Cyprus. The Turkish military talked of plans to integrate northern Cyprus should the EU allow the accession of Greek Cyprus prior to an agreed political solution covering the whole island. Turkey's decision to choose Boeing rather than Airbus for a large contract was also seen as a political response to the EU's decision.[5] The rise of the right-wing Nationalist Action Party (MHP)—which after 1998 secured a place in a new government coalition—was attributed to the EU's rejection, while itself contributing to a further hardening of Turkish positions toward Europe. Significantly, this high-level political tension frustrated many of the low-level European cooperation projects that had begun to develop, particularly in the area of good governance.

Gradually, the very extent of the standoff seemed to invite a reconsideration of attitudes on both sides. It appeared that both sides had looked into the abyss and contemplated the significance of a complete breakdown in relations and, as a result, new efforts to repair the damage soon ensued. Within the EU these efforts most notably took the form of a stronger and more explicit consideration of how the Greek and EP blocks could be circumvented. Increased frustration with Greece derived from a feeling that Athens had failed to respect its side of the bargain, other states having acquiesced to opening accession talks with Cyprus.[6] Prompted by the fourteen other member states, the Commission proposed launching a new aid package based on article 130 of the treaty, requiring, that is, only a qualified majority approval. In reaction, Greece threatened to take the Commission to court and the EP deleted credits allocated to Turkey from the 1999 draft budget.[7] A way was found of getting funding through to Turkey, however, using MEDA funds—ironic, given Turkey's lack of enthusiasm for the Barcelona Process and keenness not to be lumped together with other southern Mediterranean states. In 1999, Turkey was allocated a disproportionately high 15 percent of MEDA funds for economic reform.[8] In addition, a number of governments strongly and very publicly moved to strengthen their bilateral relations with Turkey after Luxembourg, especially Italy, Spain, and the UK; Nordic states refrained on the grounds of Turkey's democratic shortfalls. To Athens' considerable chagrin the Quintet was formed, bringing together the largest European states with Turkey, to discuss the strengthening of relations. Business organizations within Europe also took a more proactive line after the impact of the 1997 decision became evident, lobbying for a more favorable European line toward Turkey—this was true particularly of the Federation of German Industries and the Confederation of British Industry. European investment to Turkey remained negligible, well below the levels going to smaller Eastern European markets.

Within Turkey itself, after the initial hardening of attitudes, by 1999 a more tempered attitude had emerged. A new government acknowledged more openly the democratic shortfalls that needed correcting, recognizing that it was necessary and desirable for Turkey to direct its efforts toward meeting the Copenhagen criteria. The government openly supported calls from prominent judges for a fundamental reform to political institutions. A number of improvements to human rights provisions—detention conditions, human rights education—were introduced. Turkey's participation since 1987 in the European Court of Human Rights (ECHR) system had begun to entrench a culture facilitating individual petitions on specific human rights questions; by the mid-1990s the ECHR was ruling regularly against the Turkish government. The MHP came round to supporting aspects of the customs union. Perhaps most significantly, in talks with the Commission, military officials claimed that the granting of candidate status would enable them to agree to a weakening of their political role: an unequivocal commitment that Turkey could join the EU would, they claimed, provide the bulwark to Turkish secularism that they, the military, had hitherto been obliged to provide. Behind the high-politics impasse, low-level economic integration had been fostered by the customs union, for example through the harmonization of Turkish competition law to EU rules. The customs union created a dialogue between European and Turkish business representatives and encouraged Tusiad, the Turkish business organization, to begin urging the political elite to make the reforms that would enable fuller integration into the European market.

From Helsinki into the Hall of Mirrors

On the back of these trends, at the Helsinki European Council in December 1999, Turkey was accepted as a candidate, without a date set for the opening of negotiations. This marked an apparent end to the EU's ambiguity over Turkey's membership. With a clear commitment having been made, the EU could no longer expect to retain purchase over Turkey if it failed to deliver on its word. In practice, Helsinki opened a new game of bluff and double bluff, where the real intent behind each move could be presented in diametrically opposed fashion—either as genuine commitment to Turkish democracy, or as pretext for other interests.

A cluster of developments explained the EU's change of position between 1997 and 1999. First, the defeat of the PKK, after the capture of its leader Abdullah Ocalan, tempered the tension generated between Turkey and European states by the Kurdish issue. The PKK's defeat encouraged the Turkish military to conclude that they could now afford to allow more generous provision for Kurdish rights; European governments were reassured that the latter could be promoted without making likely a bloody struggle for absolute independence. Second, the change of government in Germany at the end of 1998 removed from power the Christian Democratic Union (Christlich Demokratische Union, or CDU), Europe's most skeptical party on the question of Turkish membership. Third, Greece in effect lifted its veto against Turkey's candidature. The earthquakes that struck both Greece and Turkey in 1999 ushered in a new spirit of co-operation in relations between the two adversaries. Observers suggested that Turkey's earthquake had turned the population against their government, after seeing how governmental corruption had contributed to sloppy construction standards and the inefficiency of official responses to the disaster. A change in Greek foreign minister in September 1999 brought in George Papandreou, notably more conciliatory toward Turkey. By this stage, moreover, Greece's absolute priority was to enter the European Monetary Union, encouraging it to accept trade-off compromises on issues relating to Turkey.[9]

Fourth, Turkey was able to exert new leverage from the EU's efforts to establish a European Security and Defence Policy, which Ankara could frustrate by refusing to agree to ESDP having the necessary access to NATO capabilities. This source of tension was removed, after much acrimonious debate, only at the end of 2002, when Turkey won assurances from the EU that ESDP could not be used against NATO allies and that the potential involvement of NATO partners would be assessed for each mission (the so-called Berlin-plus agreement). Fifth, European governments were eager not to be marginalized by the new rapprochement between the United States and Turkey that had developed after the 1997 Luxembourg decision. In September 1999, the United States signed a Trade and Investment Framework Agreement with Turkey, while in the US Congress the Greek lobby had increasingly been neutralized by the Jewish caucus lobbying on behalf of Turkey in the wake of an Israel-Turkey cooperation agreement.

Significantly then, Helsinki's roots lay in these factors rather than any judgment that far-reaching progress had been made on democratic reform in Turkey. Some in the EU opined that, from being discriminated against relative to Eastern European states, Turkey had now jumped ahead, the post-Communist states of Eastern Europe having had to demonstrate more sustained commitment to democracy before being formally accepted as candidates. Turkey complained that it was still being expected to reform prior to entry negotiations being opened, where in the case of Eastern European states negotiations were themselves used as part of the process of reform.

At the end of 1999 the EP unblocked a raft of aid programs to Turkey—with the condition that the Turkish government now begin to allow civil society and democracy projects.[10] Early in 2000 a new Accession Partnership was drawn up for Turkey and the EU presented a roadmap envisaging gradual change toward the beginning of negotiations. Total EC aid allocated to Turkey for 2000 was doubled from the average yearly amounts given during the late 1990s.[11] The European Investment Bank made available €6.4 billion in loans for Turkey for 2000–2007, with Commission aid set at an annual level of €177 million. In April 2000, the first EU-Turkey association council for three years was held. Aid to Turkey was more heavily Europeanized than elsewhere in the Middle East: in 2001, the Commission was Turkey's largest donor, providing $192 million; Germany gave $118 million, with no other European donor offering more than $20 million.[12]

In response to the Helsinki agreement, the Turkish government introduced a number of reforms. In May 2000, a new reformist president, Ahmet Necdet Sezer, was selected by the parliament. The 2001 national reform package introduced a raft of changes. In a program of over thirty constitutional amendments, new provisions were introduced to appoint a civilian judge to the state security courts; to restrict use of the death penalty; and to drop mention of Greece from the list of Turkey's primary security threats. The Turkish business community continued to strengthen its activity as an advocate of political change—this being the sector where the new prospect of EU accession most clearly influenced an evolution in opinion.[13]

Progress remained at best halting, however. The EU complained that reform programs lacked specifics. In 2000 Necmettin Erbakan was sent to prison, and in June 2001, Refah's successor party, Fazilet (Truth) was also banned. Harassment of Islamist civil society organizations persisted. The president of the Turkish Human Rights Association was imprisoned, while the government drew up a new list of foreigners declared persona non grata in Turkey on the grounds of their support for the Kurds. In 2001, the Turkish army spoke out more strongly against EU entry conditions, arguing that these might not be worth much sacrifice and that the EU's concept of cultural rights constituted a threat to Turkish security interests.[14] The military's reluctance to contemplate reform was hardened by the perception that the incipient ESDP risked isolating Turkey, and partially cancelled out the gains of Helsinki in the minds of the Turkish elite.[15] Restrictions were actually tightened on the publication of material judged to be against the national interest. The Ecevit government was constrained by its coalition with the MHP, which was still opposed to concessions on Kurdish rights and Cyprus.[16] Notwithstanding the reforms implemented, there were few signs of any profound change of political perspectives within the Kemalist elite. Reforms were agreed to as an instrumental adaptation only as the prospect of accession became clearer. Changes were made to basic rights issues, without fundamental reform to military-dominated power structures or to Turkey's state-centric strategic culture.[17]

Having won the signal from the EU it had so long professed to desire, Turkey did not move to ensure entirely smooth relations with Europe. Indeed, Turkish negotiators initially rejected the Helsinki offer, due to the conditions still in place relating to the Aegean and north Cyprus; the deal was secured only after an emergency visit by Solana and a telephone call from President Clinton to Prime Minister

Ecevit. EU diplomats reported that the Turkish government rankled at post-Helsinki intrusion, as it was suddenly inundated with a plethora of visits from Commission officials to launch work on accession convergence, including through public and regular dialogue with human rights groups strongly critical of the government. Many in Turkey, including in the government, remained uneasy that too much had been conceded, not only on Cyprus and the Aegean disputes with Greece, but also in terms of Turkey's acceptance that it would forgo EU freedom of movement provisions. This last provision was influential in changing German attitudes, in particular: it was suggested that far more important to Germany and other European states than the political liberalization reform packages was the Turkish government's introduction in 2002 of measures to clamp down on illegal migration from Central and South Asia into Western Europe.[18] When the French parliament pushed Turkey to recognize the Ottoman targeting of Armenians as an act of genocide, Turkey responded to this historical slight by imposing sanctions against France. The German party foundations experienced obstacles to developing projects freely in Turkey. Turkish authorities imposed restrictions on the movements of visiting MEPs and barred them from visiting prominent Kurds in prison, while the EP declared that Helsinki did not appear to have inspired any significant reform in Turkey.[19]

At this stage, focus switched away from EU conditions to Turkey's rapidly deepening financial crisis, and the reforms required by the International Monetary Fund in return for a rescue package. Germany in particular backed up the United States by funding a large rescue package, for fear of the instability that might erupt if Turkey were not to stabilize. One interpretation was that IMF reforms were more determinant and intrusive than EU conditions, affecting the "deep state" and touching on the nexus between the army, the bureaucracy, and the security services.[20] While the IMF focus was on economic but not political preconditions and reforms, when the economic crisis brought down the government it brought in its wake the most far-reaching (up to that date) package of political reforms, introduced in August 2002. This round of reforms included the lifting of emergency rule in two provinces in Eastern Anatolia. The passing of this set of changes was ironically assisted by the collapse of the government, when the antireform MHP left the Ecevit coalition.

Despite the commitment made at Helsinki, debates continued within European governments and the Brussels institutions. The Nordic states, as well as key CDU politicians in Germany, lamented the lack of conditionality prior to Turkey's candidature being accepted. Some in the EU—and in particular in the European Parliament—began advocating an "Association-plus" category for Turkey, short of full membership. Research uncovered open skepticism in some official EU quarters that Helsinki's supposed commitment was in fact definitive.[21] Concerns were raised over Turkish ownership of the nascent reform process. Piecemeal reforms had been introduced each time the EU had held out a little more of an olive branch, and thus pursued in a top-down fashion at this stage without any discernible groundswell of public pressure or engagement. Many still assumed that the Turkish elite didn't realize how intrusive preparation for membership would become and that the decision on accession was still a bridge the EU might not have to make a decision on crossing. Helsinki had formally accepted Turkey's candidature, but did not reflect agreement on how quickly or in what fashion the EU should proactively move actually to facilitate Turkey's accession.

These persisting differences suggested that Europe had still not determined the essential strategic terms in which it viewed Turkey. Views of the more skeptical European actors implied a perception of Turkey as a "security recipient" from Europe. For the more enthusiastic actors, Turkey had potential as a "security provider." For the former school of thought, Turkey was a barrier against the Islamic world; for the latter it was to be courted as a bridge to that world. The way these two groups within the EU read developments in Turkish democracy were conveniently molded to the respective security logic they each propounded. Those drawn to containment logic were those who lamented the limits to Turkish reforms. They were also the actors for whom domestic European politics weighed heavily: if in the rest of the Middle East democratization was seen as a means of potentially reducing migration, in Turkey's case it would dramatically increase migratory flows if it were to provide the country's key to the EU. Those adhering to the logic of engagement were those celebrating the far-reaching nature of change in Turkey. The attacks of 9/11 simply intensified these ongoing debates. One strand argued that the attacks made it even more urgent for the EU to embrace Turkey; most notably, German foreign minister Joschka Fischer attributed directly to 9/11 his decision to come down firmly in support of Turkish accession.[22] Another strand opined that the greater need was for realist-type security cooperation—significantly, the one concrete

decision that the EU took specifically related to Turkey in the immediate aftermath of 9/11 was to add the PKK to its list of terrorist
organizations.

Islamist Democracy and the Grand Irony

Elections in the autumn of 2003 gave victory to the Justice and
Development Party. The AKP had developed after a group of reformists split from Erbakan and the Refah-Fazilet old guard. Key to
this split was the increasing antipathy of the religious middle classes
to Erbakan's policies; the still-banned AKP leader Recep Tayyip
Erdogan moved to define the party as Islamist-oriented but principally center right, free market, and pro–small business. In contrast to
the 1996–1997 Refah government, the AKP adopted an apparently
unambiguous pro-EU and pro-democracy position. This "Damascene
conversion" reflected a realization of how EU norms could be used
to prevent the 1997 ousting of an Islamist government from happening again.[23] The EU spoke out strongly against the army's prohibition
against Erdogan's candidacy in the elections—although once again
some in Turkey saw this as less of a genuine defense of democratic
rights than another pretext for prevarication after Helsinki. Skeptics
suggested that the AKP had conceived reform in a very instrumental
sense—as a form of self-protection—and doubted whether the
Islamists had fully internalized democratic norms. Some predicted
that the party would struggle harmoniously to combine a traditional
religious identity with its modern, entrepreneurial, and democratic
constituency.

Here was a remarkable irony: the military had inched toward
accepting some reform in the late 1990s and after Helsinki as it saw
the EU as a protection against the rise in Islam, reflected in Refah's
success during the 1990s; at the same time, self-styled moderate
Islamists switched to support EU accession on the basis that European democratic norms would provide protection against the military.
Each side was minded to bet that it had more genuine cause and
stronger will to ally with European political norms than the other. A
complex nesting of "who blinks first" games had been set up: not
only between the EU and Turkey, but also within Turkey itself,
reflecting a deep intertwining of Turkish politics with EU policies.

The Copenhagen European Council in December 2002 was dominated by vigorous debate between member states on the question of

whether a date should be set for opening negotiations with Turkey. In favor of offering Turkey a firm date, the UK lined up against France, Germany, and the Commission. It was eventually agreed that progress in Turkey would be reviewed in December 2004, and if this were judged satisfactory, accession negotiations would start "as soon as possible." A firm commitment to begin negotiations had not been granted, and the Turkish government angrily accused the EU of raising the hurdle each time Turkey took another step along the path of reform. The opening of entry talks with Bulgaria and Romania, both still short of democratic consolidation, caused particular resentment in Ankara. The increasingly strongly expressed differences between member states made the divergence in strategic visions even more evident. Turkey's progress on reforms appeared to have effected a definitive rupture in the coalition, in the EU, between those genuinely concerned with democracy and those keen to exclude Turkey on identity grounds.[24]

The Copenhagen (non)decision gave grist to the mill of those suspecting the EU of still being concerned to find any way to prevent Turkey from joining the European Union. Chairman of the European constitutional convention Giscard d'Estaing's widely publicized remarks in the weeks leading up to Copenhagen, that Turkey was not a European state and should not be allowed to join, were suspected of mirroring unspoken fears pervasive in European chancelleries. Efforts by a number of member states to insert into the new European constitution reference to the EU's "Judeo-Christian roots" reinforced these fears. Polls conducted in 2002 revealed European public opinion to be in large measure hostile to Turkish accession: in all states except the UK and the Netherlands opinion was more negative toward Turkey than toward the Eastern European candidates; in all states except Spain, the Netherlands, Portugal, and Ireland, a majority of the population was opposed to Turkey's entry into the EU.[25]

With Turkey still seething from the disappointment of Copenhagen, the EU moved to invest its actions in Turkey with greater substance. The EU budget for 2003–2004 allocated Turkey an extra €250 million for accession preparations, especially on political reform. By 2003 Turkey was the second (to Serbia and Montenegro) highest recipient of Commission aid anywhere in the world.[26] A Preaccession Strategy was agreed in May 2003, with more specific conditionality and details on the new legislation required from Turkey. Under this, cooperation was for the first time to be given "an accession orientation." Despite the constant strictures on democratization since the mid-1990s, the EU recognized in this Strategy that it was only now moving "to begin" systematically to support democratic capacity building on the ground within Turkey. Aid allocations were set to increase to €300 million for 2005 and then €500 million in 2006, with democracy and institution-building initiatives for the first time identified as priorities in the distribution of these resources— although it appeared that in practice such political work would most notably take the form of twinning schemes between European and Turkish ministries and public administration bodies.[27] Funding under the EIDHR did begin to develop more political initiatives, albeit on a much smaller scale: new projects were supported on minority rights, freedom of expression, media independence, and human rights, in some cases in the face of official authorities' opposition, in some cases accepting governmental pressure not to fund more critical civil society organizations.

While the EU began to intensify its efforts, the AKP implemented further reforms. Explicitly to meet EU human rights requirements, a Reform Monitoring Group was established involving officials and NGOs, along with a system of sanctions for those in the bureaucracy, security services, and judiciary continuing to block reforms.[28] A June 2003 reform bill—the seventh harmonization package—provided for international observers at elections; authorized media broadcasts in Kurdish; lightened restrictions on the right to demonstrate; scrapped the antiterror law; and repealed an article allowing leniency for honor killings. Most significantly, the AKP government pushed through measures to reduce the political role of the military: many of the National Security Council's executive functions were downgraded to merely advisory input; the number of civilian seats on the NSC was increased to nine, against the five held by military officers; parliamentary scrutiny over the military budget was strengthened and was used in 2004 to reduce defense expenditure; and military representation in a number of civilian bodies was reduced. An eighth reform package in 2004 also enhanced the independence of key media outlets.

While political reforms deepened, the issue of Cyprus also seemed to become less of an obstacle, as Erdogan forced a deal to bring moderates into the Turkish Cypriot administration, against the will of his generals. In its concern to find a preaccession deal on Cyprus, the EU now appeared to have more of an ally in Turkey's Islamist government than in the country's pro-Western military establishment. Skeptics' assumption that Turkish truculence on Cyprus would provide another ready guarantee against accession no longer looked convincing. Indeed, a more general reversal seemed to have occurred: it was now the generals who professed the strongest doubts about EU membership, suggesting Turkey might be better aligning itself with Russia or Iran rather than the EU. A growing division was observed between, on the one hand, diplomats increasingly drawn toward working on concrete issues with and through the EU and, on the other hand, a military still more naturally comfortable cooperating with the United States. A key change in dynamics was seen to have arisen, with the Turkish population for the first time expressing greater enthusiasm for EU membership than the entrenched Kemalist elite.[29] When the Greek Cypriots voted against the UN plan for Cyprus, the AKP government could not be blamed for a lack of effort or compromise.

The Turkish government's actions in relation to the invasion of Iraq also exhibited growing moderation, but did not have an entirely positive impact on its relations with Europe. When the United States requested permission for the deployment of US troops in Turkey, the Turkish military held back its support, pushing responsibility onto the AKP for what would be a domestically unpopular decision to acquiesce to Washington's petition. The government expended considerable political capital in pushing a skeptical parliament to agree at least to US overflights.[30] The AKP then additionally claimed it had to restrain the army from sending troops into northern Iraq, to contain Kurdish fighters. The refusal of France, Germany, and Belgium to back Ankara's request for NATO to defend Turkey in the event of a spillover of the conflict in northern Iraq fostered further resentment within both the Erdogan government and the military. Turkey's postinvasion offer to deploy troops in Iraq, made at the prompting of both Washington and London, was actively opposed by key European states—even to the point of Turkey intimating that the French government had made some veiled threats over a linkage between this and the prospects for accession. By 2004, the prospect that Turkish accession would create an EU-Iraq border gave further reason for some to question the security benefit to Europe of Ankara's membership. Again, in part with its European goal in mind (and in part due to Iraqi Interim Administration ambivalence), the Turkish government relented and did not pursue its offer to send troops.

Each successive gathering of European ministers and Commission report opined—in what was becoming the stock phrase—that "significant further efforts . . . are still required" in relation to Turkey's political and economic reforms. A May 2004 Commission interim report insisted on the need for additional strengthening of parliamentary oversight of defense expenditure. European leaders were increasingly wary about being held responsible for the EU not opening accession negotiations with Turkey. In February 2004, Gerhard Schröder traveled to Ankara, in the first visit by a German chancellor for eleven years, to proclaim his support for Turkish membership. A similarly effusive visit by Tony Blair followed in May.

Other opinions began to sharpen against Turkey, however. CDU leader Angela Merkel clarified that her party favored a "privileged partnership," not full entry—thus indicating that German elections in 2006 could derail accession negotiations. Sections of Germany's Social Democratic Party also voiced increasing doubts, as did members of the Dutch government, while, as the crucial moment of decision approached, Nordic politicians became more outspoken on what they saw as Turkey's serious human rights deficiencies. The lack of a Chirac visit caused much comment in Turkey. The majority of Chirac's center-right Union for the Presidential Majority party was against Turkish accession, as were leaders of the French Socialist Party; opponents included French prime minister Jean-Pierre Raffarin and Chirac's emerging rival, Nicolas Sarkozy—most of these critics citing the likely loss of French receipts from the EU budget as a central concern. In response to this increasingly broad opposition to Turkish accession, Chirac agreed to a provision that would submit all future enlargements (after the entry of Romania and Bulgaria) to a referendum. The Austrian government also began to express reservations. The new Spanish government did not oppose the principle of Turkey's accession, but it was notably less enthusiastic to help Turkey quickly into the EU than its Atlanticist center-right predecessor had been.

Diplomats from several European states acknowledged that their governments were "hiding behind" Germany and France, the states seen as most likely to veto Turkish accession. Notwithstanding the seminal change of position in Athens and cordial relations between Erdogan and Prime Minister Costas Karamanlis, low-level tension continued between Greek and Turkish forces in the Aegean, leading Greece to lodge a formal complaint in May 2003 and adversely coloring the position of many Greek politicians.[31] The prospect of a Cypriot veto also remained; Greece threatened to block East European states' accession if the Greek part of the island were not admitted into the EU, although this was contrary to the long-held (formally, at least) EU line that it should be a united Cyprus that won entry. European sensitivities were not helped when President Bush took it upon himself to issue a judgment, at the EU-US summit of June 2004, that Turkey was ready for membership—a clear dig at European equivocation. The fact that Turkey's strongest advocate within the EU was the UK also had drawbacks by this stage, due to both the fallout from Iraq and the continuing suspicion that London was motivated primarily by a vision of Turkey's membership helping dilute European integration. It was notable, however, that much opposition to Turkish accession was couched in terms of Turkey's poverty, size, and Muslim culture.

An unseemly game of pass the buck took shape. Asked simply whether Turkey was making progress in its reforms, a French spokesman claimed it was "not for France to judge," but rather entirely in the Commission's hands. Sensing that member states were attempting to shift the entire burden of responsibility, a number of European commissioners themselves began to voice strong concerns. Commission planning clarified that even if negotiations were to begin in 2005, they were unlikely to reach conclusion for over a decade. Suggestions appeared from official sources that Turkish membership would cost up to €20 billion a year in subsidies, €10 billion for the agriculture budget alone. Opinion polls suggested rising public antipathy as the prospect of Turkey joining drew nearer: in France some polls put opposition as high as 90 percent of the population.[32] The prospect of the Commission opining in more ambiguous fashion in its judgment ahead of the December European Council would oblige member states to assume a heavier political risk with their own electorates in opting to begin negotiations.

A key question was whether a form of limited democracy was in fact viewed as optimal from the EU's perspective. Even after eight successive harmonization packages, the Turkish military retained significant powers and influence. The armed forces continued to enjoy a formal constitutionally mandated role to protect the secularism of the state. The Supreme Military Council remained exempt from judicial review, with the army in fact resisting more strongly the prospect of subordination to civilian courts because of the AKP's hold on power. The civilian defense ministry still did not exercise the same primacy over security policy as in fully democratic states, with meetings of the NSC attracting intense media coverage and debate as crucial determinants of policy. A large proportion of economic contracts also still originated with the military. When the Kurdistan People's Congress (or Kongra-Gel), successor to the PKK, commenced violent attacks in June 2004, the army's crackdown was familiar in its zeal. The military's attempts to limit some aspects of reform came in fact from a far more democracy-oriented new leadership within the armed forces. Within a framework of generally assenting to limits on its own powers, the army helped constrain AKP-proposed Islamist judges and in mid-2004 helped ensure that government plans in relation to religious schools were dropped. (These plans had purported to give graduates of religious schools equal status in access to universities).[33]

In October 2004, on the basis of its regular assessment of Turkey's preparedness for accession, the Commission recommended that accession negotiations be opened. Concerns were raised, particularly in relation to AKP plans for a new law making adultery a judiciable offense; the military's still-prominent political influence; and minority and women's rights. Proposing a provision for talks to be suspended if democratic reforms were reversed, the Commission acknowledged that the progression from entry talks to actual accession would not be as inevitable as with previous enlargements.[34] The Turkish government subsequently dropped its proposed provision on adultery but suggested that if accession talks did not offer free movement for Turkish citizens within the EU, it would reject the offer of negotiations. The European Parliament pointed to restrictions still sometimes imposed by Turkish authorities on civil society—and particular, Kurdish—organizations receiving EP delegations.[35]

At the December 2004 European Council, leaders agreed that entry negotiations would begin in October 2005. Turkish (as well as some European governments') celebration of this firm commitment was tempered by the prospect of the 10-month delay until October. Other provisions also qualified the significance of the decision. It was agreed that negotiations could be suspended by a qualified majority vote among member states, and that the possibility would remain for permanent safeguards against the free movement of Turkish citizens and for Turkey's right to cohesion and agricultural funds. The possibility of such permanent arrangements was viewed unhappily by the UK, Italy, and Belgium as tantamount to "privileged partnership" cleverly disguised as accession; these provisions had been insisted upon most strongly by France, Austria, and Denmark. Turkey would also have to agree immediately to extend the 1963 association agreement and the 1995 customs union to new entrants, implying de facto recognition of Greek Cyprus as a sovereign state. It was acknowledged that European civil society would need to be engaged to modify prevailing opposition to Turkey joining the EU. President Chirac stressed that "negotiations don't mean entry," and the French parliament pressed for Turkey's recognition of the "genocide" carried out against Armenians between 1915 and 1923 to be raised to a formal precondition to accession. The Austrian government joined its French counterpart in committing to hold a referendum on Turkish accession. Against the background of these caveats and remaining obstacles, the differential treatment of Turkey was additionally thrown into sharper relief by the pressure exerted by Germany and Austria at the December summit for entry talks with Croatia to be speeded up. The December decision was simultaneously a historic step toward possible Turkish accession and the effective end of the pretense that Turkey would be subject to conditions the equal of those applied to other current and previous candidates.

In the wake of the December decision, the Turkish government implemented a number of additional reforms. A new penal code agreed in June 2005 strengthened penalties against honor killings and torture and enhanced the protection of women's rights. However, this new law also prescribed prison sentences for journalists deemed to have insulted the nation or to have harmed national interests. By this stage President Sezer had intervened a record number of times to send religiously oriented laws back to parliament.[36] A growing number of violent attacks were carried out by the PKK and Kongra-Gel. Some European officials complained of a slowing down of the reform process, Turkey having now won its commitment to entry talks. One senior EU diplomat was quoted as opining that "Turkey no longer believes in the EU process."[37] The head of the EU delegation in Ankara lamented, "In our discussions with the Turkish authorities, we see that somehow there is not the dynamic approach which we saw before December," and complained at increasing human rights abuses on the part of security forces and a rising anti-Europeanism within sections of the Turkish population.[38] Turkey's chief accession negotiator resigned in protest at his government's equivocation. Diplomats welcomed the introduction of formal reform-oriented legislation, but alluded to delays in the implementation of such measures. As PKK violence increased, EU officials also lamented that the response of Turkish security forces demonstrated a continuing refusal to adopt a new security approach to the Kurdish question.

While the Commission published its draft framework for negotiations at the end of June, by this stage the "no" votes in the French and Dutch referendums were widely seen as rendering the prospect of Turkey acceding to the EU far more remote. This, of course, by now had little to do with the state of reforms in Turkey but much more to do with concerns internal to the European Union: if it was the apocryphal "Polish plumber" that figured most prominently in the French referendum campaign, Turkey's accession was also cited by many doubters as a specter of concern. A summer 2005 Eurobarometer poll reconfirmed that a majority of EU citizens opposed Turkish entry, with a subsequent German Marshall Fund poll suggesting that only 22 percent of Europeans favored Turkey's accession.[39] Reflecting a growing feeling of slight, Turkey's political debate changed in tone. Erdogan emphasized a switch from the Copenhagen criteria to a set of "Ankara criteria" designed to demonstrate that reforms were now driven by an internal dynamic rather the European Union.

In the weeks leading up to the October 2005 deadline a range of Cyprus-related issues emerged, revolving around the underlying question of whether Ankara's actions in relation to the Greek Cypriots would be constrained once negotiations were opened. On the question of Turkey being obliged to open its ports and airports to Cypriot craft, it was agreed that arrangements would be finalized after one year through a "rendezvous" clause. The United States intervened to gain guarantees that the Greek Cypriot administration would not complicate accession talks by seeking NATO membership. Tensions were also focused on Ankara's insistence that the extension of the customs union to new member states did not amount to formal recognition of Cyprus. While the UK presidency and European Commission urged entry talks to be opened, Jacques Chirac and Angela Merkel cited this issue in particular as reason for delay. Brussels diplomats admitted that it was by now widely recognized to have been a mistake to allow part of a divided Cyprus to join the EU.

It was agreed eventually that the issue of nonrecognition would not prevent entry talks from commencing, only for the Austrian government to then hold back its acquiescence to accession talks opening until—in a dramatic example of last-minute, late-night, EU trade-off haggling—it was agreed that negotiations would also be opened with Croatia, Vienna's long-standing Balkan client. Curiously, while formal negotiations were opened, the historical import of this move was in part drowned out by a "mood music" that was more negative and fearful than celebratory. Most EU leaders' rhetoric at and after the October summit was downbeat; some stressed how chapter negotiations would be subject to stricter benchmarks than with Eastern European states and would provide over seventy veto points. Ominously for Ankara, the formal deal that was struck clarified that eventual entry would still be dependent on the EU's capacity to absorb Turkey. Some in Brussels opined that it was still possible for Turkey itself, at some point in the negotiations, to judge that the price was too high in terms of what EU accession implied for increasingly intrusive reform requirements and the loss of national sovereignty. After the protracted rapprochement between Turkey and the EU since Helsinki, there now appeared to be a degree of hesitation from some actors on both sides.

Conclusion

From the vantage point of early 2006, one dynamic in the EU's relations with Turkey appeared increasingly prominent: many of those in the EU who had been happy to use the inducement of accession to encourage reform in Turkey were not at all immune to the temptation of looking for ways of withdrawing this reward after European transformative power had enjoyed a large measure of success. Turkey's case represented both the most successful example of this model of EU influence, but also that which took the model to—and arguably beyond—its limit. Turkey was also a case that exposed stark differences between European governments, between governments and Brussels institutions, and between the Commission and the European Parliament, and where bilateral member state policies quite openly sought to circumvent blockages at the European level; but also where the whole focus on enlargement and the transfer of "European" norms obliged governments, the Commission, and the European Parliament to persist in coordination and work through their differences until some common ground was delineated. Moreover, it was notable for being the case in which European influence was most clearly more pervasive and institutionalized than that of the United States; the latter's policy centered on military cooperation and on pushing the EU to admit Turkey as quickly as possible, far less on the minutiae of

Turkey's reform process. A pertinent question by 2006 was whether the EU "conditionality machine" had sufficed to render the momentum of Turkish reform irreversible, or whether democratic consolidation might fall victim to a backlash against the EU if and when the carrot of accession was removed.

There was an uneasy mix of competing strategic rationales in EU policies. For some actors in the EU, democratic preconditions were a stalling tactic; others arguably overstated the extent of democratic reform, as an instrumental means of bringing Turkey into the EU, concerned more that Turkey be so engaged than that it be pristinely democratic. Both groups' perspectives on Turkish democracy were in some measure—although not entirely—derived from or conditioned by this strategic thinking. Indicative of this was the fact that, beyond the carrot of European accession, concrete European efforts to assist democratic institution building in Turkey were, until very late on, both reactive and limited in scale. Those holding to the first rationale—eager to retain Turkey as a security buffer and focused on the domestic consequences of Turkish accession—could still be suspected of setting higher hurdles for Turkey than for other candidate states. The significant factor for those holding to this view was that Europe's declared principles were rather uncomfortably catching up with it: democracy had been set as a condition for membership without it appearing likely that the EU would ever be faced with a genuinely democratic Turkey; by 2006, the extent of Turkish reforms left only a few additional hurdles to surmount.

Those conversely adhering to a strategic rationale of engagement could still be suspected of setting the hurdles *lower* for Turkey, to the extent that they appeared indulgent toward a form of bounded democracy, which would improve basic rights and assuage the frustrations that lay behind Islam's rise without undermining the military-guaranteed stability of the Kemalist state. From this latter perspective, awarding accession to an Islamist-oriented government was a positive boon: the EU would gain a more credible interlocutor for the Muslim world, but within an overall constitutional structure that would still enable the army to contain potential radicalism. This was a startling irony, of course, given that membership had for long been seen—both in Turkey and the EU—as a bulwark against Islamism and a means of undercutting figures such as Erdogan. If Turkey's path toward accession was proving more tortuous than that of previous candidate states, the difference was not Islam but rather the continuing resistance to EU-mandated reforms from nationalist sections of the political elite.[40]

While it continued to be unclear whether the promises made to Turkey would be honored, and if so under what conditions, the question remained unresolved of which strategic rationale would prevail. Crucially, both sides of the argument saw 9/11 as reinforcing their respective logic. Again, 9/11 was not a watershed moment; the key changes in European policy had already occurred, linked to developments in particular in Greece, Germany, and Cyprus. But 9/11 did feed into and amplify ongoing differences within the European Union over the rightful strategy toward Turkey. The challenges of the post-9/11 international environment appeared to compound the "derived" significance attributed to the ebb and flow of Turkey's domestic reform process. Recalling Plato's metaphorical cave, Turkish democracy was the flickering shadow cast in the reflection of Europe's strategic and domestic preoccupations.

Notes

1. Cavanagh, "Turkey and the Pale Light," p. 63.
2. Arkan, "A Lost Opportunity?" pp. 19–50.
3. Cavanagh, "Turkey and the Pale Light," p. 66.
4. *Financial Times,* 17 December 1997, p. 4.
5. Yesilada, "Turkey's Candidacy for EU Membership," pp. 94–111.
6. *Financial Times,* 21 May 1998, p. 3.
7. *Agence Europe,* 24 October 1998, p. 9.
8. Commission of the European Communities, *MEDA Note de Dossier,* 2000.
9. *Financial Times,* 15 December 1999.
10. *Agence Europe,* 3 December 1999, p. 10.
11. *Agence Europe,* 10/11 April 2000, p. 12.
12. OECD DAC figures, www.oecd.org/stats.
13. Kubicek, "The Earthquake, the European Union," pp. 1–18.
14. Cizre, "Demythologizing the National Security Concept," pp. 213–229.
15. Tark, "Turkey and the European Union," pp. 61–82.
16. Yesilada, "Turkey's Candidacy for EU Membership," p. 99.
17. Tark, "Turkey and the European Union," p. 66; Schimmelfennig, Engart, and Knobel, "Costs, Commitments and Compliance," pp. 495–518.
18. Dorronsoro, "The European Union and Turkey," p. 50.
19. *Agence Europe,* 23 February 2000, p. 8, and 15 April 2000, p. 5.
20. *The Economist,* 3 May 2003, p. 48.
21. Zucconi, *Turkey's New Politics,* p. 26.

22. *The Economist,* 2 October 2004, p. 40.

23. Robins, "Confusion at Home," pp. 547–566.

24. Diez and Rumelili, "Open the Door," pp. 33–35.

25. Müftüler Bac, "Turkey in the European Union's Enlargement Process," pp. 79–95.

26. Montes and Migliorisi, *EU Donor Atlas,* p. 27.

27. Commission for the European Communities, *Pre-Accession Strategy for Turkey.*

28. *Financial Times,* 8 May 2003.

29. Triantaphyllou, "The Thirteenth Candidate—Turkey," p. 80.

30. See Robins, "Confusion at Home," pp. 564–565; Cizre, "Demythologizing the National Security Concept," p. 227.

31. Triantaphyllou, "The Thirteenth Candidate—Turkey," p. 82.

32. *Financial Times,* 10 September 2004.

33. For details on these limits to military reform, see Aydin and Fuat Keyman, "European Integration," pp. 20–21.

34. Commission of the European Communities, *2004 Regular Report on Turkey's Progress.*

35. European Parliament, *County Reports on Human Rights Practices,* p. 10.

36. *Middle East International,* no. 752, 10 June 2005, p. 21.

37. Quoted in *The Economist,* 4 June 2005, p. 31.

38. *Turkish Daily News,* 3 March 2005.

39. *Middle East International,* no. 755, 22 July 2005, p. 18; *Financial Times,* 7 September 2005.

40. Aydin and Fuat Keyman, "European Integration," p. 18.

8

Conclusion:
Europe in the Middle East

That the Middle East accounted for a greater amount of European foreign policy activity after the attacks of 9/11 was self-evident. That the region awoke acute security concerns was equally clear. If the threat of international terrorism framed such preoccupations in a general sense, the Middle East also presented more specific challenges, relating to the invasion of Iraq, the ongoing conflict between Israel and Palestine, and the actual or prospective development of WMD by countries such as Iran. Moreover, foreign policy design increasingly merged with debates over the trends conditioning Islam within Europe—a confluence shown tragically in Madrid in March 2004 and in London in July 2005. Ministerial statements became ubiquitous advocating the need for a new approach to the Middle East. As outlined in the introduction to this book, a range of questions suggested themselves to be in need of analysis, relating to Europe's capacity and willingness to take forward such a reorientation in its relations with the Middle East; the distinctiveness of European approaches to the interface between security and domestic change within the Middle East; the challenge of responding to the contrasting nature of reform processes emerging in different parts of the region; and the relationship between European and US strategies. The book has unpacked the EU's overall Middle Eastern policy into its component parts at the level of subregions and individual states, offering a detailed account of key developments in European strategies. The foregoing chapters outline the plethora of new initiatives and diplomatic efforts undertaken by European governments and the EU collectively in these areas during recent years. They raise the question of what overall observations can be offered in respect of the nature, evolution, coherence, and effectiveness of European foreign policy toward the Middle East.

The Impact of September 11

The detailed case studies of European strategies in different parts of the Middle East shed light on the impact of 9/11. They suggest that post-9/11 challenges associated with international terrorism triggered important changes in EU policies, but not an overarching paradigm shift. A concern with encouraging political modernization took shape; in some parts of the region this contained new dimensions to European policies, while in other places it built on a more established record of human rights and governance initiatives. Particularly in the Maghreb and Mashreq—the countries included within the Euro-Mediterranean Partnership—the core features of European policy since the mid-1990s were retained and developed further. The basic logic linking soft security issues to internal political conditions in Arab countries was enshrined in the Barcelona Declaration fully six years prior to the attacks of 9/11. The approach after 2001 was to deepen policy elements already initiated under the partnership, and to add incrementally to efforts that had gradually taken shape since the mid-1990s. A principal focus was on the more effective operationalization of the instruments already at the EU's disposal. Refinement rather than rupture was the maxim guiding European reaction to 9/11.

In Iran and the states of the Gulf Cooperation Council efforts were made to develop human rights dialogue on a more systematic and formalized footing, and a modest amount of reform-oriented cooperation was introduced. Here and throughout the Middle East a notable feature of European approaches was the gentle attempt to prompt the dynamics of change in the Middle East through cultural cooperation; this was one of the dimensions to European policies that was strengthened most notably after 9/11, apparently aimed at improving the "image of the other" in European and Arab conscience. The Gulf was the area where the link suggested between security and democratization convinced least in European strategic planning. This fed into an increasingly crucial internal European debate prompted by 9/11 and the invasion of Iraq, namely over the merits of the EU elaborating a broader Middle Eastern policy; as of early 2006 considerable uncertainty remained over the prospects for complementing the EU's longer-standing Mediterranean policy with a stronger "east of Jordan" framework.

Alongside the cautiously deepening focus on the political reform of the Middle East, the EU strengthened security cooperation with incumbent regimes in the region. Here, much of European policy in the wake of 9/11 appeared to have little to do with the replication of democratic norms and values, but rather more traditional power-protection security. Cooperation on counterterrorism deepened between European and Middle Eastern security and intelligence services, particularly in North Africa, the Mashreq, and the Gulf. The foregoing chapters suggest it would be wrong to argue that this was the exclusive or only meaningful element of European reaction to 9/11 and the successive terrorist incidents that subsequently came to dominate Western security concerns. Yet it was a dimension that developed, understandably no doubt, but also in a more immediate and concrete fashion than policies zeroing in on the underlying political causes of terrorism and instability—despite this latter issue being routinely declared the European priority.

In conjunction with such trends, in parts of the region clear priority was accorded to issues perceived to be of direct strategic concern, in a way that also sat uneasily with frequently made claims that EU policy was in a more sophisticated manner aimed at the underlying roots of terrorism than was US strategy. Policy toward Iran, Syria, and Libya, in particular, unequivocally accorded priority to containing the development of weapons of mass destruction; pressure on political reforms was sacrificed for progress on what was seen to be the more pressing objective of gaining formal guarantees on WMD. Most clearly in Iran this was approached as an either/or choice, when arguably the key potential lay in nonproliferation and political reform proceeding in mutually reinforcing tandem.

In some parts of the region, the evolution of policy was conditioned most strongly by factors other than those related directly to 9/11. In the Palestinian Territories a reassessment of policy had been encouraged by the outbreak of the Al-Aqsa Intifada; the retightening of Israeli control over the West Bank and Gaza; and the unfolding of domestic Palestinian politics. In Turkey, momentum had been injected into the preaccession process by political changes in Turkey itself, as well as in a number of European states. In Iran, policy had shifted as the balance between reformists and conservatives had fluctuated back and forth. In all these cases, factors fostered by 9/11 fed into ongoing policy developments, but the major determinants were domestic—to both the Middle East and Europe. The impact of 9/11 was felt indirectly through the filter of these domestic developments. In relation to Iraq more specifically, the attacks of 9/11 in themselves occasioned little change in European policy preferences; here the causal chain was that the US administration opportunistically used 9/11 to bolster what was an already coveted strategy of regime change, to which European governments were then obliged to respond.

The One and Many European Policies in the Middle East

In general terms the European strategy for supporting incipient political change in the Middle East combined relatively indirect bottom-up approaches, on the one hand, with support for elite-guided reform measures on the other. Such strategies were developed in their most structured way in the Maghreb and Mashreq. Within the Euro-Mediterranean Partnership efforts intensified to encourage political change; but the elaboration of such policies was in key ways sufficiently nonspecific for their impact, and indeed their real intent, to be open to some doubt. What might be described as reform support with caveats applied in a number of different dimensions.

The central focus of European initiatives was on social development and economic liberalization, but moves in these fields were not engineered specifically with a view to crafting an associated decentralization of political power. In particular in Syria and Libya, policy was centered to an overwhelming degree on purely economic reform. EU-backed cultural dialogue expanded and was conceived as a means of stimulating the inculcation of democratic values, but was invariably related to political objectives in tenuous fashion. Support increased for civil society organizations pressing for human rights improvements, but only officially registered NGOs received funding. Security sector reform projects were initiated, but they contained relatively intangible political reform elements. In states such as Morocco, Algeria, and Jordan support was forthcoming for governments' controlled incorporation of moderate, pro-regime Islamist parties. In all these areas it was often difficult to determine that there was genuine liberalizing intent behind Arab elites' reforms; where this was so, the EU tended to accord regimes the benefit of the quasi-reformism doubt.

Critical European interjections were at best tepid in relation to the specific and most identifiable signs of autocracy and the further tightening of restrictions on political rights that was witnessed in some countries; in some instances, such as in Tunisia, such pressure if anything slackened in the period following 9/11. A move toward the use of positive democratic conditionality was signaled as a key development in European policy, but the design and use of this principle was loose. Where aid initiatives, conditionality, and diplomatic pressure were deployed they tended to focus around a general set of core human rights rather than the underlying politics of change in different national settings. Policies were probably most gradualist in the Gulf, where the model centered on support for improvements in governance standards and women's rights, along with a strengthening of parliaments that themselves advocated reform within existing regime parameters. In the GCC the model of gradualist political reform also flowing from technocratic and development-related engagement found less echo in European policy.

The elite-oriented prism that guided reform efforts was particularly evident in Palestine. When the EU did, belatedly, develop a sustained institutional reform strategy in the Occupied Territories, this was seen in terms of boosting state capacity and enhancing particular elements of the political spectrum, with a scattering of civil society projects as an addendum. There was a relatively direct conceptualization of institutional reform in terms of measures that could contribute in an immediate sense to improvements in security. European support for a more prime-ministerial political system was instrumentally aimed at circumventing the ailing and increasingly divisive figure of Yasser Arafat, and did not fully survive the PLO leader's death. The EU professed an all-inclusive model of political participation in the Occupied Territories, but in practice attitudes toward Hamas were ambivalent and changeable—accounting in part for the EU's acute predicament after the January 2006 elections. In Iran a similar model prevailed of reform support being pursued through President Khatami. To some extent Khatami's presence was both boon and bane for the EU, offering a foothold for modest amounts of cooperation in areas such as judicial reform, but also diverting European attention from other emerging centers of liberal activism that arguably embodied greater future potential.

In Turkey European positions on the nature of political reform were entangled in and conditioned by debates over accession. At the EU level a comprehensive model for Turkish reform was projected, but in some measure this said more about concerns internal to the European Union than about thinking on Turkey itself. It was difficult to rebut completely the suspicion that such stringent and broad-ranging democratic conditions served at least in part as a means of continually delaying entry talks as Turkey introduced its successive packages of reforms. At the same time, and conversely, the very prospect of having Turkey inside the EU led some European governments to an implicit support for a model of reform that did not completely undo the Kemalist legacy and institutions. As of early 2006, these competing dynamics were still precariously balanced within overall European strategy.

In short, threads of a standard European approach developed across the Middle East, but this was injected with varied elements specific to the distinctive nature of trends and challenges in different parts of the region. Such variation suggested a calibration of value-based EU strategy to material interest calculations, as opposed to a uniquely ideationally driven reproduction of European norms. If the normative dimension was present in European foreign policy, a significant factor was the way in which this was given differential expression by country-specific strategic deliberation. That the nature of its policy in the Middle East rendered the EU a distinctive type of international actor, in this sense at least, was open to doubt.

This diversity of policy was, crucially, compounded by another prominent feature of European strategies, namely their propensity to counterbalance US approaches. This was seen in Iran, Turkey, Syria, and Yemen; but it was most obviously the case in Iraq, where the strategy of noncoalition member states, and to some extent the Commission, was far more focused on pressing the United States to leave than on the challenges facing the design of Iraq's new political system. In Palestine, the approach adopted toward the PA reflected in part the widely perceived imbalance of US policy toward the Israeli-Palestinian conflict. The United States was the ghost at the European feast. EU strategies were in part a reflection of (often internally differing) perceptions on US policy, sometimes as much as they were of European judgments on the internal politics of Middle Eastern countries themselves. While not offering exhaustive detail on US initiatives, the case studies suffice to suggest that it would be unduly simplistic to reduce the comparison between EU and US policies in the Middle East to any generalized or overarching difference in approach; clear points of transatlantic divergence in some parts of the region coexisted with significant overlap between US and European strategies on questions related to political reform and security.

The European Hydra

The detailed study of European policies across the component parts of the Middle East reaffirms the complex nature of European "actorness." The foregoing chapters uncover the ways in which the balance between national and collective EU initiatives varied across different Middle Eastern countries. Overall, European action flowed from a multilevel and multiactor foreign policy system that embraced and facilitated a variety of dynamics. In some places, on some issues, significant differences of opinion persisted or emerged between national governments; in these cases bilateral diplomacy and aid initiatives constituted a key component, if not the bulk, of European foreign policy. In other places, on other issues, convergence and Europeanization were the more dominant dynamics.

Iraq was, of course, the clearest case where national governments were chief protagonists, whether in support of or in opposition to the US-led invasion; and here the bitterness left by the debates leading up to the March 2003 invasion took on a trenchant stubbornness well after the transfer of sovereignty to a new Iraqi government, when much similarity could be detected between European states on political and economic reconstruction imperatives. Beyond Iraq, collective EU engagement was most sporadic and least structured in the states of the Gulf Cooperation Council; in this area some European governments maintained strong bilateral interests, while other member states—backed up to some degree by the Commission—were not strongly enthusiastic about an overall EU focus being diverted from elsewhere to this region. Here again, the national-level diplomacy, security cooperation, and aid initiatives of some governments were at least as substantial as the engagement offered through EU-level instruments. If in parts of the Middle East the often-remarked institutionalized continuity of European approaches was evident, political change at the national level also injected elements of more direct revision; the change of government in Spain in March 2004 was, for instance, felt not only in Iraq but also in the subsequent evolution of Euro-Mediterranean relations.

Probably the two most Europeanized areas of policy were found in Palestine and the broader Mediterranean. Differences remained between European governments in these areas, of course—on conditionality, the nature of support for political reform movements, levels of future MEDA aid, trade liberalization, and, in Palestine, over more specific questions like the engagement of Hamas and the relationship between institutional reform and Arab-Israeli final settlement negotiations. But these were the areas where the weight of collective EU instruments was strongest in relation to those of member states. Initial differences over the putative European Neighbourhood Policy were resolved in large measure, and the latter established itself as a common framework for future relations with a number of Arab states. In Morocco, Algeria, and Tunisia, French and Spanish diplomacy in particular often appeared to cut across declared EU-level objectives; but in other cases, such as Lebanon in 2005, French efforts represented a form of vanguard for broader European influence. Here and elsewhere in the Middle East, even where there were clear differences between member states, the very pervasiveness of the machinery of EU coordination demonstrated itself capable of grinding out common positions and smoothing the roughest edges of national diplomatic tensions. Even in Iraq, while governments were spitting diplomatic venom at each other, they were also agreeing to the cautious beginnings of a common EU contribution to postinvasion reconstruction and a strategy for inducing troubled Iraq into Europe's network of regional partnerships.

The relationship between prominent national-level European initiatives and collective EU instruments often contained a finely balanced mix of divergence and convergence. This was demonstrated in policies toward Iran. Familiar north-south differences within the EU over human rights were overlain here by British-Franco-German nuclear diplomacy, separate again from Communitarized trade negotiations. To a greater extent than might have been predicted, these diverse fragments did cohere into a relatively unified overall European strategy toward the Islamic republic. Turkey was even more of a curiosity: the primary focus on EU accession made this one of the most Europeanized areas of policy; yet it was also one where major differences of opinion persisted between governments, between different Brussels institutions, and within member states themselves. If a notable degree of convergence had sufficed to open the door to Turkish accession, by 2006 the first steps in entry talks appeared to be forcing out into the open some very real opposition that had for some time been shoehorned into a common European strategy.

The Limits to European Presence

Finally, the question remained of whether this multiplicity of European actorness and these threads of a new approach to security and to political, social, and economic change accorded the EU any meaningful presence in the Middle East. Again, the answer to this question differed across different parts of the region. Such presence was, unsurprisingly, most elusive in Iraq. Here coalition members gained little influence, even in the minor way that their modest contributions to the overall US-led alliance might have merited; the UK was in particular increasingly frustrated in this sense, its influence limited to the south of Iraq. But neither did the option *not* to participate in the coalition win the French or Germans, or later the Spanish, credibility within Iraq, or much impact over international strategy. The EU's tentative offer of trade incentives and regional partnership as the main plank of future European influence looked incongruent in the midst of Iraq's gruesome afflictions. Outside Iraq, it was in other parts of the Gulf that Europe's traction remained weakest; in GCC states the EU appeared to have neither the incentives nor the resource base to exert significant influence.

In contrast, the prospect of accession clearly gave the EU primary influence in Turkey—even if the carrot of EU entry was not, at least until relatively late on, backed up by significant and proactive engagement and assistance on political reform within Turkey. More generally, in other parts of the Middle East the common situation was that the EU positioned itself strongly to play a significant role, which then failed to materialize fully. Probably more than any other state in the Middle East, Iran appeared to be in need of an alliance with the EU; and to some extent European governments used this to good effect, becoming the primary international presence that won from the Iranian regime some degree of self-limitation in relation to its nuclear activities. But European influence failed to use this as a base from which to cajole Iran into more firmly rooted arrangements, predicated upon a broad-ranging partnership and sponsorship of a regional security framework. The EU offered Iran a number of incentives that were far-reaching and ingenuous; arguably, this example simply reaffirmed the limited role of external factors per se. It was also the case, however, that the EU limited its own potential influence over Iran in two important ways: first, by failing to roll its different levels of activity together into an overall vision that embraced issues of political reform; and second, in allowing tensions with the United States to weaken its ability to entice Washington into a more constructive engagement with Iran—when the EU did finally succeed in convincing the Bush administration to adapt its strategy, the momentum behind Iranian conservatives' return to power had already taken hold. The ultimately limited European impact on Iran was particularly disappointing as here there was an initial, internally driven reform dynamic around which external support could be molded.

In Palestine, too, it might have been hoped that the European Union's prominent role in keeping the PA afloat would have translated into more pervasive political influence. The EU's presence here was subtle and low key, impacting reforms that were linked to the areas covered by its own aid programs and to the transparency and capacity of basic services delivery. The Bush administration provoked: its direct attack on Arafat's leadership predictably led Palestinians to rally around the symbolic leader of the independence struggle, but it also acted as a catalyst for political-level debates in the Occupied Territories. The EU's more surreptitious approach was less evident at this level, but more relevant at the level of specific financial, governance, and administrative reforms. In light of the profound implications of the January 2006 elections, it must be asked whether the EU could have done more to leverage reforms, improve economic livelihoods, and thus contain the rise of Hamas. The EU traded pressure over Israel for involvement in an international diplomacy that was increasingly nonexistent; and a broader focus on Palestinian democracy for cooperation with a nominally pro-peace leadership that was increasingly unable to meet the prerequisites to peace.

Flowing from the most structured policy framework in the Middle East, the European dimension was certainly a factor increasingly present in domestic political debates within the Arab states included in the Euro-Mediterranean Partnership. Again, it was salutary to note that after many years of this institutionalized cooperation with Europe, the highest-profile international presence in new political reform debates in the Maghreb and Mashreq was that of the United States. The policies of the Bush administration were almost universally disliked within the region; but, as elsewhere, it was the United States' explicit rhetorical commitment to democratization that had the catalytic impact, not the EU's more carefully couched talk of "shared norms and values"—and this was so even in states where in objective terms the European presence and weight was far greater than that of the United States. European influence was again of a secondary order: the fear of a tough new US democracy promotion policy was what made regimes look to make tactical adjustments; it was then most commonly through the European prism that cooperation and technical advice entered the picture as a means of facilitating such reform in more practical terms. The EU played a form of "before and after" influence in the southern Mediterranean. On the one hand, it had gently begun to shift debate in its Arab partners in a way that cultivated some fertile ground for internalization of the more abrupt change in US rhetoric; on the other hand, it provided a kind of incentivizing cover for elites to cooperate on limited governance reforms in a way they perceived to be self-serving.

This, then, condenses some of the central points to have emerged from this study of European policy in the Middle East: intense new European activity took shape after 9/11 in the Middle East, some genuinely aimed at supporting democratic reform, but other elements cut across this declared objective even more adversely than previously; the multiplicity of European actorness was increasingly in evidence; a balance was struck between uniform values and country-specific variation in the Middle East; and, while European policy sought to position itself to play a more defining role in the region, the conditioning shadow of US policies also lengthened. The Middle East was a case particularly illuminating of the strengths and weaknesses of European foreign policy coordination and action. It also remained the case presenting the most acute dilemmas and doubts in relation to shaping the widely posited relationship between security and democracy. Certainly, as of early 2006, the challenges associated with the region remained as pressing as, and were if anything more complex than, when terrorists slammed their planes into the Twin Towers on 11 September 2001.

Bibliography ─────────────────────

Abrahams, M. "When Rogues Defy Reason: Bashar's Syria," *Middle East Quarterly* 10, no. 4 (2003): 45–55.

Agencia Española de Cooperación Internacional. *Plan Anual de AECI 2005,* Madrid, AECI.

Aliboni, R. "The Geopolitical Implications of the European Neighbourhood Policy," *European Foreign Affairs Review* 10, no. 1 (2005): 1–16.

———. "An Italian Perspective on Future EU-GCC Relations," *GCC-EU Research Bulletin,* no. 1 (March 2005): 10.

———. "Promoting Democracy in the Euro-Mediterranean Partnership: Which Political Strategy?" Euromesco Report, November 2004.

Allaf, R. "Point of No Return," *World Today* 60, no. 11 (2004): 12–14.

Aoun, E. "European Foreign Policy and the Arab-Israeli Dispute: Much Ado About Nothing," *European Foreign Affairs Review* 8 (2003): 289–312.

Arkan, H. "A Lost Opportunity? A Critique of the European Union's Human Rights Policy Towards Turkey," *Mediterranean Politics* 7, no. 1 (2002): 19–50.

Asseburg, M. "The EU and the Middle East Conflict: Tackling the Main Obstacle to Euro-Mediterranean Partnership," *Mediterranean Politics* 8, no. 2 (2003): 174–193.

———. "From Declaration to Implementation? The Three Dimensions of European Policy Towards the Conflict," in M. Ortega, ed., *The European Union and the Crisis in the Middle East,* Chaillot Papers no. 62. Paris: EU Institute for Security Studies, 2003.

Asseburg, M., and V. Perthes, ed. "The European Union and the Palestinian Authority: Recommendations for a New Policy," *Stiftung Wissenschaft und Politik S421* (Ebenhausen, SWP), 1998.

Attina, F. "The Euro-Mediterranean Partnership Assessed: The Realist and Liberal Views," *European Foreign Affairs Review* 8 (2003): 181–199.

Aydin, S., and E. Fuat Keyman. "European Integration and the Transformation of Turkish Democracy," Working Paper no. 2. Brussels: Center for European Policy Studies, EU-Turkey, 2004.

233

Baabood, A. "Dynamics and Determinants of the GCC States' Foreign Policy, with Special Reference to the EU," in G. Nonneman, ed., *Analyzing Middle East Foreign Policies.* London: Routledge, 2005.

Balfour, R. "Italy's Policies in the Mediterranean," in H. Amirah Fernández and R. Youngs, ed., *The Euro-Mediterranean Partnership, Assessing the First Decade.* Madrid: Real Instituto Elcano, 2005.

———. "Rethinking the Euro-Mediterranean Political and Security Dialogue," Occasional Paper no. 52. Paris: EU Institute for Security Studies, 2004.

Barber, B. "Democracy and Terror in the Era of Jihad and McWorld," in K. Booth and T. Dunne, ed., *Worlds in Collision: Terror and the Future of Global Order.* London: Routledge, 2002.

Bellin, E. "The Political-Economic Conundrum: The Affinity of Economic and Political Reform in the Middle East and North Africa," Working Paper no. 53. Washington, DC: Carnegie Endowment for International Peace, 2004.

Bertelsmann Foundation—Centre for Applied Research. *The EU and the GCC: A New Partnership.* Gutersloh: Bertelsmann, 2002.

Biscop, S. "The European Security Strategy and the European Neighbourhood Policy: A New Starting Point for a Euro-Mediterranean Security Partnership?" paper presented at the EUSA 9th Biennial Conference, Austin, Texas, 31 March–2 April 2005.

Boniface, P. "French Policy in the Gulf: Opportunities, Challenges and Implications," paper presented at the International Interests in the Gulf Region, Emirates Center for Strategic Studies and Research, 2004.

Booth, K., and T. Dunne. "Worlds in Collision," in K. Booth and T. Dunne, ed., *Worlds in Collision: Terror and the Future of Global Order.* London: Routledge, 2002.

Brumberg, D. "Liberalization Versus Democratization: Understanding Arab Political Reforms," Working Paper no. 37. Washington, DC: Carnegie Endowment for International Peace, 2003.

Brumberg, D., and L. Diamond. "Introduction," in L. Diamond, M. Plattner, and D. Brumberg, ed., *Islam and Democracy in the Middle East.* Baltimore: Johns Hopkins University Press, 2003.

Burgat, F. *Face to Face with Political Islam.* London: I. B. Tauris, 2003.

Byman, D. "Constructing a Democratic Iraq," *International Security* 28, no. 1 (2003): 47–78.

Byman, D., and K. Pollack. "Democracy in Iraq?" *Washington Quarterly* 26, no. 3 (2003): 119–136.

Cameron, F., and E. Rhein. "Promoting Political and Economic Reform in the Mediterranean and Middle East," European Policy Centre Issue Paper, no. 33, 18 May 2005.

Carnegie Endowment Forum. *Toward Democracy in Palestine: Learning from Other Countries,* July 2002, www.ceip.org.

Carothers, T., and M. Ottaway. "Middle East Democracy," *Foreign Policy,* November–December 2004.

Cavanagh, Hodge. "Turkey and the Pale Light of European Democracy," *Mediterranean Politics* 4, no. 3 (1999).

Checkel, J. "Why Comply? Social Learning and European Identity Change," *International Organization* 55, no. 3 (2001): 553–588.

Chourou, B. "Security Partnership and Democratisation: Perception of the Activities of Northern Security Institutions in the South," in H. G. Brauch, A. Marquina, and A. Biad, ed., *Euro-Mediterranean Partnership for the Twenty-First Century.* Basingstoke: Macmillan, 2000.

Cizre, U. "Demythologizing the National Security Concept: The Case of Turkey," *Middle East Journal* 57, no. 3 (2003): 213–229.

Cofmann Wittes, T. "The Promise of Arab Liberalism," *Policy Review* (June/ July 2004): 61–76.

Commission of the European Communities. *Algérie: Document de Stratégie 2002–2006.* Brussels: Commission of the European Communities, 2002.

———. *Communication from the Commission to the Council and the European Parliament: The Madrid Conference on Reconstruction in Iraq,* COM(2003)575. Brussels: Commission of the European Communities, 1 October 2003.

———. *Communication from the Commission to the Council and the European Parliament: Reinvigorating EU Actions on Human Rights and Democratisation with Mediterranean Partners,* COM(2003)294. Brussels: Commission of the European Communities, 2003.

———. *Communication to the Council on Commission Proposals for Action Plans Under the European Neighbourhood Policy,* COM(2004)795. Brussels: Commission of the European Communities, 9 December 2004.

———. *Egypt: Country Strategy Paper 2002–2006.* Brussels: Commission of the European Communities, 2002.

———. *EIDHR Programming Document 2005–2006,* COM(2004)4474. Brussels: Commission of the European Communities, 2004.

———. *EIDHR Programming Update 2004.* Brussels: Commission of the European Communities, 2004.

———. *EMP Syria National Indicative Programme 2005–2006.* Brussels: Commission of the European Communities, 2004.

———. *The EU and the Gulf Cooperation Council.* 2002. http://europa.eu .int/comm/external_relations/gulf_cooperation/intro/index.htm.

———. *The European Union and Iraq: A Framework for Engagement,* COM(2004)417. Brussels: Commission of the European Communities, 2004.

———. *Implementation of the Democracy and Human Rights Initiative 1996–1999.* Brussels: Commission of the European Communities, 2000.

———. *Iraq: Assistance Programme 2005.* Brussels: Commission of the European Communities, 2004.

———. *MEDA Regional Indicative Programme 2002–2004.* Brussels: Commission of the European Communities, 2002.

———. *Pre-Accession Strategy for Turkey.* Brussels: Commission of the European Communities, 2003.

———. *Regional and Bilateral MEDA Cooperation in the Area of Justice, Freedom and Security,* Information Note. Brussels: Commission of the European Communities, February 2004.

————. *A Strategic Partnership with the Mediterranean and the Middle East.* Brussels: Commission of the European Communities, 2003.

————. *Strengthening the EU's Relations with the Arab World.* Brussels: Commission of the European Communities, December 2003.

————. *Tenth Anniversary of the Euro-Mediterranean Partnership: A Work Programme to Meet the Challenges of the Next Five Years.* Brussels: Commission of the European Communities, April 2005.

————. *2004 Regular Report on Turkey's Progress Towards Accession,* COM(2004)656. Brussels: Commission of the European Communities, 6 October 2004.

Conclusions of the London Meeting on Supporting the Palestinian Authority, 1 March 2005, www.fco.gov.uk.

Cooper, R. *The Breaking of Nations: Order and Chaos in the Twenty-First Century.* New York: Atlantic Monthly, 2003.

Council of the European Union. *European Security Strategy: A Secure Europe in a Better World.* Brussels: Council of the European Union, December 2003.

Council on Foreign Relations. *In Support of Arab Democracy: Why and How.* New York: Council on Foreign Relations, 2005.

Crowe, B. "A Common European Foreign Policy After Iraq?" *International Affairs* 79, no. 3 (2003): 533–546.

Crystal, J. "Political Reform and the Prospects for Democratic Transition in the Gulf," Working Paper no. 11. Madrid: FRIDE, 2005.

Dawisha, A. "Iraq: Setbacks, Advances, Prospects," *Journal of Democracy* 15, no. 1 (2004).

Dawisha, A., and K. Dawisha. "How to Build a Democratic Iraq," *Foreign Affairs* 82, no. 3 (2003): 36–55.

Department for International Development. *Country Assistance Plan: Palestinian Territories 2004–2006.* London: Department for International Development.

————. *Iraq Country Strategy Paper,* February 2004. London: Department for International Development.

————. *Iraq Update,* no. 48, August 2003. London: Department for International Development.

————. *Iraq Update,* no. 8, June 2005. London: Department for International Development.

————. *Middle East and North Africa: Regional Action Plan,* 2003. London: Department for International Development.

————. *Regional Action Plan: MENA,* Consultation Draft, June 2003. London: Department for International Development.

DG Coopération Internationale et Développement. Documents Stratégiques Pays: Liban, 2002. Official statement of the ministry, www.diplomatie .gouv.fr.

Diamond, L. "What Went Wrong in Iraq?" *Foreign Affairs* 83, no. 5 (2004): 50.

Diez, T. "Constructing the Self and Changing Others: Reconsidering 'Normative Power' Europe," *Millennium: Journal of International Studies* 33, no. 3 (2005): 613–636.

Diez, T., and B. Rumelili. "Open the Door," *World Today* 60, no. 8–9 (2003): 33–35.

Dodge, T. "A Sovereign Iraq?" *Survival* 46, no. 3 (2004): 39–58.

———. "US Intervention and Possible Iraqi Futures," *Survival* 45, no. 3 (2003): 103–122.

Dodge, T., G. Luciani, and F. Neugart. *The European Union and Iraq: Present Dilemmas and Recommendations for Future Action.* Gutersloh: Bertelsmann, 2004.

Dorronsoro, G. "The European Union and Turkey: Between Geopolitics and Social Engineering," in R. Dannreuther, ed., *European Union Foreign and Security Policy: Towards a Neighbourhood Strategy.* London: Routledge, 2004.

Dosenrode-Lynge, S., and A. Stubkjaer. *The European Union and the Middle East.* London: Sheffield Academic, 2002.

Dunne, M. "Libya: Security Is Not Enough," Carnegie Endowment for International Peace, Policy Brief 32, Washington, DC, 2004.

Ebeid, H., and K. El Kady. "The Politics of Arab Reform: International, Regional and Domestic Dialectics," paper presented at launch of the Arab Reform Initiative, Cairo, 21 December 2004.

Ehteshami, A. "Reform from Above: The Politics of Participation in the Oil Monarchies," *International Affairs* 79, no. 1 (2003): 53–75.

El-Affendi, W. "The Elusive Reformation," *Journal of Democracy* 14, no. 2 (2003): 34–39.

Emerson, M., and G. Noutcheva. "From Barcelona Process to Neighbourhood Policy—Assessments and Open Issues," Working Document. Brussels: Center for European Policy Studies, 2004.

Emerson, M., and N. Tocci. "The Rubik Cube of the Wider Middle East," CEPS Report. Brussels: Center for European Policy Studies, 2003.

Emirates Center for Strategic Studies and Research. *International Interests in the Gulf Region.* Abu Dhabi: Emirates Center for Strategic Studies and Research, 2004.

Enhali, A., and O. Adda. "State and Islamism in the Maghreb," *Middle East Review of International Affairs* 7, no. 1 (2003): 66–76.

EU Council Secretariat. "EU Assistance to Palestinian Civilian Police," Background Note, 20 April 2005.

Euro-Mediterranean Human Rights Network. *Barcelona Plus 10 and Human Rights,* Position Paper, 1 March 2005.

———. *Rule of Law, Democracy and the Euro-Mediterranean Partnership,* report from the Human Rights Workshop at the Civil Forum, Marseilles, 10–12 November 2001, p. 81.

Euromesco. *Barcelona Plus: Towards a Euro-Mediterranean Community of Democratic States.* Lisbon, 2005.

European Parliament. *County Reports on Human Rights Practices: Turkey 2004.* Brussels, 2005.

Everts, S. *Engaging Iran: A Test Case for European Union Foreign Policy.* London: Centre for European Reform, 2004.

———. "Iran: The Next Big Crisis," *Prospect* 48, no. 93 (December 2003): 46–49.

————. *Shaping a Credible European Union Foreign Policy.* London: Centre for European Reform, 2002.

Feliu, L. "A Two Level Game: Spain and the Promotion of Democracy and Human Rights in Morocco," *Mediterranean Politics* 8, no. 2 (2003): 90–111.

Foreign and Commonwealth Office. "Achieving a Common Vision: A UK Contribution to the Future of the Barcelona Process," mimeo. London: FCO, 2005.

Fukuyama, F. "The US vs. the Rest," *New Perspectives Quarterly* 19, no. 4 (2002): 8–24.

Fuller, G. "Islamists in the Arab World: The Dance Around Democracy," Working Paper no. 49. Washington, DC: Carnegie Endowment for International Peace, 2004.

Gause, F. G., III. "How to Reform Saudi Arabia Without Handing It to Extremists," *Foreign Policy,* September–October 2004.

Gillespie, R. "Spain and Morocco: Towards a Reform Agenda?" Working Paper no. 7. Madrid: FRIDE, 2005.

————. "Spain and the West Mediterranean," Economic and Social Research Council Working Paper. ESRC, 2001.

Ginsberg, R. *The European Union in International Politics: Baptism by Fire.* Lanham, MD: Rowan and Littlefield, 2001.

Greenstock, J. "What Must Be Done Now?" *The Economist,* 8 May 2004, pp. 24–26.

Griegerich, B., and W. Wallace. "Not Such a Soft Power: The External Deployment of European Forces," *Survival* 46, no. 2 (2004): 163–182.

Grunert, A. "Loss of Guiding Values and Support: September 11 and the Isolation of Human Rights Organisations in Egypt," *Mediterranean Politics* 8, no. 2 (2003): 133–152.

Hafez, M. *Why Muslims Rebel: Repression and Resistance in the Islamic World.* Boulder: Lynne Rienner, 2002.

Hawthorne, A. "Middle Eastern Democracy: Is Civil Society the Answer?" Working Paper no. 44. Washington, DC: Carnegie Endowment for International Peace, 2004.

Heisbourg, F. "Iran: The Moment of Truth—A European Perspective," in *Iran: The Moment of Truth,* Working Paper no. 20. European Security Forum, IISS-CEPS, Brussels, June 2005.

Hinnebusch, R. "Globalization and Generational Change: Syrian Foreign Policy Between Regional Conflict and European Partnership," in G. Nonneman, ed., *Analyzing Middle East Foreign Policies.* London: Routledge, 2005.

————. *The International Politics of the Middle East.* Manchester: Manchester University Press, 2003.

Hobsbawm, E. "Spreading Democracy," *Foreign Policy,* September–October 2004.

Holden, P. "The European Community's MEDA Aid Regime: A Strategic Instrument of Civilian Power?" *European Foreign Affairs Review* 8 (2003): 347–363.

Hollis, R. "Europe and the Middle East: Power by Stealth?" *International Affairs* 73, no. 1 (1997): 15–29.

———. "Iraq: The Regional Fallout," RIIA Briefing Paper. London: Royal Institute of International Affairs, February 2003.

Ibrahim, S. E. "Reviving Middle Eastern Liberalism," *Journal of Democracy* 14, no. 4 (2003): 9–10.

Indyk, M. "Back to the Bazaar," *Foreign Affairs* 81, no. 1 (2002): 75.

———. "A Trusteeship for Palestine?" *Foreign Affairs* 82, no. 3 (2003): 51–70.

International Crisis Group. *Dealing with Hamas,* Middle East Report no. 21. International Crisis Group, Brussels, 2004.

———. *Governing Iraq.* International Crisis Group, August 2003.

———. *Iran: Discontent and Disarray.* International Crisis Group, October 2003.

———. *Iraq's Transition on a Knife Edge,* Middle East Report no. 27. International Crisis Group, Brussels, April 2004.

———. *Islamic Social Welfare Activism in the Occupied Palestinian Territories: A Legitimate Target?* International Crisis Group, Brussels, 2003.

———. *Islamism in North Africa I: The Legacies of History,* Briefing. International Crisis Group, Brussels, April 2004.

———. *Middle East Endgame I: Getting to a Comprehensive Arab-Israeli Peace Settlement.* International Crisis Group, Brussels, July 2002.

———. *A Middle East Roadmap to Where?* International Crisis Group, Brussels, May 2003.

———. *Reconstructing Iraq,* Middle East Report no. 30. International Crisis Group, Brussels, September 2004.

———. *Saudi Arabia Backgrounder: Who Are the Islamists?* Middle East Report no. 31. International Crisis Group, Brussels, 2004.

———. *Syria Under Bashar (I): Foreign Policy Challenges,* Middle East Report no. 23. International Crisis Group, Brussels, 18 February 2004.

———. *Syria Under Bashar (II): Domestic Policy Challenges,* Middle East Report no. 24. International Crisis Group, Brussels, February 2004.

———. *Yemen: Coping with Terrorism and Violence in a Fragile State,* Middle East Report no. 8. International Crisis Group, Brussels, 2003.

Jennings, R. S. "The Ghosts of Baathists Past and the Predicament of Civil Culture in Iraq," Arab Reform Bulletin no. 2/5. Washington, DC: Carnegie Endowment for International Peace, May 2004.

Jones, S., and M. Emerson. "European Neighbourhood Policy in the Mashreq Countries: Enhancing Prospects for Reform," Working Document no. 229. Brussels: Center for European Policy Studies, September 2005.

Kagan, R. *Of Paradise and Power: America and Europe in the New World Order.* New York: Alfred Knopf, 2003.

Kampfner, J. *Blair's Wars.* London: Free Press, 2004.

Kelly, J. "New Wine in Old Wineskins: Promoting Political Reforms Through the New European Neighbourhood Policy," *Journal of Common Market Studies* 44, no. 1 (2005): 29–55.

Kepel, G. *Bad Moon Rising: A Chronicle of the Middle East Today.* London: Saqi, 2003.

———. *Jihad: On the Trail of Political Islam.* Cambridge, MA: Harvard University Press, 2002.

Khan, M. "Prospects for Muslim Democracy: The Role of US Policy," *Middle East Policy* 10, no. 3 (2003): 79–89.

Kirchner, E., and J. Sperling. "The New Security Threats in Europe: Theory and Evidence," *European Foreign Affairs Review* 7, no. 4 (2002): 423–452.

Koch, C. "GCC-EU Relations," in Gulf Research Center, *Gulf Yearbook 2004.* Dubai, UAE: Emirates Center for Strategic Studies and Research, 2005.

Kubicek, P. "The Earthquake, the European Union and Political Reform in Turkey," *Mediterranean Politics* 7, no. 1 (2002): 1–18.

———, ed. *The European Union and Democratization.* London: Routledge, 2003.

Lacroix, S. "Between Islamists and Liberals: Saudi Arabia's New 'Islamo-Liberal' Reformists," *Middle East Journal* 59, no. 2 (2004): 344–364.

Langhor, V. "An Exit for Arab Autocracy," *Journal of Democracy* 13, no. 3 (2002): 116–122.

Lannon, E. "Parlements et societé civile dans la securité euro-méditerranéenne," Euromesco Paper no. 19, 2002, www.euromesco.net.

Leonard, M. *Why Europe Will Run the 21st Century.* London: Fourth Estate, 2005.

Leveau, R. "La France, L'Europe et la Méditerrannée: un espace à construire," *Politique étrangère* 67, no. 4 (2002): 1019–1032.

———. "France's Arab Policy," in L. Brown, ed., *Diplomacy in the Middle East.* London: I. B. Tauris, 2001.

Lewis, B. *The Crisis of Islam: Holy War and Unholy Terror.* London: Weidenfeld and Nicolson, 2003.

Lia, B. "Security Challenges in Europe's Mediterranean Periphery—Perspectives and Policy Dilemmas," *European Security* 8, no. 4 (1999): 27–56.

Litwak, R. *Rogue States and U.S. Foreign Policy: Containment After the Cold War.* Baltimore: Johns Hopkins University Press, 2000.

Lucas, R. "Deliberalization in Jordan," *Journal of Democracy* 14, no. 2 (2003): 137–144.

Luciani, G. *An EU-GCC Dialogue for Energy Stability and Sustainability.* Florence: European University Institute, 2005.

Luciani, G., and F. Neugart. *Toward a European Strategy for Iraq.* EUI/RSC Policy Paper. Florence: European University Institute/Robert Schumann Center, 2003.

———, ed. *The EU and the GCC: A New Partnership.* Florence: European University Institute-Bertlesmann, 2005.

MacGinty, R. "The Pre-War Reconstruction of Post-War Iraq," *Third World Quarterly* 24, no. 4 (2003): 601–617.

Magan, A. "Building Democratic Peace in the Eastern Mediterranean: An Inevitably Ambitious Agenda," Working Paper no. 9. Stanford, CA: Center on Democracy, Development, and the Rule of Law (Stanford University), 2004.

Manners, I., and R. Whitman. "The 'Difference Engine': Constructing and Representing the International Identity of the European Union," *Journal of European Public Policy* 10, no. 3 (2003): 380–404.

Matlary, J. H. *Intervention for Human Rights in Europe.* Basingstoke: Palgrave, 2002.

Menéndez, I. "Arab Reform: What Role for the European Union?" Egmont Paper no. 8. Brussels: Royal Institute for International Relations, 2005.

Ministère des Affaires Etrangères. *Pour une Gouvernance Démocratique: Document d'orientation de la politique française de la co-opération.* Paris: MAE, 2003.

Monar, J. "Institutional Constraints of the European Union's Middle Eastern and North African Policy," in S. Behrendt and C. Hanelt, ed., *Bound to Cooperate: Europe and the Middle East.* Gutersloh: Bertelsmann, 2000, pp. 209–243.

Montes, C., and S. Migliorisi. *2004 EU Donor Atlas.* Brussels: Commission of the European Communities, 2004.

Moosbauer, C. "Relations with the Persian Gulf States," in V. Perthes, ed., *Germany and the Middle East: Interests and Options.* Berlin: Heinrich Böll Foundation, 2002.

Moshaver, Z. "Revolution, Theocratic Leadership and Iran's Foreign Policy: Implications for Iran-EU Relations," in G. Nonneman, ed., *Analyzing Middle East Foreign Policies.* London: Routledge, 2005.

Müftüler Bac, M. "Turkey in the European Union's Enlargement Process: Obstacles and Challenges," *Mediterranean Politics* 7, no. 2 (2002): 79–95.

Niblock, T. *Pariah States and Sanctions in the Middle East: Iraq, Libya, Sudan.* Boulder: Lynne Rienner, 2001.

Nonneman, G. "Saudi-European Relations 1902–2001: A Pragmatic Quest for Relative Autonomy," *International Affairs* 77, no. 3 (2001): 631–661.

Norton, A. R. "Political Reform in the Middle East," in L. Guazzone, ed., *The Middle East in Global Change.* Basingstoke: Macmillan, 1997.

Noutcheva, G., N. Tocci, B. Coppieters, T. Kovziridze, M. Emerson, and M. Huysseune. "Europeanization and Secessionist Conflicts: Concepts and Theories," in G. Noutcheva, N. Tocci, B. Coppieters, T. Kovziridze, M. Emerson, and M. Huysseune, ed., *Europeanization and Conflict Resolution.* Ghent: Academia, 2004.

Noyon, J. *Islam, Politics and Pluralism: Theory and Practice in Turkey, Jordan, Tunisia and Algeria.* London: Royal Institute for International Affairs, 2003.

Ottaway, M. "Iraq: Without Consensus Democracy Is Not the Answer," Policy Brief no. 36. Washington, DC: Carnegie Endowment for International Peace, 2005.

Patten, C. "Engagement Is Not Liberal Mush," *New Perspectives Quarterly* 19, no. 2 (2002): 36–38.

Patten, Chris. *Not Quite the Diplomat.* London: Allen Lane, 2005.

Pei, M., and S. Kasper. "Lessons from the Past: The American Record in Nation-Building," Policy Brief. Washington, DC: Carnegie Endowment for International Peace, 2003.

Piccone, T. *Defending Democracy.* Washington, DC: Democracy Coalition Project, 2004.

Powell, C. "A Long, Hard Campaign," *Newsweek,* 15 October 2001.

Rheinhardt, U. J. "Civil Society Cooperation in the EMP: From Declarations to Practice," Euromesco Paper no. 15, 2002, www.euromesco.net.

Ridolfo, K. "Assessing Iraq's National Conference," Arab Reform Bulletin no. 2/8. Washington, DC: Carnegie Endowment for International Peace, September 2004.

Robins, P. "Confusion at Home, Confusion Abroad: Turkey Between Copenhagen and Iraq," *International Affairs* 79, no. 1 (2003): 547–566.

Roy, O. *The Failure of Political Islam.* London: I. B. Tauris, 1994.

———. "Islam in the West: The Westernization of Islam?" presentation at FRIDE, Madrid, 16 May 2005, www.fride.org.

Royal Institute of International Affairs. "Iraq in Transition: Vortex or Catalyst?" Briefing Paper no. 04/02. London: Royal Institute of International Affairs, September 2004.

Sarsar, S. "Can Democracy Prevail?" *Middle East Quarterly* 7, no. 1 (2000): 47.

Savage, B. "The EU and the GCC: A Growing Partnership," GCC-EU Research Bulletin no. 1. Dubai: Gulf Research Centre, March 2005.

Sawers, J. "Transforming Iraq," valedictory article by UK special envoy to Iraq, 2 August 2003, www.fco.gov.uk.

Schimmelfennig, F. "The Community Trap: Liberal Norms, Rhetorical Action, and the Eastern Enlargement of the European Union," *International Organization* 55, no. 1 (2001).

Schimmelfennig, F., S. Engart, and H. Knobel. "Costs, Commitments and Compliance: The Impact of EU Democratic Conditionality on Latvia, Slovakia and Turkey," *Journal of Common Market Studies* 41, no. 3 (2003): 495–518.

Schmid, D. "France and the Euro-Mediterranean Partnership: The Dilemmas of a Power in Transition," in H. Amirah Fernández and R. Youngs, ed., *The Euro-Mediterranean Partnership, Assessing the First Decade.* Madrid: Real Instituto Elcano, 2005.

Schnabel, A. "Democratization and Peacebuilding," in A. Saikal and A. Schnabel, ed., *Democratization in the Middle East: Experiences, Struggles, Challenges.* Tokyo: United Nations University Press, 2003.

Sedelmeier, U. "Collective Identity," in W. Carlsnaes, H. Sjursen, and B. White, ed., *Contemporary European Foreign Policy.* London: Sage, 2004.

Smith, K. "The EU, Human Rights and Relations with Third Countries: Foreign Policy with an Ethical Dimension?" in K. Smith and M. Light, ed., *Ethics and Foreign Policy.* Cambridge: Cambridge University Press, 2001.

Smith, M. E. "Toward a Theory of European Union Foreign Policy-Making: Multi-Level Governance, Domestic Politics, and National Adaptation to Europe's Common Foreign and Security Policy," *Journal of European Public Policy* 11, no. 4 (2004): 740–758.

Soetendorp, B. "The EU's Involvement in the Israeli-Palestinian Peace Process: The Building of a Visible International Identity," *European Foreign Affairs Review* 7, no. 2 (2002): 283–295.

Spencer, C. "Rethinking or Reorienting Europe's Mediterranean Security Focus," in W. Park and G. Wyn Rees, ed., *Rethinking Security in Post–Cold War Europe*. London: Longman, 1998.

Springborg, R. *Multiple Candidate Elections in Egypt: Diverting Pressure for Democracy*. FRIDE, March 2005, www.fride.org.

Takeyh, R. "Iran at a Crossroads," *Middle East Journal* 57, no. 1 (2003): 42–56.

———. "Uncle Sam in the Arab Street: Mideast Democracy and American Interests," *The National Interest* (Spring 2004): 45–51.

Tanner, F. "NATO's Role in Mideast Defence Cooperation and Democratization," *International Spectator* 34, no. 4 (2004): 101–113.

———. "North Africa: Partnership, Exceptionalism and Neglect," in R. Dannreuther, ed., *European Union Foreign and Security Policy: Towards a Neighbourhood Strategy*. London: Routledge, 2004.

———. "Security Cooperation: A New Reform Orientation?" in H. Amirah Fernández and R. Youngs, ed., *The Euro-Mediterranean Partnership, Assessing the First Decade*. Madrid: Real Instituto Elcano, 2005.

Tark, Oguzlu. "Turkey and the European Union: The Security Dimension," *Contemporary Security Policy* 23, no. 3 (2002): 61–82.

Tarock, A. "Iran–Western Europe Relations on the Mend," *British Journal of Middle Eastern Studies* 26, no. 1 (1999): 41–61.

Tessler, M. "The Influence of Islam on Attitudes Towards Democracy in Morocco and Algeria," in A. Saikal and A. Schnabel, ed., *Democratization in the Middle East: Experiences, Struggles, Challenges*. Tokyo: United Nations University Press, 2003.

Tocci, N. "Does the European Union Promote Democracy in Palestine?" in M. Emerson, *Democratisation in the European Neighbourhood*. Brussels: Center for European Policy Studies, 2005.

———. "The European Neighbourhood Policy: Responding to the EU's Post-Enlargement Challenges?" *International Spectator* 40, no. 1 (January–March 2005).

———. "The Widening Gap Between Rhetoric and Reality in EU Policy Towards the Israeli-Palestinian Conflict," Working Document no. 217. Brussels: Center for European Policy Studies, January 2005.

Tonra, B., and T. Christiansen. "The Study of European Union Foreign Policy: Between International Relations and European Studies," in B. Tonra and T. Christiansen, ed., *Rethinking European Union Foreign Policy*. Manchester: Manchester University Press, 2004.

Triantaphyllou, D. "The Thirteenth Candidate—Turkey: Whither Its March Towards the European Union?" in J. Batt, D. Lynch, A. Missiroli, M. Ortega, and D. Triantaphyllou, ed., *Partners and Neighbours: A CFSP for a Wider Europe,* Chaillot Paper no. 64. Paris: EU Institute for Security Studies, 2003.

United Nations. *Arab Human Development Report 2002*. New York: United Nations, 2002.

————. *Arab Human Development Report 2003*. New York: United Nations, 2003.

————. *Arab Human Development Report 2004*. New York: United Nations, 2005.

US State Department. *The National Security Strategy of the United States.* Washington, DC: State Department, September 2002.

————. *Supporting Human Rights and Democracy: The US Record 2004–2005*. Washington, DC: State Department, 2004.

Vasconselos, A. "The EU and Iraq," in W. Posch, ed., *Looking into Iraq,* Chaillot Paper no. 79. Paris: EU Institute for Security Studies, 2005.

Volpi, F. "Regional Community Building and the Transformation of International Relations: The Case of the Euro-Mediterranean Partnership," *Mediterranean Politics* 9, no. 2 (2003): 145–164.

White, B. *Understanding European Foreign Policy.* Basingstoke: Palgrave, 2001.

Willis, M., and N. Messari. "Analyzing Moroccan Foreign Policy and Relations with Europe," in G. Nonneman, ed., *Analyzing Middle East Foreign Policies.* London: Routledge, 2005.

Wilson, R. "EU-GCC Relations: Towards a Free Trade Agreement and Beyond," in C. Hanelt, F. Neugart, and M. Peitz, ed., *Future Perspectives on Europe-Gulf Relations.* Gutersloh: Bertelsmann, 2000.

World Values Survey 2001–2005. Stockholm: World Values Association.

Yesilada, B. "Turkey's Candidacy for EU Membership," *Middle East Journal* 56, no. 1 (2002): 94–111.

Youngs, R. "Democracy and Security in the Middle East," FRIDE Working Paper no. 21. Madrid: FRIDE, 2006.

————, ed. *Survey of European Democracy Promotion Policies 2000–2006.* Madrid: FRIDE, 2006.

Zakaria, F. "No Security, No Democracy," *Newsweek,* 24 May 2004.

Zucconi, M. *Turkey's New Politics and the European Union.* Rome: Ethnobarometer, 2003.

Index _____

Abbas, Mahmoud, 106, 146, 152, 155–157, 166; election victory of, 163; reforms of, 164–165
Abdullah, Crown Price of Saudi Arabia, 183, 184, 187
Ahmadinejad, Mahmoud, 15, 67, 82, 90–91
Algeria: civil society in, 119, 120; counterterrorism cooperation of, 14, 121; democratic and human rights reform in, 11, 118– 120; European aid programs in, 120–122; European-backed government reforms in, 118–122; government incorporation of Islamist parties in, 224; judicial reform in, 120; Neighbourhood Action Plan, 121; presidential elections (2004), 120; relations with France, 119–121; security-oriented political reform in, 119; trade liberalization in, 121, 122
Allawi, Ayad, 43–45, 47
Amsterdam treaty, 200
Ana Lindh Euromed Foundation, 107, 108
Arab-Israeli conflict: Euro-Mediterranean Partnership and, 98, 107–108; European strategy toward, 19; and Middle East policy debates, 18; and peace process, 126–127, 151–156; US and, 151–153
Arab states, pro-democracy reforms in, 11. *See also specific states*
Arafat, Yasser: death of, 145, 146, 163; European governments' stance toward, 155; governance of, 147, 149, 153–156, 161; US demonizing of, 152, 161, 162
Assad, Bashar al-, autocratic government of, 129–131, 133, 136
Aznar, José María, 117, 120

Bahrain: democracy projects in, 178; free trade agreement with US, 182; parliamentary training project in, 192; political reform and reversals in, 11, 175, 181; and trade liberalization, 172. *See also* Gulf Cooperation Council states
Barcelona Process/Declaration, 99, 100, 108, 139, 140; democracy and human rights focus in, 102; and European Neighbourhood Policy, 111–113; and "soft" reforms, 96
Berlusconi, Silvio, 155
Blair, Tony, 79, 91, 137, 163–164, 212; Iraq policy of, 34–36, 46, 54, 57

Bouteflika, Abdelaziz, 14–15, 118–121
Brahimi, Lakhdar, 41
Bremer, Paul, 36, 37, 40, 49–50
Broader Middle East and North Africa Initiative (BMENA), 8, 103; Forum on the Future, 105–106, 112
Bush administration: and Arab-Israeli conflict, 151–153; Egyptian policy of, 123, 125; Iran approach of, 72–74, 79, 84, 91, 230; Iraq policy of, 33, 35, 36, 39; Maghreb and Mashreq policy of, 230; Middle East policy of, 6, 8, 111; Palestinian policy of, 164–166; political reform perspective of, 23; Saudi Arabia policy of, 185; Syria policy of, 130, 133, 134; and Turkey's accession to the EU, 213

Chirac, Jacques, 116, 118–121, 128, 137, 153; Iraq policy of, 38, 48; and Turkey's accession to the EU, 212, 215, 216
Clinton administration: Iran policy of, 70; Iraq policy of, 33; and Turkey's accession to the EU, 205
Common Foreign and Security Policy (CFSP), 147; Common Strategy for the Mediterranean, 97; and European unity in Iraq, 33; and Europe's Mediterranean preference, 179–180; policy divide in, 179–180; reforms to, 20
Copenhagen European Council, and Turkey's accession negotiations, 208–209
Crooke, Alistair, 157

Democratization: as EU condition, 226; and inculcation of democratic values, 224, 225; US versus EU rhetoric on, 230–231. *See also specific countries and regions*

Denmark: hard-line policy on Iran, 68; human rights dialogue with Iran, 85; and Saudi political reform, 189; Wider Middle East Initiative of, 7
Department for International Development (DfID), 35; Iraq projects of, 58; Yemen assessment of, 192
de Villepin, Dominique, 38, 40–41, 79, 156, 158, 176

Ecevit, Bülent, 205–206
Egypt: association council in, 124; civil and economic reforms in, 123, 124; democracy in, 10, 123; EIDHR funding for, 123; and election monitoring, 125–126; EU aid to, 98, 123; European-backed reforms in, 122–126; al-Ghad Party, 10, 12; government repression and limited reforms in, 12–13; human/women's rights issues in, 123–125; Neighbourhood Action Plan in, 125, 127; NGO law restrictions in, 123–124; relations with US, 122–124; trade policy, 124
Egyptian Human Rights Organization, 123
Erbakan, Necmettin, 200–201, 205
Erdogan, Recep Tayyip, 197, 208; government of, 210–212, 216
Euro-Arab Dialogue, creation of, 19
Euromed Internal Market Programme, 109
Euro-Mediterranean free trade area, 96–98, 110
Euro-Mediterranean Human Rights Network, 102
Euro-Mediterranean Partnership (EMP), 44; and Arab-Israeli conflict, 98, 107–108, 148; autocratic governments and, 97, 98; and counterterrorism cooperation, 99–100, 104; democratization and human rights focus in, 96,

97, 99, 101–102, 107, 109–111, 113–114; and economic liberalization, 96, 109–111; formal commitments of, 96–99, 101; and infrastructure funding, 109; justice and home affairs pillar of, 100–101; linking of economic/political reform strategies in, 110–111; and migration controls, 101; moderate Islamists' inclusion in, 108–110; partner states of, 95; political and security issues in, 97–101, 104–105, 110–113; soft/apolitical initiatives in, 96, 106–109; and trade relations, 97–98. *See also* MEDA democracy funding

Euromed Parliamentary Forum/Assembly, 106, 108

European Commission: and Gulf states funding policy, 175–177, 179–181; and Iraq reconstruction aid, 55, 56, 62; and Palestinian aid distribution, 164; and Turkey's accession to the EU, 214

European Court of Human Rights (ECHR) system, Turkey's participation in, 202

European Initiative for Democracy and Human Rights (EIDHR), 8, 56, 88, 128, 147, 179, 181

European member states: bilateral diplomacy/aid initiatives of, 227; foreign policy coordination between, 19–20; and Kurdish rights in Turkey, 203; and Turkey's accession, 202, 207, 209, 212, 213. *See also specific states*

European Neighbourhood Policy (ENP), 7–8, 95, 109, 111–115. *See also specific countries and regions*

European Parliament (EP), 201, 206; Arab-Israeli conflict and, 150–151; and EU-Turkey customs union, 199–200; and Turkey's accession, 214

European Security and Defence Policy (ESDP), 20, 49, 62, 100, 105, 205; and Berlin-plus agreement, 204

European Security Strategy, 20

European Union Coordination Unit for Palestinian Police Support (COPPS), 159

European Union Middle East policy: advocacy for broadening, 179–180, 193; and change through cultural cooperation, 222; conditionality in, 23; containment-based, 2, 4; country-specific strategic deliberation in, 226; cultural dialogue in, 224; of democratization and human rights promotion, 4, 6–8, 21, 22, 24, 140, 224, 225; domestic determinants of, 223–224; duality in, 19; and elite-guided reforms, 224; and EU influence and capacity to react, 25; of gradual and bounded reform, 140, 194; on human rights, 4, 225; limited influence of, 229–231; Mediterranean preference in, 179–180; national-level European initiatives in, 227–228; and nation building, 2; and nonproliferation initiative, 100; normative dimension in, 140, 230–231; of partnership-based reform, 112; and political Islam, 4; and political will, 24–25; post-9/11 critique of, 21–22; and restrictions on political rights, 225; and security risks, 2; and security through mutual understanding, 140; September 11 impact on, 8–9, 222–224; social/economic development focus of, 224; soft/apolitical approach in, 22–23, 96, 106–109, 139; traditional power-projection security focus of, 223; and US policies, 8, 25, 226–227; women's rights focus in, 189. *See also specific regions and states*

Fatah political party, 161–163, 165, 166, 168
Fischer, Joschka, 79, 90
5+5 Dialogue, 101, 139
France: and EU role in Gulf states, 180; Iran relations with, 68–70, 88; Iran's nuclear development agreement with, 79–83; and Iraqi transfer of power, 38–41; Iraq sanctions and, 33–34; and security training in Iraq, 54; and Syrian interference in Lebanon, 134–135; troop deployment to Iraq, 48–49; Turkey's sanctions against, 206; and Turkey's accession to EU, 212; and UN Oil for Food program, 33–34
Friedrich Ebert Stiftung, Syrian initiatives of, 131, 132
Front Islamique du Salut (FIS), 121

Generalized System of Preferences (GSP) trade provisions (EU), 42
Germany: and GCC states' reforms, 178; Iran's nuclear development agreement with, 79–83; Iran's relationship with, 61–62, 70, 90; Task Force for Dialogue with the Islamic World, 7; and Turkey's accession to the EU, 212
al-Ghad Party (Egypt), 10, 12
Greater/Broader Middle East Initiative, US proposal for, 8, 177, 179–180
Greek Cyprus: accession prospects for, 201; Turkey's relations with, 215, 216; UN plan for, 211
Gulf Cooperation Council (GCC) states: autocratic containment of Islamist radicals in, 171; and bilateral links to EU, 182; and bottom-up governance reform, 174–175; and broader Middle East initiative, 177, 179–180; civil society in, 174, 181;

Cooperation Agreement with EU (1988), 172; counterterrorist cooperation/projects in, 171, 176, 177; customs union, 175, 181; democracy issues in, 176, 178; development aid to, 173, 180–181; economic/trade cooperation and liberalization in, 172–173, 175–176, 181; EU defense links and arms sales to, 173–175; and EU-GCC free trade area, 173, 175–177, 181–182, 186; EU political involvement in, 182; European states' bilateral cooperation with, 177–183; human rights issues in, 174, 176, 177, 182; migration issues in, 177; oil and defense diplomacy in, 172–175, 181; post-9/11 European policy and representation in, 175–190, 227; reform-oriented cooperation in, 222; security and defense cooperation/reforms in, 171, 175–178; women's support and training programs in, 178–179. *See also* Saudi Arabia; *specific states*

Hamas, 225; election participation of, 145, 146, 165–166, 168; EU/European governments' relations with, 157–158; listed as terrorist organization, 157, 165, 166; national support for, 161; social benefits provided by, 149, 157, 158
Hariri, Rafik, 135, 136
Hizbollah, 74, 135, 136, 159; European diplomatic dialogue with, 134; Syrian support for, 131
Human rights, and Western discourse/policies, 4, 5. *See also specific regions and states*
Hussein, Saddam, 34; and weapons inspections, 34

International Atomic Energy Agency (IAEA): and Iran

inspections and censure, 78–84; vote to refer Iran to UNSC, 67
International Monetary Fund (IMF), 60
International Task Force on Palestinian Reform, 149
Iran, 67–92; civilian nuclear energy program of, 79; and democracy, 11, 67, 68, 74, 86–87, 89; economic and trade liberalization in, 69–70, 72; economic control by conservative *majlis* in, 88; elections (June 2005), 90; electoral manipulations in, 87; elite-oriented reforms in, 225; European strategy in, 75–76, 228; EU's limited influence in, 229–230; freedom movement in, 70–71, 77; government's gradual reform efforts in, 70–71; human rights issues/dialogues in, 71, 73–76, 84–85, 88–91; IAEA inspections in, 78–84; internal political development in, 83–91; intra-Iranian dissension in, 70–72, 76–77; nuclear-related activities in, 77–83, 89, 223; post-9/11 EU partnership with, 71–77; referral to UNSC, 80, 83; reform assistance to, 71, 75–76; rule of law projects in, 87, 91; security focus in, 78; strategic importance of, 69; trade and cooperation agreement in, 79, 81; uranium enrichment program of, 79–83; US relations with, 68, 72–75, 86–87, 92; and WTO entry, 72–73, 81, 82, 90
Iran Democracy Act, US proposal for, 86–87
Iraq: aid conditions in, 61; Baathist political/security participation in, 34, 37, 38, 50, 52; Coalition Provisional Authority in, 36–38, 41, 50, 52; debt relief, 44; democracy, 31, 34–36, 38, 41, 45, 48, 56; economic/trade liberalization in, 42; elections/electoral process in, 37–39, 43, 45–47; and ethnically-based politics, 47–48; EU containment policy in, 32, 33; EU long-term strategy for, 42–43; European postinvasion challenges in, 13, 34–36; Europe's limited influence in, 229; human rights issues/funding in, 50, 53, 56, 57; international NGOs roles in, 58–59; judicial reform and rule of law in, 42; Kurdish autonomy issue in, 31; member states' engagement/deployment in, 43–50; military deployments in, 54–55; national voting in, 11; nuclear issue in, 34, 35; police reform in, 51–55; political conditionality in, 45; postconflict security challenges in, 48–55; and post–Gulf War conditions and aid flows, 32–33; regime change policy for, 33, 34; rule of law mission in, 46, 62; sanctions, 33–34; security sector focus/reforms in, 47, 50–55; sovereign interim government of, 36–37; state building/reconstruction, 39, 55–63; Sunni representation in new government of, 46–47; trade and cooperation agreement in, 45; transfer of power in, 36–41; UN roles in, 38–41, 50; US policy in, 32–41, 43, 46–52, 56–57
Iraq Country Strategy, 58
Iraqi Governing Council (IGC), 41, 52; authority of, 36, 37; elections and, 39; and European military presence, 49–50
Iraq Liberation Act, 33
Islah Islamist party (Yemen), 190
Islam: and European foreign policy, 221; political Islam and democracy, 16–17; social reformist, 17–18
Islamic Action Front (Jordan), 126
Islamic Jihad, 161

Islamist Party of Justice and
Development (Morocco), 14
Islamist Refah (Welfare) party, 201
Istanbul Cooperation Initiative
(ICI), 177–178
Italian-Libyan Security Committee,
139

Jafari, Ibrahim al-, 46
Jordan: controlled political reform
in, 14; elite-guided reforms in,
127, 129; EU aid program
in, 126, 127; government-
incorporated Islamist parties in,
224; judicial reform in, 127; and
Middle East peace process, 126–
127; security cooperation in, 127
Justice and Development Party
(AKP) (Turkey), 197, 208

Khamenei, Ayatollah, 74, 86
Khatami, Mohammed, 225; EU
rapprochement with, 67–69;
gradual political reforms of,
68–72, 77; nuclear program
development and, 81, 84–86
Kurdistan People's Congress
(Kongra-Gel), 214, 215
Kurdistan Workers Party (PKK),
199, 214, 215
Kuwait: limits on reforms in, 13;
political and human rights reform
in, 11; women activists' training
in, 178. *See also* Gulf Cooperation Council states

Lahoud, Emile, 134
Lebanon: Cedar revolution in, 10;
consociational democracy in,
135, 136; democratic and reform
dynamics in, 15; EU aid to, 134;
Neighbourhood Action Plan in,
135; reform funding in, 135–136;
security cooperation in, 134;
sovereignty, 15; Syrian rule in,
133–135
Libya: abandonment of nuclear
program in, 136, 138; accession

to EMP, 137; economic and
security sector reforms in, 136,
138, 224; European engagement
and aid in, 136–139; European
Neighbourhood Policy and, 137,
139; human rights violations/
conditions in, 137; lifting of
sanctions against, 136–138; and
migration cooperation, 138; US
human rights dialogue with, 137;
WMD and containment policy
in, 223
Libyan Islamic Group, persecution
of, 137

Maghreb and Mashreq states,
95–140; Agadir agreement in,
109; aid allocations to, 101;
bilateral forums on human rights
in, 127; consolidation of European influence in, 139–140;
cultural and social initiatives in,
107–109; democracy promotion
in, 102–103; election monitoring
in, 106; "elite-bounded" reform
in, 96; EU influence in, 230–231;
European Neighbourhood Policy
in, 7–8, 109, 111–115; European
political dialogue with, 98–99;
Governance Facility for reform
in, 105–106; government-
controlled reform in, 115–129;
Maghreb-wide governance
initiative in, 103–104; police
force sensitivity training in, 105;
political reform funding and
strategies for, 101–111; post-9/11
approaches to, 99–111, 139;
regional disarmament and WMD
control process in, 100; security
sector reform in, 104–105; and
subregional economic liberalization in, 109–110. *See also*
Euro-Mediterranean Partnership;
specific states
MEDA democracy funding: Algerian
policing project of, 119; of
human rights projects, 126; in

Iraq, 61; in Maghreb and Mashreq, 97, 98, 100, 101, 102, 103–104, 109–110; in Occupied Territories, 147, 164; in Syria, 131–132; and Turkish economic reform, 202
Mediterranean Dialogue/ Partnership, 100, 105; GCC exclusion from, 178
Merkel, Angela, 212, 216
Middle East Free Trade Zone, US proposal for, 80
Middle East monarchies, reform in, 10
Middle East Partnership Initiative (MEPI), 6, 8, 104
Middle East region: controlled political liberalization in, 13–14; democracy-migration link in, 5; democratization in, 10, 17–18; dynamics of political change in, 9–18; economic and political liberalization in, 15–16; and EU-US differences, 20–21; impact of violent conflict in, 18; level of political freedom in, 9; limits to political opening in, 12; patrimonial-style rule in, 16; political and social reformist Islamic agendas in, 16–18
Millennium Challenge Account, 117
Mohammed VI, King of Morocco, 115, 116, 117
Morocco: bilateral Neighbourhood Action Plan in, 116; civil society groups in, 115; democracy in, 117; European-backed reforms in, 115–118; human rights and press restrictions in, 116, 118; Islamist parties in, 224; political liberalization in, 13, 117; progress on human/women's rights in, 10; reform funding in, 115–116, 118; Reinforced Dialogue in, 116; Spain's relations with, 117–118
Movement for Islamic Reform (MIRA), 188
Mubarak, Gama, 123–124
Mubarak, Hosni, 122–125

Muslim Brotherhood, 10, 14, 108, 123, 125
Muslims, support for democracy among, 12

National Council of the Iranian Resistance (NCIR), 70
Nationalist Action Party (MHP), 201, 202, 206
National Liberation Front Party (Algeria), 14
North Atlantic Treaty Organization (NATO), 8; Istanbul Cooperation Initiative, 177–178, 190; Mediterranean Dialogue/Partnership, 100, 105, 178
Nour, Ayman, 125

OECD-UNDP good governance initiative, 178
Oman, civil service reform in, 178
Operation Desert Fox, 34
Operation Ulysses, 101
Organisation for Economic Cooperation and Development (OECD), 7
Organization of the Petroleum Exporting Countries (OPEC), and European integration, 19
Oslo peace accords, 98, 145; Mediterranean regimes' support for, 97

Palestine Liberation Organization (PLO), 147
Palestinian Authority (PA): account- ability of, 154; association agree- ment, 147, 148; credibility and legitimacy of, 149; EU aid conditions and priorities in, 146–150, 153–155; European arms transfers to, 150; European Neighbourhood Action Plan, 164; financial transparency focus in, 162; and Gaza withdrawal, 159–160; legal system reform in, 159; 100 days reform plan, 149; political reforms in, 145, 155,

164; security focus in, 154; support for Abbas, 163

Palestinian Islamist organizations: radicalization of, 149; welfare programs of, 147, 157

Palestinian Legislative Council (PLC), 150, 155

Palestinian Occupied Territories, 145–168; Al-Aqsa Intifada in, 145, 148, 149; civil society funding/priorities in, 147–149; counterterrorist strategies in, 157; democracy and governance allocations to, 154; democratic reforms in, 11, 152–153, 155, 161, 163, 164, 167, 168; elections in, 161, 162, 164–166; elite-oriented reforms in, 225; emergency/humanitarian relief in, 146, 153; EU funding and reform approach in, 146–151, 226, 229–230; and EU policy, 150, 167–168; human rights issues/initiatives in, 154, 155; institutional reform in, 145, 146, 153–156, 161–164, 167; NGO/civil society funding in, 154; peace process in, 145, 146, 148, 162; reform require-ments for, 163–164; Roadmap toward final settlement in, 151–156; security cooperation/imperatives in, 149, 154, 156–160, 164; support for statehood in, 147–148, 151, 152; welfare support in, 147, 157, 158

Party of Justice and Development (PJD) (Morocco), 116

Patten, Chris, 6, 7, 42, 102, 151

People's Mujahideen (MKO), 70, 86–87, 89, 90; listed as terrorist organization, 86

Powell, Colin, 37, 118

Prodi, Romano, 106, 109, 136–137

Qaddafi, Muammar, 136–139

Al-Qaida, 183, 184

Qatar, government-instigated reforms in, 175. *See also* Gulf Cooperation Council states

Qurei, Ahmed, 156, 161

Rafsanjani, Ali Akbar Hashemi, 76–77, 90

Rapid Reaction Force, 150–151

Rapid Reaction Mechanism, 139; and third country nonproliferation commitments, 130–131

Rule of law programs, 104; Iraq mission for, 46, 62

Rushdie, Salman, 68–69

Sadr, Moqtada al-, 44, 51

Saleh, Ali Abdallah, 190–193

Saudi Arabia: counterterrorism cooperation of, 185, 187–188; European governance and reform assistance to, 187–190; European arms sales to, 174; foreign direct investment in, 173; and free trade agreement with the EU, 186; government brutality and corrup-tion in, 13, 184; human rights and civil society reforms in, 183–184, 189; market-regulating role of, 185; National Dialogue in, 183; political Islam in, 183; political reform dialogue in, 11, 190; post-9/11 security coopera-tion of, 186–187; terrorist attacks in, 183; and trade liberalization, 172; women's and workers' rights in, 184, 189; and WTO accession/conditions, 186, 188, 190

Schröder, Gerhard, 82, 137, 176, 189, 212

September 11 terrorist attacks: EU versus US view of, 21; and Middle East political liberalization, 1–9, 222–224

Seville European Council, 101

Sezer, Ahmet Mecdet, 205

Sharon, Ariel, 145, 149, 156, 159–161, 163, 165

Sistani, Ali al-, 40

Solana, Javier, 7, 20, 42, 46, 80–82, 157, 158, 160, 182, 205

Spain: and EU's Mediterranean focus, 180, 187; Iran policy of,

87–89; Iraq policy of, 45; Morocco relations with, 117–118; Tunisian policy of, 128, 129; and Turkey's accession to the EU, 212, 213
Strategic Partnership with the Mediterranean and Middle East, 7, 177, 179, 180, 182
Straw, Jack, 69, 77, 79, 81, 87, 182, 187
Syria: democracy and human rights focus in, 130, 133; elite-oriented reform in, 133, 224; EU association agreement with, 129–133, 135; European and US policy in, 129–136; Kurdish activism in, 133; reform-oriented funding in, 131–132; US sanctions against, 130; WMD and containment policy in, 223; WTO entry of, 131

Trade and Investment Framework Agreement (US-Turkey), 204
Treaty on the Non-Proliferation of Nuclear Weapons (NPT), and Iran's nuclear-related activities, 77–78, 80, 81
Tunisia: democracy and human rights funding in, 128; elite-oriented reform in, 128–129; EU aid to, 98, 128, 129; political repression in, 129
Turkey, 197–219; accession of, 197, 200–201, 203–215, 218, 225–226, 228; and accession opposition, 209, 213, 216; aid programs for, 204; AKP Islamic government/reforms in, 208, 210–211, 214; arms flows to, 199; association agreement/ council, 198, 204, 215; civil society projects in, 200; cooperation projects in, 201; customs union, 199–200, 202–203, 210, 215; Cyprus issues in, 201, 205, 210–213, 216; democratic reforms in, 15, 197, 198,

200–202, 207–210, 214, 218; and economic integration, 202–203; and EU freedom of movement provisions, 206; EU funding for, 201–202; EU member states' bilateral relations with, 202; European investment in, 202; European strategy and influence in, 217–218, 228, 229; and EU security logic, 198, 207–208; funding priorities in, 210; government-initiated reforms in, 205; government repression in, 205; Greece relations, 203; harassment of Islamist civil society organizations in, 205; human rights violations/reforms in, 199, 200, 202, 206, 210, 215; IMP political reforms in, 206; institutional reforms in, 202; Iraq invasion and, 50, 211; Kurdish rights issue in, 198–200, 203, 205, 210, 216; limits and nature of reforms in, 207; military training aid for, 200; nationalist security culture in, 15; ousting of Islamist government in, 200–201; political reforms in, 10, 211, 213–215; and US policy and relations, 198–199, 204, 217–218

United Arab Emirates: elections in, 11; and trade liberalization, 172
United Kingdom (UK): Arab reform strategy of, 7; Iran relations of, 68–70, 91; Iran's nuclear development agreement with, 79–83; Iraq aid and institution building of, 57–60; Iraq containment policy of, 34; and Iraqi postconflict political process, 35–40; Libya policy of, 136, 138; oil-for-arms sales to Saudi Arabia, 174; and Saudi political reform, 187–188; and Turkey's accession to the EU, 213
United Nations: Arab Development Report, 176; Oil for Food

program, 33–34; role in Iraq,
38–41, 50
United Nations Commission on
Human Rights, and Iranian
human rights abuses, 85
United Nations Development
Programme (UNDP), 7; good
governance initiative of, 188
United States: Gulf states policy of,
172, 174, 179–182, 191, 194; and
Iran's nuclear-related activities,
78; Israeli-Palestinian conflict
and, 156, 157, 161; Morocco
policy of, 116–118; and Palestinian statehood, 150; Saudi Arabia
policies of, 185; Syria and
Lebanon policies of, 129, 131,
135; and Syrian-EU association
agreement, 130; US–Middle East
free trade area proposal, 111. *See
also* Bush administration
United States Agency for International Development (USAID),
6, 149; democracy funding of, 125

Venice Declaration, 19

Western Middle East policies,
historical perspective on, 3–4
Women's rights, Middle East
reforms for, 10, 123, 124
World Trade Organization, Iran's
bid for membership in, 72–73

Yemen: civil society and women's
rights reforms in, 191, 192;
cooperation agreement in, 190;
counterterrorist challenges in,
190–192; EU aid to, 190–193;
European development policies/
funding in, 172, 192; governance
reforms related to WTO entry
in, 191; international assistance
to, 193; parliamentary training
project in, 192; political dialogue
on human rights in, 191; political
reform policies in, 13, 172,
186, 190–193; political
repression in, 190; security-
oriented cooperation in, 190–
192; US policy in, 180, 191,
194
Yemeni Socialist Party, 190

About the Book _____

In the wake of September 11, the European Union proclaimed a new commitment to encouraging processes of political liberalization in the Middle East, and a plethora of initiatives were introduced to that end. Richard Youngs offers a thorough analysis of the policies actually followed by the EU—by national governments, as well as collectively—in the intervening several years.

Drawing on official documents and extensive interviews with key policymakers, Youngs assesses EU policies implemented throughout the Middle East: in Iraq, Iran, the Maghreb and Mashreq, the Palestinian Territories, the Gulf states, and Turkey. His analysis sheds light not only on the EU's strengths and weaknesses as an international actor, but also on the impact of external factors on political change and on the hotly debated topic of the relationship between democracy and security.

Richard Youngs is senior researcher at the Fundación para las Relaciones Internacionales y el Diálogo Exterior (FRIDE) in Madrid and lecturer in the Department of Politics and International Studies at the University of Warwick, UK. His publications include *International Democracy and the West: The Role of Governments, NGOs and Multinationals* and *The European Union and the Promotion of Democracy: Europe's Mediterranean and East Asian Policies.*